IN TEACHERS' HANDS

SUNY Series, Educational Leadership
Daniel L. Duke

In memory of
Nancy Faires Conklin,
a scholar and friend.

IN TEACHERS' HANDS

Investigating the Practices of Classroom Assessment

RICHARD J. STIGGINS
NANCY FAIRES CONKLIN

Sponsored by Office of Educational Research and Improvement
U.S. Department of Education

State University
of New York
Press

This publication is based on work conducted by the Northwest Regional Educational Laboratory sponsored wholly, or in part, by the Office of Educational Research and Improvement (OERI), U.S. Department of Education, under Contract Number 400-86-006. The content of this publication does not necessarily reflect the views of OERI, the Department, or any other agency of the U.S. Government.

Published by
State University of New York Press, Albany

© 1992 State University of New York

For information, address State University of New York
Press, State University Plaza, Albany, N.Y., 12246

Library of Congress Cataloging-in-Publication Data

Stiggins, Richard J.
    In teachers' hands : investigating the practices of classroom
  assessment / Richard J. Stiggins and Nancy Faires Conklin.
      p.   cm.
    Includes bibliographical references (p.   ) and index.
    ISBN 0-7914-0931-7 (alk. paper) : $47.50. — ISBN 0-7914-0932-5
  (pbk. : alk. paper) : $15.95
    1. Educational tests and measurements—United States.   2. Grading
  and marking (Students)—United States.   I. Conklin, Nancy Faires.
  II. Title.
  LB3051.S8535   1992
  371.2'6—dc20   91-12704
                                                                   CIP

10 9 8 7 6 5 4 3

CONTENTS

PREFACE

These are times when citizens and educators alike are embracing the idea that schools should team with other important social institutions to make sure students attain the specific learner outcomes that will make them productive citizens. Thus our schools increasingly are held accountable not just for providing quality programs in the hope that students will benefit, but for making sure those programs benefit students in specific ways.

In this context, it has become absolutely essential that educators not only understand the nature of the outcomes students are to attain, but also know how to translate those achievement targets into appropriate, high-quality assessments. Evidence abounds that these requirements are not being met. It is not that we have failed to conduct sound educational assessments in recent years. To the contrary, outstanding advances have been made in psychometric theory and in the practical aspects of school testing. Both the status and the state of the art in large-scale testing programs have leaped forward in recent years, with the help of highly visible school accountability movements and the rapid development of computer technology. Unfortunately, however, these advances have either had few implications for the classroom teacher, or those implications have not found their way into teachers' hands. This is most unfortunate, because the schooling process includes far more day-to-day classroom assessments than large-scale assessments and those classroom assessments have a far greater impact on students than do large-scale tests.

It is the premise of this book that the imbalance in our attention to large-scale assessment versus classroom assessment results from a lack of clear understanding of classroom measurement processes. Due to a lack of classroom-level research, we fail to understand the assessment task demands faced by teachers. The apparent extreme complexity of classroom assessment environments and issues has served as a barrier that has kept researchers from conducting the needed research.

The purpose of this volume is to describe a program of research on classroom assessment intended to confront this complexity. Over the past decade, we have been with teachers and students watching through measurement eyes as the teaching and learning process unfolds, trying to understand classroom assessment in all of its depth and color. Only teachers are in the unique position of being able to obtain and evaluate a long-term, comprehensive sample of student achievement. The questions we addressed during this research were how and how well do teachers take advantage of this opportunity.

Over the years, many Northwest Regional Educational Laboratory (NWREL) staff members and others have contributed to the completion of this research program. They include Nancy Bridgeford, who helped to lay the foundation through her work as a key member of the team that conceived the research, completed the early survey studies and conducted the first few case studies of classroom assessment environments; Karen Reed Wikelund, who participated extensively in the field research and provided valuable leadership in translating complex results into readable, usable information; Maggie Griswold, whose data analysis and summary skills saved time and effort and brought cohesiveness to the presentation; and Celeste Brody, Nels Doeleman, Dave Frisbie, Phil Griswold, Karen Nelson, and Lynde Paule, all of whom served on the field research staff along the way. Thanks to all for clear thinking and hard work.

Thanks also to Dave Frisbie, Bill Schafer, Peter Airasian and Dan Duke for reviewing early drafts of the manuscript and offering suggestions that improved the focus of our description, and to Sharon Lippert who, as always, demonstrated her patience and extreme competence in merging diverse research reports into a high-quality manuscript.

Our understanding of the nature and quality of classroom assessment environments and the task demands of classroom assessment are in their infancy. Further, we have very little understanding of how to prepare teachers to meet those demands. We will not be fulfilling our responsibility to students until we competently and confidently prepare their teachers to assess. For this reason, our work continues.

CHAPTER 1

Exploring Classroom Assessment

In this book, we describe a journey of discovery. Assessments of student achievement command in excess of a billion dollars of educational resources in the US each year and are becoming very prominent forces in the setting of educational policy at international, national, state and local levels. Yet we still have so much to learn about whether or how these assessments really influence students' learning. To fill some of the gaps in our assessment wisdom, several years ago, we set out on a journey to explore the nature, quality and influences of one as yet unexplored part of this vast and growing assessment world: those assessments developed and used by teachers in their classroom on a day-to-day basis. This book details what we found. It can be read as if it were a journal in which we describe our travels: the people we met along the way, the assessment practices they use, their feelings about those assessments, how they use their assessments and their assessment-related needs.

We departed on this journey because these are times of profound change in education—times of "school improvement," and the pursuit of educational excellence. Clearly our innovations cannot succeed, we surmised, if assessments of educational outcomes are inadequate. But what assessments need to be of high quality? Is it just the highly visible, politically important standardized tests that must be sound? They certainly seem to command sufficient research and development resources to ensure high quality. But, we asked ourselves, what about the rest of the assessments that shape student learning: teachers' classroom assessments? Do they need to be of high quality too? Are they sound now? They seem to be so critical to student well-being. Not only are they one of our indicators of educational *outcomes*, but these classroom assessments also are part of the very instructional *treatments* that produce the desired outcomes.

However, our initial forays into the research literature on the nature and quality of classroom assessment (described in detail in Chap. 2) revealed very few meaningful studies, and those that had been completed foreshadowed the possibility of serious quality control problems.

And so, armed with our intense curiosity and a supply of research tools, we launched our adventure into a process of understanding. We began with research methods that relied on interviews and questionnaires. These provided us with a general outline of teachers' assessment practices. But we wanted and needed a much higher resolution picture. So we turned to indepth studies of classroom assessment environments using ethnographic research methods (after we labored to learn about these methods). As these more powerful methods allowed us to move from broad strokes to finer lines, our focus began to improve and details began to emerge.

In time, we came to understand that our adventure and the insights it was producing were allowing us to create an ever sharper and more colorful portrait of what appeared to be a sleeping giant—the truly huge and complex world of classroom assessment. As the picture gained clarity, we were forever transformed both as researchers and professionals in the field of educational measurement.

We were startled by the complexity of what we found and awed by the scope of teachers' need for help. We were encouraged by their desire to improve their assessments. We were both tantalized and frightened by the anticipation of what might result if the giant awoke and demanded to be served. But, from the outset, we were committed to making that happen. This volume represents our attempt to sound the alarm.

THE CRITICAL ROLE OF ASSESSMENT IN TIMES OF CHANGE

As we enter the decade of the 1990s, reforms are sweeping education as never before. Most of the basic underlying assumptions and key ingredients of the teaching and learning process are being reexamined (Shulman 1986). In effect, we are reconsidering everything from the knowledge and skills that comprise the teaching profession to the very way we organize schools and use instructional time. At the same time, we are conducting an equally intense and every bit as important reexamination of the role and training of school administrators, as we strive to come to terms with the meaning of the concept of instructional leadership.

The one constant during this reevaluation of education is the fact that schools and educators are to be held accountable for students' attainment of educational outcomes. School reforms are to be tested in terms of their impact on students. This fact has stimulated several very exciting developments.

For example, virtually every professional association of teachers in every subject matter area spent considerable time and effort at the national level in the 1980s defining the achievement targets they want students to hit. The clarity and quality of the resulting goal statements is far superior to those developed in the past. Clearer targets are easier for students to hit and easier to assess well.

In addition, concern for accountability has given rise to innovative thinking about alternative forms of assessment. New forms of paper and pencil and performance assessment are emerging. This will provide for the proper translation of a broader array of valued outcomes into sound assessment.

The optimist says assessment will drive instruction in the future and new and better assessments are being developed to do the job. But the cautious optimist says this will only happen if educators at all levels understand the difference between sound and unsound assessment and can integrate sound assessments into the instruction process in effective ways. As our research results will reveal, there is reason to believe that neither teachers nor administrators—those who make schools happen—can meet these standards.

The challenge we faced in initiating this program of research was to find ways to help them. None of the currently popular school reforms, whether they be "outcome-based education," the "restructuring of schools," "instructional theory into practice (ITIP)," special programs for "at-risk youth," or any other attempt at innovation, can be (or has been) properly evaluated unless and until they have been evaluated in terms of their ability to help more students hit more clearly articulated and carefully assessed achievement targets.

We can only build a foundation of solid understanding of critical assessment issues with and for practitioners if we come to understand the real-world assessment demands they face. We build our emerging structure of school reform and improvement on a foundation of sand if we choose to remain uninformed about the nature, role and quality of classroom assessment.

A ROAD MAP

Our journey into the domain of classroom assessment was long and complex. For this reason, we provide a road map here at the outset to assist the reader. The chapters that follow describe a series of studies in the order in which they were carried out. Each study was influenced by those that preceded it and, in turn, influenced those that followed. The road map provided below outlines each study in terms of the question(s) of interest, why the questions were important, the research methodology employed and a very brief overview of results. The story that unfolds for the reader evolves very much as it did for us as we progressed along the way.

We began our investigations in the early 1980s with a comprehensive analysis of prior research on school testing with the intent of gleaning important insights about assessment in the classroom. In Chapter 2, we detail the results of our initial exploration of the literature. Two bodies of work were tapped, research on the use of tests in schools and research on the teaching and learning process. In the latter case, we concentrated on the emerging research on teacher decision making in the classroom and their use of assessment data in that context.

Our first conclusion was that the literature was shallow. Almost every study of school testing focused on the use of standardized test results in schools. Classroom assessment drew very little attention. However, two key points seemed to emerge. Teachers assess a great deal and student well-being in the classroom hinges on the quality of teachers' assessments. We also found evidence of quality control problems with classroom assessments and clear indications that the educational measurement community is unaware of some fundamental differences between assessment in the context of large-scale testing programs and assessment in the classroom.

This led us to our first exploration of classroom assessment processes, described in Chapter 3. We relied on two forms of teacher self-report data collection methods to help us begin to understand the assessment experience from the teachers' perspective. First, we conducted a national survey of teachers' uses of and concerns about paper and pencil assessment methods, performance assessments and published, standardized tests. Second, we enlisted several teachers to serve as research partners. They kept daily journals in which they described important assessment events in their classrooms.

The results provided our first insights into the student characteristics teachers assess, why they assess, and how they do so. We also were able to detect differences in assessment approaches across teachers teaching at different grade levels and in different subject matter areas. However, paradoxically, we found that individual teachers are quite stable in their assessment methods, even when they assess in different subjects. In addition, our first investigation provided our first clear evidence that teachers are concerned about the quality of their own assessments.

This start told us what teachers *say* they do by way of assessment. We wanted to know more about what they *actually* do. So we moved beyond self-report data to the direct observation of classroom assessment process. In Chapter 4, we describe our first attempt to see assessment happening for ourselves. Three members of the NWREL research staff—all of whom had sound assessment backgrounds, but none of whom had prior public school teaching experience—became participant observers for ten weeks in three separate and quite different sixth-grade classrooms. Our mission was to describe achievements assessed, purposes for assessment, methods, results, and use of assessment results.

We obtained our first detailed portraits of immense complexity of classroom assessment environments. We surmised that the reason prior assessment researchers had not delved into this arena must have been the fear of trying to come to terms with and make sense of this immense complexity. The similarities and differences we found in our three observational experiences provided many long and enjoyable hours of story telling at weekly research team meetings. We were awed and fascinated.

In an initial attempt to come to terms with the complexity we found, we endeavored to create a written framework to use in profiling the important aspects of what we came to refer to as "classroom assessment environments." Our profiling scheme is presented in detail in Chapter 5. It breaks classroom assessment environments down into fine detail, covering eight major dimensions and dividing those into over 400 specific features. We were determined to come to terms with the complexity. We were certain our framework could be used to analyze the assessment environment in any classroom.

In Chapter 6 we describe our initial attempts to do just that. We took the framework to school and profiled the assessment environments in eight high school classrooms, two each in four subject matter areas: mathematics, science, social studies and language arts. We sought to describe each environment thoroughly and test the sensitivity of the framework to differences across classrooms.

Limitations in space did not permit us to include all of the profiles in this volume. However, in Chapter 6, we present one complete profile and compare it to the profile of another class on another subject taught by the same teacher. The results illustrate the extreme complexity of this aspect of classroom life, but also reveal in sharp detail how that complexity can be described so as to capture both their richness and variation.

And then to fill-in some detail about the remaining six classroom profiles, we devote Chapter 7 to describing the contrasts we found among the remaining assessment environments. This chapter reveals the sensitivity of the profiling process to differences across classrooms and portrays more clearly than ever before the richness of school testing when considered from the classroom perpective. In effect, in this presentation, we turn the spotlight on aspects of assessment in schools not previously examined and are able to reveal both strengths and weaknesses in the assessments of these teachers.

In Chapter 8 we present our first attempts to take parts of the framework and study each with more powerful microscopes. One such attempt relied on classroom observations and assessment document analysis to describe teachers' assessments of student thinking across ten grades and in four different subject matter areas. The other used similiar information-gathering strategies to uncover precise details about the extent to which the report card grading practices of a small number of high school teachers conform to suggested principles of sound grading practice. We use these two studies to illustrate the kind of detail needed to understand both the assessment competencies teachers need and the extent to which those competencies often are missing.

In the final two chapters, we explore the implications of the classroom assessment research we have completed to date. Chapter 9 addresses implication for the professional preparation of teachers. We spell out in detail both what it is that teachers and their supervisors need to know about assessment in order to manange classroom assessment environments effectively, and how little they are taught about this topic in undergraduate, graduate, preservice and inservice training programs. Specific action programs are proposed to change this critical aspect of teacher preparation.

And in Chapter 10 we explore the implications of our work for assessment policy and future research on classroom assessment. Policy issues addressed include standards for teacher and administrator licensing and certification, standards for the evaluation of teacher performance, the development of building and district staffing plans to help teachers meet the challenges of classroom assessment, and the allocation of limited assessment resources to assure the quality of both large-scale standardized and classroom assessments. In addition, we seek to stimulate additional research on classroom assessment by identifying and discussing important questions about classroom assessments, their quality and use that remain unanswered.

With this map in mind, then, explore with us the meaning and importance of high-quality classroom assessment.

CHAPTER 2

The Research Context

This research effort took root in the early 1980s in a measurement research and development environment that was totally dominated by concern for issues related to the design, development and improvement of large-scale standardized assessments. In fact, one might speculate that large-scale assessment priorities had dominated the field so thoroughly for so long that scholars had failed to even sense, let alone acknowledge, there might be a different set of priorities related to other uses of assessment, such as in the classroom.

Scholars in any field of inquiry adopt a set of conventions for research design and concept development to increase their communication efficiency and research productivity. Those conventions define the dominant paradigm for that field of study:

> a paradigm is an implicit, unvoiced and pervasive commitment by a community of scholars to a conceptual framework. In a mature science, only one paradigm can be dominant at a time. It is shared by that community and serves to define proper ways of asking questions . . . [and of identifying] those common "puzzles" that are defined as the tasks of research [in that field] (Shulman, 1986, p. 4).

What paradigm has guided scholarship in educational measurement? Available evidence suggests that the dominant view has regarded measurement in education as a means of documenting student achievement by using collections of standardized paper and pencil test items. As we began our research, we found evidence of the dominance of this conceptualization in research reported in scholarly journals and in published standards of accepted professional practice.

At that time, nearly all major studies of testing in the schools had focused on the role of standardized tests (Airasian, Kellaghan, Madaus, and Pedulla, 1977; Fyans, 1985; Goslin, 1967; Kellaghan, Madaus and Airasian, 1982; Lortie, 1975; Rudman et al., 1980; Salmon-Cox, 1981; Sproul and Zubrow, 1982; Stetz & Beck, 1979; and Tollefson et al., 1985). Further, in a special 1983 issue of the *Journal of Educational Measurement* on the "state of the art integrating testing and instruction," the editor introduced the issue as follows:

> Linking testing and instruction is a fundamental and enduring concern in educational practice . . . . Fundamental questions about how well achievement test items reflect both student knowledge and the content of instruction are clearly at the heart of the matter . . . [yet] The contributors [to this special issue] were asked to limit their conception of achievement testing to include standardized achievement tests, curriculum embedded or locally developed domain-referenced and proficiency tests, and state assessments. *Thus, teacher-made tests . . . were systematically excluded* [italics added] (Burstein, 1983, p. 99).

Further, the only written standards on acceptable testing practice were the *Standards for Educational and Psychological Tests* (Standards, 1985) that detail the ethical responsibilities of publishers of standardized paper and pencil tests. In addition, the primary source of public analysis of educational tests was the Buros *Mental Measurements Yearbook* series, which deals only with published tests.

The dominance of this measurement paradigm over the past four decades testifies to its utility. As Coffman (1983) and Calfee and Drum (1976) point out, it has afforded education an image of scientific precision and ultimately has fostered a tradition of scientific inquiry in educational research and psychometric theory. Politically, it has given educational measurement a visible role as the criterion of effectiveness of schools in our society. The coin of the realm in determining the value of schools was and is the standardized test score.

However, when we viewed the totality of teachers' classroom assessment activity, it became clear that the dominant measurement paradigm was too narrow and restrictive. The kind of measurement referenced under that paradigm represented only a small fraction of the assessments that take place in schools and that influence the quality of schooling and student learning. Unfortunately, due to the narrow scope of measurement research at that time, we knew little about the nature, role, or quality of the preponderance of school assessment: that which is developed and used by teachers in the classroom.

Although we were in an outstanding position to construct and administer high-quality, large-scale testing programs in the early 1980s, we were far less able to teach teachers how to address the task demands of the day-to-day measurement of student achievement. Measurement is an integral part of the classroom environment. It is a part of the pedagogical process teachers can learn to use effectively, like classroom management and instructional strategies. In short, it is far more than an outcome variable. Yet our scholarship had shed little light on classroom assessment.

Clark and Peterson (1986), after reviewing extensive research on the relationship between teacher behavior and student achievement, were able to draw conclusions about only one small facet of effective teacher-developed assessment practices: the management of oral questioning during recitation or discussion. Those most deeply immersed in the vast and growing body of research on teaching conclude: "In general, the kinds of tests we use are inconsistent with, and in many cases irrelevant to, *the realities of teaching*" (Shulman, 1980, p. 69).

Similarly, Lazar-Morris, Polin, May, and Barry (1980) concluded their comprehensive review of research on testing in the schools as follows:

> In-class assessments made by individual teachers have yet to be examined in depth. How these and other assessments are united with teacher instructional decision-making processes and how they affect classroom organization and time allocation to other objectives are areas that should be explored. Teachers place greater reliance on, and have more confidence in, the results of their own judgments of stu-

dent performance, but little is known about [these] kinds of activities (pp. 24–25).

A similar synthesis of research on testing in high schools, conducted by Haertel et al. (1984), led to the conclusion that we know a good deal about teachers' attitudes about norm-referenced, standardized tests, but little else about teacher or student perceptions of the day-to-day tests used in schools.

The unfortunate consequence of this neglect of classroom assessment was that the measurement field was not in a position to take advantage of a golden opportunity to contribute to current school improvement efforts by improving classroom assessment. This, then, was the measurement research environment that framed the series of studies reported herein.

However, our search of the professional literature did allow a few brief glimpses with classroom assessment process through two back windows. One perspective came to us from research on school testing and the other from research on the role of teacher decision making in the domain of research on the teaching/learning process. We summarize the insights derived from both in this chapter.

INSIGHTS FROM RESEARCH ON TESTING

Although research on testing in the schools has tended to concentrate on the role of standardized tests, a few studies provide insights into the nature of the classroom assessment environment. These studies are reviewed in this section, focusing on what they tell us about the nature of classroom assessment, the relative importance of various types of assessment in the classroom, the quality of classroom assessments, and prevailing teacher and student attitudes toward assessment.

Available research provides some very limited insight into the *nature* of classroom assessment. Airasian (1984) summarizes some key dimensions of classroom assessment that have been the focus of inquiry:

- There appear to be two sets of characteristics measured in class-rooms: scholastic variables and social variables (Airasian, Kellaghan and Madaus, 1977; Herbert, 1974; Pedulla, Airasian and Madaus, 1980).

- The relative importance assigned to these two factors varies with grade level, and with social factors seen as more important in elementary school (Salmon-Cox, 1981).

- Teachers "size up" students as individuals, group them very quickly, and these initial estimates remain quite stable (Airasian, Kellaghan, and Madaus, 1977; Rist, 1970).

- Students appear sensitive to these early teacher assessments, learn their positions in the "pecking order" of the class, and respond accordingly (Morrison and McIntyre, 1969; Rist, 1970).

- Teachers interact differently with students they perceive to be of high or low ability (Brophy and Good, 1974).

- Teachers can accurately predict student test performance and thus use standardized test results to corroborate their own judgments (Kellaghan, Madaus, and Airasian, 1982).

Three in-depth studies of the characteristics of teacher-made tests have been conducted. Fleming and Chambers (1983) analyzed nearly 400 teacher-developed tests including thousands of test items and drew these conclusions about the qualities of teachers' paper and pencil tests:

- Teachers use short-answer questions most frequently in their test making.

- Teachers, even English teachers, generally avoid essay questions, that represent slightly more than 1% of all test items reviewed.

- Teachers use more matching items than multiple-choice or true-false items.

- Teachers devise more test questions to sample knowledge of facts than any of the other behavioral categories studied.

- When categories related to knowledge of terms, knowledge of facts, and knowledge of rules and principles are combined, almost 80% of the test questions reviewed focus on these areas.

- Teachers develop few questions to test behaviors that can be classified as ability to make applications.

- Comparison across school levels shows that junior high school teachers use more questions to tap knowledge of terms, knowledge of facts, and knowledge of rules and principles than do elementary or senior high school teachers. Almost 94% of their questions address knowledge categories, versus 69% of the senior high school teachers' questions and 69% of the elementary school teachers' questions (p. 32).

In another study, Carter (1984) studied the test development skills of 310 high school teachers and reported that teachers had great difficulty recognizing items written to measure specific skills, especially higher order thinking skills. She also reported that teachers learned to write original items at higher skill levels very slowly and felt insecure about their test making capabilities.

Other studies of testing in the schools reveal the relative *importance* teachers attach to various assessment types. For instance, they rely on their own assessments as the primary source of information on student achievement. This point is illustrated in research by Morine-Dershimer (1979) and Joyce (1979a, 1979b), as summarized by Shulman (1980). The investigation focused on teacher reactions to performance data provided by a state-mandated diagnostic testing program. Test results detailed individual student performance on specific objectives and suggested materials for remediation. After allowing teachers several days to process the results, interviewers contacted the ten teachers to explore how the information was used. Not one of the ten teachers in the study had even looked at the results. They already knew the needs of their students and were certain the new tests would provide no new insights.

Studies conducted at the Center for the Study of Evaluation (Dorr-Bremme and Herman, 1986 and Yeh, 1978) suggest that, depending on grade level, one-third to three-quarters of assessments used in classrooms are teacher-developed (see Table 2.1). Those assessments include far more than collections of paper and pencil test items. In an earlier study, Herman and Dorr-Bremme (1982) reported that nearly every survey respondent in a national study reported that "my own observations and students' classwork" were a crucial or important source of information.

In another study, Salmon-Cox (1980) concluded that teachers,

TABLE 2.1
TIME ON DIFFERENT TESTS, AS A PERCENTAGE OF THE
TOTAL STUDENT TIME DEVOTED TO TEST-TAKING

Type of Test	Elementary Teachers		Tenth Grade English Teachers	Tenth Grade Mathematics Teachers
	Reading	Math		
Tests which form part of a statewide assessment program	3%	3%	5%	1%
Required minimum-competency tests	1	2	1	1
Tests included with curriculum materials	28	35	8	17
Other commercially published tests	17	18	6	3
Locally developed- and district-adopted tests	13	8	5	2
School- or teacher-developed tests	37	35	74	76

Source: Dorr-Bremme and Herman (1986), p. 18, reprinted by permission.

when talking of how they assess their students, most frequently mention "observation." Clearly, she contends, this favored technique is quite different from the kind of information provided by standardized tests. In a subsequent study, Salmon-Cox (1981) found that, of eighty-seven high school teachers she interviewed, 44 percent reported using their own tests for evaluating students, 30 percent used interaction, 21 percent relied on homework, 6 percent used observation and one reported using standardized tests. Further, Kellaghan, Madaus, and Airasian (1982) concluded their international research on use of standardized test information by suggesting that such information is a secondary criterion in teacher judgment. Teachers in their study stated that the most common grouping criteria were the teachers' own observations and tests.

Research on testing in the schools has provided very little information concerning the quality of teacher-developed assessments. Further, that which is available is quite narrow in scope. For instance, we can infer that some teacher-developed assessments have validity, since they allow some teachers accurately to predict student performance on standardized achievement tests (Fyans, 1985; Kellaghan et al., 1982). Further, teachers often feel their tests are valid (Farr & Griffin, 1973).

However, there are some indications of problems with quality. For instance, Fleming and Chambers (1983) and Carter (1984) cite a need for teachers to write better test items, particularly items that are less ambiguous and require more of students than the simple recall of facts and information. Fleming and Chambers also offer some preliminary evidence that teacher-developed tests are very short; that is, they contain a minimal number of items.

Gullickson's (1982; Gullickson and Ellwein, 1985) studies of midwestern teachers' testing strategies provide further evidence of a lack of quality control strategies. For example, few of the teachers he surveyed computed summary statistics needed to evaluate test performance. Most limited test questions to short-answer and matching, testing lower cognitive levels. Few teachers took time to improve their tests, and usually reused items without careful item analysis. Overall, Gullickson concluded that teachers have not been taught how to evaluate their test items, take necessary steps to improve quality, or accurately set criterion levels for student performance. Further, they do not value statistical analysis of test items as a helpful strategy in the classroom (Gullickson, 1984a, 1984b).

Although most research on testing in the schools has focused on attitudes toward standardized tests, a few studies allow us to draw some conclusions about teacher and student attitudes toward classroom assessment. Some of those attitudes are reflected in the patterns of test use among teachers. Teachers value assessments that provide information relevant to the decisions they may face. Interviews of thirty-five elementary school teachers conducted by Salmon-Cox (1980) illustrate this point. The teachers judged students even in the absence of formally communicated information. They sometimes gave social and background characteristics greater emphasis than ability. And observation of students was the most frequent mode of assessment for these teachers. Salmon-Cox (1981) concluded that "teacher preference, in effect, is for continuous movies, with sound, while a test score or even a profile of scores, is more akin to a black and white photograph."

This conclusion is reinforced in data reported by Dorr-Bremme and Herman (1986) in which a national sample of teachers rated the importance (4 pt. scale, 4 high) of various forms of assessment in making various classroom decisions. As seen in Table 2.2, clearly they prefer their own assessments and rely most heavily on teacher observation and opinion.

Student attitudes about standardized tests have been studied to some extent, but again until very recently, researchers have expressed little interest in exploring student perceptions of teacher-developed assessments. A study of standardized tests by Stetz and Beck (1979) included some student-directed questions about classroom assessment. Their results suggest that students are more concerned about teacher-made than standardized tests. Most students thought teacher-made tests were harder, and twice as many got nervous before a teacher-made test. The analysis by Haertel et al. (1984) of questionnaire responses of over 600 high school students provides a more comprehensive perspective. They concluded that:

> Students conceive of tests as limited to formal, paper and pencil assessments, usually asking objective questions, and quite separate from ongoing instruction. The purpose of testing is primarily to assign marks and grades. While students consider tests important and are willing to work to earn high scores, they see tests as requiring mostly memorization, perhaps to the detriment of other types of learning.
>
> Students understand that there should be more to schooling outcomes than answering multiple-choice questions; over half recognize that many important ideas are not tested at all. Nonetheless, while students may feel that they know more than their test scores show, they are most comfortable with the familiar true-false and objective types of items; they dislike testing formats that require more extensive response (p. 29).

TABLE 2.2
IMPORTANCE OF TEST RESULTS AND OTHER INFORMATION
IN CLASSROOM DECISIONS

Decision Area	Standardized Test Batteries	District Continuum or Minimum Competency Tests	Tests Included with Curriculum	Teacher-Made Tests	Teacher Observations/ Opinions
			—Elementary—		
Planning teaching at beginning of the school year	2.53	2.60	—	—	3.39
Initial grouping or placement of students	2.51	2.59	2.91	3.12	3.58
Changing a student from one group or curriculum to another, providing remedial or accelerated work	2.52	2.52	3.04	3.12	3.66
Deciding on report card grades	1.62	1.81	2.89	3.38	3.69

			—Secondary—		
Planning teaching at the beginning of the school year	2.22	2.38	—	—	3.59
Initial grouping or placement of students	2.28	2.46	2.48	3.04	3.84
Changing students from one group or curriculum to another, providing remedial or accelerated work	2.52	2.59	2.67	3.27	3.61
Deciding on report card grades	1.36	1.45	2.29	3.65	3.68

Source: Dorr-Bremme and Herman (1986), p. 39, reprinted by permission.

Fortunately, we did not have to rely only on research on school testing to inform us about classroom assessment. We also could turn to the rapidly growing body of research on the teaching process and teacher decision making for additional insights.

INSIGHTS FROM RESEARCH ON TEACHING

Research on teaching has focused on relationships between teacher behavior and student outcomes, relationships between student behavior and learning, classroom processes, and or the cognitions of students and teachers as instruction proceeds (Shulman, 1986). Although contemporary research on teaching has not focused specifically on effective classroom assessment, it does provide some interesting, useful insights to supplement what research on testing has shown us about the nature of the classroom assessment environment.

Summaries of research on teaching compiled by Shavelson and Stern (1981), Clark and Peterson (1986), Shulman (1986), and Berliner (1987) instruct us in two ways. First, by providing a window into teacher decision-making processes, they allow us to see the complexity of the teacher's classroom assessment task. Second, by using this window we can explore the nature and role of assessment before, during, and after instruction. From this vantage point we can see the great challenges teachers face in accurately assessing student characteristics.

For instance, research on teaching tells us that assessment is unquestionably one of teachers' most complex and important tasks. Each investigation of the teaching process arises out of a model or conceptualization of teaching and learning. Every model of effective teaching requires that teachers base their instructional decisions on some knowledge of student characteristics. We begin to comprehend the complexity of classroom assessment as we explore the amount of assessment, the range and frequency of teachers' decisions and the plethora of student characteristics teachers must consider in making those decisions.

There is a vast amount of information available to teachers on student achievement during the instructional process. For instance, based on a review of several studies, Gall (1970) estimates the average frequency of questions posed for students in elementary science and social studies lessons to be 150 per hour. These data, combined with the constant flow of assignments, quizzes, tests, and projects, creates an immense flow of information. The teacher's task is to cull through the available data for that information that can serve best in decision making contexts. Berliner (1987) provides a concise summary of the relationship between teacher questioning strategies and student achievement.

Investigations of classroom practices have tended to focus on three major types of decisions, each placing significantly different measurement demands on teachers. These are: preinstruction (preactive, planning) decisions, interactive decisions (made during instruction), and postinstructional decisions. Shavelson and Stern (1981) summarized thirty studies of teacher decision making, identifying the type of instructional decision teachers faced in each and the salient cues those teachers considered in making those decisions. Salient cues represented the specific student characteristics considered. Sixty-six such cues were listed across all studies.

Classifying these cues as representing academic, social, or personality student characteristics, and crossing these with the preinstructional, interactive and postinstructional categories of group decisions, we can develop a frequency count reflecting (a) the extent to which teachers must be able to measure more than academic achievement, and (b) how factors considered vary as a function of the nature of the decision (see Table 2.3).

When faced with planning decisions, teachers placed greatest reliance on academic and ability variables. Decisions made during instruction had antecedents in social interaction with academics, and decisions rendered after instruction considered a variety of salient cues. Clearly teachers were measuring more than achievement. Other student characteristics considered by teachers were such social characteristics as disruptiveness, work habits, consideration, group mood, and participation. Teachers also considered such personal characteristics as motivation, self-esteem, openness, sense of humor, attentiveness, family background, and attitudes.

From a measurement perspective, perhaps the most important point of these lists of nonacademic student characteristics is that these factors are not considered by teachers just in managing dis-

TABLE 2.3
FREQUENCY OF STUDENT CHARACTERISTICS REPORTED IN
RESEARCH BY TYPE AND DECISION CONTEXT STUDIES

| | Decision Context | | | |
Characteristic	Planning	During Instruction	After Instruction	Total
Academic	15	11	2	28
Social	5	15	3	23
Personal	6	4	5	15
Total	26	30	10	66

Summarized from Shavelson and Stern, 1981.

ruptive behavior. They play a role in planning instruction, managing interactive exchanges, and making evaluative judgments about students. Further, when teachers gather information about these factors, they have no published standardized tests or guidelines on which to rely. They are left to their own devices with little support or training.

Most models of interactive decision making posit the teacher observing some form of student behavior or performance and comparing it to a standard to see if it is within tolerance (Clark and Peterson, 1986; Shavelson and Stern, 1981; Yinger, 1977). These decisions occur frequently. For instance, Clark and Peterson synthesized six studies and concluded that teachers make an interactive decision on average every two minutes. To understand the measurement implications of this pace and the importance for learners, consider that in half of these decisions teachers have antecedent thoughts based on concerns about the learner, including comparisons of behavior, knowledge, and so forth, with expectations or standards (Clark and Peterson, 1986, and Marland, 1977). In this context, the teacher must either assess very rapidly with validity and reliability, or rely on an existing reservoir of valid, reliable information. Surely this is an assessment and information processing task of immense proportions.

Teachers use a wide range of interactional cues to assess their students. However, ethnographic research on classroom interaction suggests that many of these teacher judgments inappropriately incorporate the level of congruence between student behavior and teacher expectation, resulting in potential misdiagnosis of student ability and achievement. Erickson (1977) has described this interactional congruence factor as "assessment of the intellectual competence of children on the basis of social performance" (p. 64), and found that teachers use cues such as the ways children sit, talk, listen, and respond to instructions to develop a "typology" of the kinds of students in the class.

There is an abundance of ethnographic research demonstrating how children's interactional behavior in the classroom varies according to the conversation rules and the patterning of parent-child communication in the home. Among American Indian children, for example, direct questioning will commonly evoke silence, whether or not the child knows the answer, since assertive demonstration of knowledge is not seemly in the Indian home (DuMont and Wax, 1969; Philips, 1972). Analogously, unwillingness to dispute a claim or engage in debate may not justify a teacher judgment that an Indian child is inadequately prepared for discussion or unable to analyze the problem posed; familial and tribal interaction patterns rely on much less direct, nonpersuasive ways of expressing dissent and differing from authority figures (Cooley, 1979). African-American children tend also to respond to known-answer questions with silence, especially in test-like situations (Heath, 1982, 1983; Labov, 1970, 1972).

Hawaiian children tend to interrupt each other, co-creating narrative, a pattern that appears to some teachers as off-task and disruptive (Watson-Gegeo and Boggs, 1977). Like their peers and parents, African-American children prefer to tell stories that chain a lengthy series of events together, indirectly defining their theme, rather than creating a narrative around a single topic that is quickly stated as the explicit center of their story (Michaels and Cook-Gumperz, 1979). Teachers in their study concluded that the African-American children could not develop narratives.

Especially for such children, but indeed for all youngsters, the "hidden curriculum" (Gearing and Epstein, 1982) of the early grades is the achievement of an interactional style that is congruent with teacher expectations of on-task behavior. Children must learn to tread the unclear line between too much and too little communication, between responses that are too slow and too fast. Gearing and Epstein found that students' ability to perceive subtle shifts in their teacher's interactional style was a critical factor in the assessment of their general ability. Students who immediately detected when their teacher shifted from a presentation monologue to an answering-soliciting mode were rewarded with positive feedback, whereas those students who did not so quickly perceive the unspoken style shift were unable to compete successfully in word games, and were judged slow learners.

Schultz and Florio (1979) reported that kindergarten students were expected to deduce how they were to behave from their teacher's physical movements throughout the classroom. Unconsciously the teacher used her position in the room as a signal. The teacher judged the youngsters who did not promptly respond to her nonverbal signal indicating, for example, the end of free play and the beginning of clean up or work time, as less promising students.

Mehan (1979, 1980, 1982) has investigated such shifts in behavior required of students if they are to keep up with teachers' interactional expectations. Success in interactional routines such as turn-taking, he argues, is a critical factor in assessment, regardless of students' mastery of the material. Mehan (1982) contrasts the "content" of classroom instruction with the "form." A student may know the content required by the teacher, but failure to wait for his or her turn or failure to bid to answer are both assessed negatively.

> If a student provides correct content without proper form, the student will be sanctioned. A history of such inappropriate behavior can lead the teacher to treat the student negatively. If a student attends to form without an equivalent concern for content, that student loses opportunities to express knowledge. A history of lost opportunities can lead a teacher to believe that a student is inattentive, unexpressive, and the like. It is in this arena that teachers' expectations are built up, and worked out interactionally (p. 80).

As if interactive decision making were not complex enough, we must also consider the pre- and postinstructional decisions teachers face. In this case, however, the research holds a surprise. Although planning is a complex enterprise for teachers, work conducted by Zahorik (1975), Yinger (1977), and others (summarized by Clark and Peterson, 1986) reveals that teachers tend not to focus on assessments of student characteristics when they plan. Nor do they focus on goals and objectives. The instructional activity is most often the planning unit. Teachers focus on activities and content—what they will do and cover. Shulman (1980) explores the implications of these data for measurement and evaluation:

> For years, those of us in educational research, especially in evaluation and measurement, have been insisting that teachers learn to think straight educationally. By that we mean they have to learn to think of outcomes stated in terms of behavioral objectives. However . . . teachers appear not to evaluate their day-to-day activity in terms of general assessments of achieved outcomes, but rather attend to variations in student *involvement*. When we ask teachers, "What did you achieve today?" they are inclined to say, "Well, we covered three more pages of math and the kids were really involved." We then become critical and berate teachers for not thinking in terms of objectives—which ones they achieved and which not. I believe we have to treat the teachers' observations as data rather than as sources for blame. That is how teachers evaluate what they do (p. 70).

When teachers do focus on student characteristics during planning, it is often only early in the year and is done very quickly and efficiently. Calderhead (1983) and Salmon-Cox (1980) point out that experienced teachers become very proficient at using available information to understand their new class almost before it arrives in the classroom. However, these rapid conclusions based on scant data can have detrimental effects. Peterson and Barger (1985) suggest that teachers may become fixed on initial impressions based on unreliable, inaccurate information, and use subsequent data to maintain a consistent picture of the student.

Given this impressive array of decision contexts and student characteristics, teachers must act decisively to make the assessment task manageable. Research on teaching provides some clues as to how they do this. Simon (1957) suggests that, when faced with an overload of information to process, teachers simplify their view of reality to create a manageable task. Teachers find thinking strategies that allow them to process and store information efficiently, often as a reflex action.

For example, teachers sometimes reduce the number of assessments by tapping group rather than individual data. Dahlof and Lundgren (1970) found teachers identifying a "steering group," a subset of students in the class with whom they could check for dependable information on whether to repeat instruction or proceed to the next topic. Jackson (1968) illustrated the nature of some of the group cues teachers use:

> Oh, look at their faces . . . they look alert, they look interested, they look questioning. They look like they're anxious to learn more about it. . . . And other times you know you haven't done a good job when they look blah or disinterested or [show an] I don't care attitude (p. 22).
>
> A theatrical sense is something that you can't learn, but a good actor can sense his audience. He knows when a performance is going well or not going well, simply by the feeling in the air. And it's that way in the classroom. You can feel when the kids are resistant (p. 122).

As mentioned earlier, it appears that teachers gather information quickly and form it into impressions of student ability very early in the school year (Calderhead, 1983). Once those judgments are made, assessment of ability ceases, leaving those impressions in place and allowing the teacher to move on to other aspects of assessment. There is also evidence that teachers turn to characteristics that are most easily measured, such as social behavior and task completion, that often become as crucial as achievement in classroom assessment (Weiner and Kukla, 1974). And when teachers measure achievement they focus on those levels of achievement best measured with item formats that are efficient to use, such as recall of facts (Fleming and Chambers, 1983).

Shavelson, Caldwell, and Izu (1977) conducted a laboratory-based experiment to determine whether teachers reconsider their initial estimates of student abilities when presented with new information, and whether they consider the reliability of information when making judgments. Teachers did revise estimates of students when presented with new, differing information and showed appropriate sensitivity to the reliability of information sources. Similarly, some studies, such as Kellaghan et al. (1982) and Fyans (1985), comment favorably on teachers' ability to correctly judge students' achievement and estimate students' performance on standardized tests.

Other studies, however, recount numerous problems in teachers' judgments. For example, Brophy and Good (1970) conclude that teachers' expectations of students clearly correlated with differential patterns of interaction between teacher and student. After coding the behavior of teachers and students, the researchers noted that teachers consistently favored perceived high achievers over perceived low achievers in demanding and reinforcing quality performance. Students perceived as high achievers were more frequently praised when correct and less frequently criticized when incorrect or unable to respond. Later, Good and Brophy (1978) verified these results and further indicated that teachers were totally unaware of their differing levels of interchange with students whom they judged to have different abilities.

Weinshank (1980), in a multiphased investigation of the clinical problem-solving skills of reading and learning disability specialists, discovered surprisingly low diagnostic and remedial reliability among specialists. Weinshank noted that the mean agreement between any two clinicians on a given case was no more than would have occurred by chance. Surprisingly, clinicians were almost as unlikely to agree with themselves when presented with a replicate case, as they were with other clinicians.

Rudman et al. (1980) also recounted similar investigations that substantiate low reliability in diagnostic evaluations of students by reading specialists. Research by Gil and Freeman (1980) confirms the inadequacy of teachers' judgment procedures in natural and laboratory settings. After observing and interviewing teachers, the researchers concluded that teachers lack information-processing strategies to make complete, specific diagnoses.

Whitmer (1983), in studying the judgment process of five elementary school teachers during marking, found an emphasis on completion of tasks rather than quality of outcomes. These teachers failed to consider the level of task difficulty in grading students or to weight tasks or assignments in deriving summative grades.

Their emphasis on expediency and simplicity in grading, often at the expense of discrimination about student work, reinforces the assumption that teachers' evaluation practices lack rigor and possibly appropriateness.

These findings from research on teaching are preliminary, arising from a few studies that focus on a narrow set of subjects and grades. Very few teachers have been studied with respect to the reliability of their assessments and judgments. But there exists the danger of fallible assessment information, especially in the fast-paced assessment and decision making world described in this research. In this case, the impact will fall directly on the achievement of individual learners and their academic and personal self-concept.

THE UNMET CHALLENGE

Regardless of the depth of information in these summaries, at least one point became obvious: Teachers trained only in paper and pencil measurement methods face real difficulties. Both oral questions and performance assessments (observations and judgments) play key roles in classroom assessment. There are fundamental, far-reaching differences between the science of standardized testing and the assessment demands of the classroom. We had been aware of these differences for decades and still in the early 1980s had failed to address them.

In 1943, Scates clearly articulated key discrepancies between the science of measurement and classroom assessment. We take the liberty of quoting extensive passages from the paper because they vividly convey issues that seem still to be neglected.

> In the main, science is concerned with abstracting a specific element out of a complex—with isolating a character that is common to a group of objects, and freeing the character from restrictions of immediate circumstance. The teacher's concern is just the opposite. He is working with variable individuals to build a variable product (p. 3).
>
> The scientist may be satisfied with a series of cross-sectional observations; the teacher must be aware of continuing behavior. The scientist is primarily analytical, seeking the elemental, the universal,

the permanent; the teacher is primarily constructive, seeking to produce an artistic whole that is unique and changeful (p. 4).

The scientist must be strictly uniform, insofar as he can, in his observations. He must have an observational instrument which will reflect the same trait or quality in every instance and in the hands of every observer. . . . The teacher, on the other hand, with much greater tolerance granted him, has no such interest in either objectivity or precision. . . . Impersonal observations may have a more universal quality but they are also more barren. . . . [Thus] the things that science wants *out* of its observations the teacher wants *in* (pp. 5–6).

Formal testing cannot be continuous, but the need for watchful observation and interpretation (on the part of the teacher) is continuous. . . . Some tendencies (among students) are revealed by only fleeting manifestations. . . . The teacher must detect changes in attitude, in effort, in cooperative spirit as quickly as they begin to manifest themselves. . . . An author cannot wait until his book sells to write the second chapter; an artist cannot wait until his picture is judged before deciding its composition; and a teacher cannot wait until his pupil is tested before deciding what to do the next hour or the next day (p. 7–8).

The test maker who begins his thinking with the teacher's problems and utilizes technical principles where they will aid, without letting the principles warp his product out of conformity to the practical needs, is bridging the gap between the two situations. But the test maker or the textbook writer who approaches the problem of appraisal by asserting his convictions that all units on a scale must be equal, that a test must be objective, highly reliable, and statistically valid . . . is just not focusing on the practical problem (p. 13).

The question that guided the research reported in the chapters that follow is, what is the "practical problem" to which Scates refers? Precisely what are the task demands of classroom assessment? What are the active ingredients in the assessment dimension of a classroom assessment environment? How do (should) those ingredients vary across grades, subjects, teachers and/or differing levels of student achievement? What do teachers need to know to manage classroom assessment environments effectively and efficiently? Are they trained to do so? And how might we improve their competence and confidence in assessment, if such improvement is needed?

These and other similar issues were not of interest to the field of measurement research at the time we began our program of research. We conducted the research presented in subsequent chapters in part to provide preliminary answers to these questions and in part to focus attention on the unmet challenge of ensuring the quality of classroom assessment day-to-day in all classrooms and schools.

CHAPTER 3

Assessment from the Teacher's Viewpoint

As a first step in answering some of the questions posed at the end of Chapter 2 about the nature and quality of classroom assessment environments, we invited teachers from a range of grades, subjects, and school districts to describe their current patterns of assessment use and concerns about assessment by either (1) completing an extensive questionnaire, or (2) keeping a journal describing assessment practices.

The frequency of use of published tests, teachers' own paper and pencil tests, and structured and spontaneous performance assessments were described, as well as teachers' confidence with each of these methods, the extent to which they rely on the results, and the assessment purposes served by each. When questionnaire responses and journal entries were summarized across teachers, the results suggested that the foundation of classroom assessment consists primarily of teacher-developed assessments, with performance assessment serving as one of the primary tools. Grade level and subject affect assessment practice, but teachers do not appear to differentiate assessment method by purpose of the assessment. Teachers express confidence in their assessment practices, but also voice serious concerns suggesting that improvement may be needed.

In this chapter, the methods and results of the survey and journal studies are presented, along with conclusions drawn from these teachers' self-report data.

STUDY 1: A SURVEY OF TEACHERS' ASSESSMENT PRACTICES*

This research was designed to provide a detailed focused look at teachers' preferences for different assessment tools—published tests, their own paper and pencil objective tests, and performance assessments—the purposes for which each is used, and the reliance teachers place on each as they make judgments about their students.

Research Methodology

Teachers Surveyed. The study probed assessment practices of a stratified sample of teachers selected from eight districts across the country, varying in size and geographic location. Five districts were urban, three suburban; three were in the East, two in the Northwest, and three in the West. Each district was to recruit forty-eight volunteer teachers to complete a comprehensive questionnaire on classroom assessment. Twelve teachers were to be recruited from each of four grades (2, 5, 8, and 11). Of those twelve teachers at each grade level, three were asked to describe the methods they used in measuring writing skills, three the methods used to assess speaking skills, three science skills, and three math achievement. Thus, each respondent described assessment methods in only one subject, and at only one grade level. At elementary levels, respondents were typically responsible for teaching all subjects. At high school levels, respondents were English, speech, math, and science teachers.

All districts responded with completed survey questionnaires; however, the number of completed forms differed substantially across districts. A total of 228 completed questionnaires were received. The respondents were distributed almost equally across grades and subjects.

Although 228 responses represented less than our desired sample of 384, the group was sufficiently large to permit analysis.

---

*This represents a brief synopsis of research reported in much greater detail in Stiggins and Bridgeford (1985).

However, the sample size precluded an analysis of responses by subject area within each grade level—eighth grade science assessment, for example. Analyses of the responses were limited to grade and subject totals (i.e., main effects) only.

The Types of Classroom Assessment Explored. One goal of this research was to determine the role and relative importance of several types of measurement in the classroom: (a) *the teachers' own paper and pencil objective tests,* defined to include teacher-developed multiple-choice, true/false, matching and short answer fill-in tests; (b) *published tests,* defined to include both standardized objective achievement tests and objective tests supplied as part of published text materials; and (c) *performance assessment,* defined as the observation and rating of student behavior as products in contexts where students actually demonstrate proficiency (Stiggins, 1984).

In the research, we distinguish between structured and spontaneous performance assessments. The former is planned and systematically designed to include prespecified purposes, exercises, observations, and scoring procedures. The latter arises spontaneously from the naturally occurring classroom environment and leads the teacher to a judgment about an individual student's level of development.

Performance assessments have several important characteristics. First, students are called upon to apply the skills and knowledge they have learned. Second, performance assessment involves completion of a specified task (or tasks) in the context of real or simulated assessment exercises. Third, the assessment task or product completed by the examinee is observed and rated with respect to specified criteria, in accordance with specified procedures.

To ensure that teachers understood the meaning of each type of assessment covered in the questionnaire (reproduced in Appendix A), they were provided with concise definitions of teacher-made objective tests, published tests, structured performance tests, and spontaneous performance assessments at the beginning of the questionnaire. In each case, the teacher was asked to supply an example of each kind of test from his or her experience. If the example revealed that the teacher did not understand the definitions of and distinctions between assessment types, that teacher's responses were not included in the analysis. A small number of booklets from each district (usually 2 or 3) were eliminated for this reason.

Levels of Use. One major set of questions probed teachers' use of each specific assessment option. To determine the extent to which each assessment option was used, we used an adaptation of a scaling system developed by the University of Texas Research and Development Center in Teacher Education (Hall and Loucks, 1978) to pinpoint teachers' level of use of each of the four alternative assessment methods. As a result, each respondent was classified as being at one of these levels of use with respect to each assessment option: nonuse, comfortable use, or refining use. Scaling on the teachers' level of use was accomplished by having the respondent answer a branching series of questions about their use of each test type.

Teachers then were asked to describe the relative importance of different test options as a function of their specific purposes for testing; that is, for diagnosis, grouping, grading, evaluating instruction, and reporting achievement results. Each teacher was given 100 points to distribute across the assessment options to show importance for a given purpose. The most important method received the highest number of points.

Types of Concern. We also investigated teachers' concerns about each individual type of test by adapting the "levels of concern model" developed at the University of Texas Research and Development Center (Hall, George, and Rutherford, 1977). This model helps uncover teachers' perceptions of their own assessment needs by asking teachers to identify their primary concern (e.g., lack of information, management issues) about each type of classroom assessment. Each teacher was asked to identify his or her primary concern for each type of test by selecting from among these optional concerns: (a) lack of information, (b) competence—level of skill or experience, (c) time management—amount of time taken, (d) consequences—reactions of students, (e) collaboration—establishing relationships with other teachers, and (f) test improvement and more effective use. Teachers could also report no major concern with respect to any of the assessment types. After selecting a concern, the teachers were asked to specify why that particular one was primary for them.

Results

Results are summarized in several parts. First, we report teachers' patterns of test use and the relative weight teachers assigned to different test types for different purposes. The analysis then turns to teachers' concerns about assessment and reasons for those concerns. The third part of the analysis addresses teachers' use of structured performance assessments, focusing specifically on quality control procedures. In all three cases, data are explored across test type (teacher-made objective, published, structured performance assessment, and spontaneous performance assessment), grade level (2, 5, 8, and 11), and subject area (writing, speaking, science, and math).

The overall goal of the analysis is to describe the classroom assessment practices—use, preferences, attitudes, and role of performance assessment—of these 228 volunteer teachers. Because these teachers may not be representative of the general teacher population and because the practices described reflect what teachers say they do—not necessarily what they actually do—inferences about the testing practices of all teachers are not justified.

To explore the significance of differences in proportions across grade levels and school subjects, contingency analyses were conducted. Each analysis focused on a component of Tables 3.1, 3.2, and 3.3, crossing a set of response categories (e.g., nonuse, anticipated use, etc., of teacher-made objective tests in Table 3.1) with grade or subject. Thus, Table 3.1 included eight analyses and Tables 3.2 and 3.3 included ten analyses each. Discussion of differences focuses only on those components yielding significant X^2, noting those rows showing greatest differences across grade or subject.

Patterns of Test Use. Table 3.1 reports the percentage of respondents at each category on the level of use scale.

Looking first at *teacher-made objective tests*, about half of

TABLE 3.1
LEVEL OF USE BY TEST TYPE, GRADE AND SUBJECT
(in percent of respondents)

Level		Grade				Subject*			Total
		2	5	8	11	WR	SP	SC	MA	Sample
	N	57	58	58	55	58	61	50	59	228

Teacher-made Objective Tests

Level	2	5	8	11	WR	SP	SC	MA	Total
Nonuse	34%	26	17	11	28	31	14	14	26
Use	58	55	53	47	47	40	61	51	49
Refinement	9	19	15	15	14	9	14	20	14

$X^2 = 22.52, p < .01$ $X^2 = 17.07, p < .01$

Published Tests

Level	2	5	8	11	WR	SP	SC	MA	Total
Nonuse	34	29	45	53	41	57	44	17	41
Use	58	63	45	39	45	41	42	76	52
Refinement	9	9	11	8	14	2	14	7	9

$X^2 = 16.65, p < .01$ $X^2 = 52.20, p < .01$

Structured-performance Assessment

Level	2	5	8	11	WR	SP	SC	MA	Total
Nonuse	17	10	16	8	6	17	11	16	12
Use	68	65	62	57	70	62	59	61	63
Refinement	15	26	23	36	25	17	29	24	25

$X^2 = 14.47$, N.S. $X^2 = 10.23$, N.S.

Spontaneous-performance Assessment

Level	2	5	8	11	WR	SP	SC	MA	Total
Nonuse	2	2	0	11	2	3	6	4	4
Use	86	88	84	70	84	88	74	79	82
Refinement	13	11	17	19	14	8	19	18	14

$X^2 = 17.79, p < .01$ $X^2 = 10.71$, N.S.

* WR stands for Writing, SP for Speaking, SC for Science, MA for Mathematics

these teachers report comfortable use. This holds across grades and subjects. The other half of the teachers vary in level of use. For instance, use of teacher-made objective tests tends to increase steadily as grade increases (i.e., nonuse percent declines). Further, math and science teachers tend to use their own objective tests slightly more than writing and speaking teachers.

Regarding *published tests,* again, nearly half report that they use these tests with relative ease, with most of the others reporting that they do not use them at all. There appears to be slightly more use in early grades and appreciably more use in math relative to other subjects.

The levels of use for *performance assessment*—structured and spontaneous—differ from the paper and pencil tests. Eighty-eight percent of these teachers report some use of structured performance tests. Sixty-three percent report comfortable use, with another quarter refining their use of these assessments. Nearly 95 percent of respondents report use of spontaneous performance assessments, with nearly 80 percent reporting comfortable use. All of these patterns seem relatively constant across grades and subjects.

Table 3.2 summarizes the relative importance teachers assigned to the various test types for diagnosing the strengths and weaknesses of individual students, grouping for instruction, assigning grades, evaluating the effectiveness of an instructional treatment and reporting results to parents. Because teachers assigned higher percentages to the methods that contribute most to each decision, these data are hereafter called "reliance percentages" in describing and interpreting the results. The higher the reliance percentage, the more weight given to a type of test for that purpose.

In analyzing the role of each test type for different test purposes certain consistent patterns emerge. For example, teachers indicate they use their own objective tests more frequently than other assessments for all purposes. However, teachers also report heavy reliance on both types of performance assessments. Published tests consistently play a secondary role. Clearly, teacher-made tests dominate.

With a few exceptions, these are relatively stable patterns across grades and subject areas. Across grade levels, teacher-made objective tests and structured-performance tests gradually increase

TABLE 3.2
ROLE OF TEST TYPE AS A FUNCTION OF PURPOSE FOR
ASSESSMENT, REPORTED BY GRADE AND SUBJECT
(in percent of respondents)

Purpose		Grade				Subject*				Total
		2	5	8	11	WR	SP	SC	MA	Sample
	N	57	58	58	55	58	61	50	59	228
Diagnosing OBJ*		25%	27	33	37	24	24	41	34	31
PUB		20	25	12	13	19	14	15	21	17
ST PA		24	23	27	35	37	26	23	22	27
SP PA		32	26	28	15	20	35	21	24	25
		$X^2 = 20.70$, N.S.				$X^2 = 19.53$, N.S.				
Grouping OBJ		26	27	32	32	20	24	36	38	29
PUB		29	32	21	19	28	21	20	30	25
ST PA		18	22	23	32	34	21	20	19	24
SP PA		28	19	24	14	18	33	24	12	22
		$X^2 = 15.22$, N.S.				$X^2 = 28.34$, $p < .01$				
Grading OBJ		29	36	43	48	34	33	46	44	39
PUB		19	22	8	9	14	11	12	20	15
ST PA		23	22	28	34	36	27	24	20	27
SP PA		28	20	17	10	16	24	18	16	19
		$X^2 = 27.41$, $p < .01$				$X^2 = 14.17$, N.S.				
Evaluating OBJ		30	35	36	39	31	33	44	35	35
PUB		19	24	12	14	18	11	15	25	17
ST PA		21	22	32	29	36	28	19	20	26
SP PA		30	20	19	18	15	29	22	20	22
		$X^2 = 13.82$, N.S.				$X^2 = 20.93$, N.S.				
Reporting OBJ		29	30	38	44	29	30	45	38	35
PUB		22	29	14	10	20	14	17	26	19
ST PA		25	23	30	31	35	28	22	23	27
SP PA		26	18	18	14	17	28	18	13	19
		$X^2 = 19.89$, N.S.				$X^2 = 19.32$, N.S.				

* OBJ stands for teacher-made objective tests, PUB for published tests, ST PA for structured-performance assessment, and SP PA for spontaneous-performance assessment.

in importance whereas reliance on published and spontaneous performance tests declines. With respect to subject areas, math and science teachers appear to give more emphasis to their own objective tests, whereas writing teachers rely on structured-performance tests and speaking teachers emphasize the use of spontaneous performance tests.

Concerns About Assessment. Table 3.3 reports teachers' types of concern about different kinds of tests. The percentage of teachers selecting each category as her or his primary concern is reported.

Note that nearly three-quarters of these teachers expressed some concern about their own tests. By far the most common concern about teacher-made objective tests focused on test improvement, reflecting teachers' desire to improve their use of this kind of test. The other common concern is management, reflecting uneasiness with the amount of time required to manage this mode of assessment in the classroom. These teachers tend to be less concerned about a lack of information about these tests, their competence in using them, the student reactions to their use, or collaborating with others in using them. These patterns of concern vary with grade and slightly with subject. For example, about 50 percent of the second grade respondents expressed some concern, while 85 percent of the eleventh grade teachers did so. There is an increasing concern about improvement and management of teacher-made objective tests as grade increases, and for math and science teachers in contrast to writing teachers.

The reason for the teachers' concern about time required to develop and use their own tests is that it interferes with instructional time. Teachers who indicated uneasiness about the objective tests they developed and used posed such questions as: Are my tests effective? How can I make them better? Do they focus on students' real skills? Are they challenging enough? Do they aid in learning?

Fewer teachers expressed specific concerns about published tests. Of those expressing some concern, most were uneasy about (a) student reactions, and (b) improving test use. More eleventh-grade teachers seemed concerned about consequences than teachers at other grades. Concern for improvement is greatest at the eighth-grade level and in speaking assessment relative to other subjects.

TABLE 3.3
SUMMARY OF TYPE OF CONCERN ABOUT ASSESSMENT
BY TEST TYPE, GRADE, AND SUBJECT
(in percent of respondents)

Concern		Grade				Subject			Total
		2	5	8	11	WR	SP	SC	MA	Sample
	N	57	58	58	55	58	61	59	59	228

Teacher-made Objective Tests

Concern	2	5	8	11	WR	SP	SC	MA	Total
No concern	46%	22	30	15	31	35	20	25	28
Lack of information	5	—	—	—	3	2	—	—	1
Competence	2	2	2	—	—	2	2	2	1
Time management	14	22	18	22	24	15	22	15	19
Consequence	—	7	5	7	9	7	2	2	5
Collaboration	4	3	—	7	3	2	2	7	4
Improvement	30	43	45	49	29	38	51	49	42

$X^2 = 26.18$, p $< .01$ $X^2 = 15.65$, N.S.

Published Tests

Concern	2	5	8	11	WR	SP	SC	MA	Total
No concern	41	31	42	38	38	37	32	45	38
Lack of information	5	9	5	9	10	8	10	—	7
Competence	—	3	—	—	2	—	—	2	1
Time management	13	12	5	6	7	5	10	14	9
Consequence	20	17	14	33	19	15	28	22	21
Collaboration	2	3	4	4	3	2	2	5	3
Improvement	20	24	30	11	21	33	18	12	21

$X^2 = 26.61$, p $< .01$ $X^2 = 22.81$, p $< .01$

Structured-performance Assessment

Concern	2	5	8	11	WR	SP	SC	MA	Total
No concern	50	33	35	24	29	44	25	42	35
Lack of information	4	—	4	—	3	2	2	—	2
Competence	4	4	7	2	3	—	10	4	4
Time management	20	21	16	26	21	12	27	25	21
Consequence	2	11	9	6	7	10	10	—	7
Collaboration	—	4	7	6	5	3	2	5	4
Improvement	20	28	23	38	31	29	25	25	27

$X^2 = 19.35$, p $< .01$ $X^2 = 14.97$, N.S.

(continued)

TABLE 3.3 (*Continued*)

Spontaneous-performance Assessment									
No concern	59	48	39	39	41	58	39	46	46
Lack of information	2	2	2	6	3	2	2	4	3
Competence	2	5	7	6	5	3	10	2	5
Time management	9	10	2	4	10	3	6	5	6
Consequence	2	7	5	9	5	5	6	7	6
Collaboration	2	—	2	7	2	2	4	4	3
Improvement	24	28	44	30	33	27	33	33	31
	$X^2 = 13.25$, $p < .01$				$X^2 = 5.65$, N.S.				

Those concerned about student reactions to published tests tended to view these tests as invalid, undependable, too long, and so on, and thus anticipated that the tests were not helpful to students. Those concerned about improving test use viewed published tests as time-consuming, not matching their instruction, failing to reflect true student characteristics, and generally not meeting important instructional needs such as identifying material to teach or reteach.

Expressions of concern about structured performance assessments were similar to those for teacher-made objective tests: improving quality and time management were most crucial. Some grade-level trends appear, with indications that concern for improving such assessments and using them more effectively increases with grade level.

Spontaneous performance assessments elicit the fewest expressions of concern, with only half of the respondents reporting some concern. Most of these were concerned with improvement of the assessments. Again, the frequency of this concern seemed to gradually increase with grade level.

STUDY 2: TEACHERS' CLASSROOM ASSESSMENT JOURNALS

Teachers' responses to the survey questionnaire offered insight into the complexity of the assessment task they face daily in their classrooms. In order to probe more deeply into teachers' assessment practices, attitudes toward assessment, and ability to administer and evaluate valid student assessments, teachers in a graduate course in educational measurement were asked to reflect on their assessment activities as an ongoing process.

Methodology

The teachers were given the following assignment:

> Over the next ten weeks, please keep a journal describing the assessment activities and environment in your classroom. The purposes of this assignment are to (a) raise your level of awareness of how and why you measure student characteristics, and (b) provide me with a profile of how you use your knowledge and skills in the assessment arena.

> The journal is to provide a succinct record of the most important assessments and evaluations you conduct. Therefore, to make the assignment manageable, you are to make only one journal entry each week. That entry is to be made at the end of each week and is to describe the single most important assessment you conducted over the previous week.

> *Important Note.* Please be advised that the most important assessment you conduct need not be a paper and pencil quiz or test— although it may be. The basis of the assessment might be an observation and professional judgment on your part. Further, the assessment need not be a group test. It might focus on an individual student or small group of students. Finally, the assessment need not necessarily be a measure of academic achievement. It might focus on personality, social or affective characteristics. These are all possible candidates for the assessments you describe.

> More specifically, select the most important assessment you conducted and describe it in terms of the following points:

> 1. State the purposes for the assessment and the reason for its importance,

> 2. Summarize what you wanted to measure (e.g., recall of science facts),

3. Describe how you measured it (e.g., true-false tests, observation, etc.) and why you selected that method,

4. Specify the origin of the assessment (e.g., you developed it, text-book, etc.), and

5. Comment on how it worked and how you might revise it in the future.

The twelve elementary (K–6) and twenty secondary and middle school teachers (7–12) who kept journals represented all grade levels and a variety of subjects, both core academic subjects and areas such as art and physical education. Thus, a great diversity of assessment situations was portrayed in journal entries.

Analysis of Journals. The thirty-two journals included some 290 individual assessment activities. In summarizing these, we focused on two major issues: (1) how teachers described the assessments and their outcomes in respect to purposes, methods and characteristics of the assessment; and (2) what specific issues or perspectives they raised about their own assessment process and their classroom assessment environment. Descriptions are summarized below. We recorded the specific characteristics of elementary and secondary teachers' assessments in order to understand what kinds of assessments were being conducted and what teachers relied on most frequently. Five dimensions of the assessment activity were considered:

- what purpose teachers most frequently described and how those purposes differed from elementary to secondary programs,
- what characteristics, such as achievement or aptitude, were being assessed,
- the assessment strategies used,
- special dimensions of the test, that is whether it was planned or spontaneous, obtrusive or unobtrusive, and
- how the assessment was recorded.

Results

A Composite Picture. Although the characteristics of teachers' assessments varied considerably across grade level and subject area, teachers' important assessments were strikingly similar.

For elementary teachers, determining students' mastery was the typical assessment purpose. Student achievement rather than social characteristics, aptitude or personality were the key focus of attention, and observation methods were used more frequently than objective tests. In addition, these elementary teachers usually used progress reports rather than grades or anecdotal records to monitor students' progress. This differed from the typical secondary assessment.

Secondary teachers were preoccupied with grading. They too focused on student achievement or mastery rather than other personal or social characteristics. Secondary teachers were most likely to use a teacher-developed test, planned in advance, rather than other assessment strategies, and results of the assessment were regularly recorded as a grade in the grade book. The following comments and accompanying tables describe each assessment dimension and teachers' responses more thoroughly.

Purpose. Table 3.4 summarizes teachers' purposes for conducting assessments. These range from assigning grades to diagnosing, grouping, and evaluating instruction. In their journals, both elementary and secondary teachers focused almost exclusively on three assessment purposes: assigning grades, judging students' mastery of material, and diagnosing individual and group needs. As Table 3.4 indicates, teachers seldom mentioned other purposes such as sizing up students, grouping, or feedback to parents in these journal entries. In the assessments, teachers' most frequent purpose was grading or determining student mastery (64%). Diagnosing needs was mentioned in only 18 percent of the journal entries, while only 9 percent of secondary entries noted that evaluating instruction was a purpose of the assessment.

Traits Measured. These teachers were primarily interested in judging student achievement. Eighty-three percent of the assessment entries discussed this characteristic; 17 percent recounted evaluating other characteristics such as social abilities or aptitude. As Table 3.5 illustrates, the only other characteristic noted with some frequency is social functioning, e.g., interactions with others, etc. Overall, seven percent of the entries, fairly evenly divided between elementary and secondary teachers, discussed assessing this

TABLE 3.4
ASSESSMENT PURPOSE*

	Elementary		Secondary		Total	
	N	%	N	%	N	%
Assign grades	7	6	73	36	80	25
Diagnose individual and group needs	26	21	33	16	59	18
Sizing up	5	4	—		5	2
Grouping	5	4	2	1	7	2
Selection for program	7	5	3	2	10	3
Feedback to parents	4	3	2	1	6	2
Evaluation of instruction	3	2	18	9	21	6
Control and motivate	1	1	7	4	8	2
Feedback to managers	—		2	1	2	1
Communicate expectations	—		—		—	
Mastery	67	54	60	30	127	39

*Some assessments involved multiple purposes.

characteristic. Interestingly, very few teachers mentioned assessing critical thinking skills in their journal entries; in fact, few referred to the cognitive level of their test questions despite the emphasis in this course on assessing higher cognitive thinking skills. In judging achievement, most teachers appeared to use a criterion-referenced system; only a few indicated that their assessments compared students to one another (norm-referenced system).

Strategies. In this sample, a majority of the key assessment events at both elementary and secondary levels relied on performance assessment (Table 3.6). These were equally divided between product and behavior observation. Of the paper and pencil methods used, clearly, teacher-developed instruments dominated, followed by text-embedded and standardized tests.

Planning of Assessment. This category attempted to describe whether the assessments were planned in advance or were spontaneous, such as an informal observation of a student.

TABLE 3.5
STUDENT CHARACTERISTICS ASSESSED

	Elementary		Secondary		Total	
	N	%	N	%	N	%
Achievement mastery (undefined)	59	48	86	51	145	50
Achievement—criterion-referenced	33	26	46	27	79	27
Achievement—norm-referenced	9	7	9	5	18	6
Aptitude	7	6	4	2	11	4
Higher-cognitive functioning	1	1	2	1	3	1
Social characteristics of individual	11	9	11	6	22	7
of group	—		—		—	
Personality characteristics	1	1	2	2	3	1
Unspecified	1	1	2	2	3	1
Other	1	1	7	4	8	3

TABLE 3.6
ASSESSMENT STRATEGIES USED

	Elementary		Secondary		Total	
	N	%	N	%	N	%
Paper-&-pencil instruments						
Standardized tests	18	16	8	4	26	9
Text-embedded tests	12	10	11	6	23	8
Teacher-developed tests	20	18	53	28	73	24
Performance assessments						
Behavior observation	34	30	57	29	91	29
Product observation	29	26	52	27	81	26
Other	—		12	6	12	4

TABLE 3.7
DEVELOPMENT OF ASSESSMENTS

	Elementary		Secondary		Total	
	N	%	N	%	N	%
Objective tests were:						
Planned	51	94	69	88	120	91
Spontaneous	3	6	9	12	12	9
Performance assessments were:						
Planned	30	59	52	55	82	57
Spontaneous	19	41	41	45	60	43

The overwhelming majority of objective tests and quizzes described in these journals, were planned (Table 3.7). In a few instances, however, teachers talked about giving a quick checkup quiz to measure students' progress. With performance assessments, on the other hand, nearly half were spontaneous, informal observations.

Assessment Record. Teachers' assessment records, as described in Table 3.8, indicate that grades in the gradebook were far and away the most frequent type of record maintained by these teachers. A much smaller percentage describe assessments that involved feedback other than a grade. In addition, a substantial number of teachers did not mention their method of recording assessment results, probably because this aspect of the assessment was not specifically requested in the assignment. When teachers described results they usually discussed how well the students did on the test rather than what record they maintained of results. Few teachers maintained any written records or files of students' work apart from a grade in the gradebook.

In sum, the most important assessments described by these elementary and secondary teachers show the following characteristics. The assessment's purpose, regardless of grade level, primarily focused on judging students' achievement for assigning grades; only 18 percent of these entries discussed using their assessments

TABLE 3.8
THE FORM OF ASSIGNMENT RECORDS

	Elementary		Secondary		Total	
	N	%	N	%	N	%
Grade in book (progress report)	40	38	78	46	118	43
Permanent record	12	11	4	2	16	6
Written comment (form)	13	12	19	11	32	11
Verbal comment	8	8	17	10	25	9
Nonverbal comment	4	4	4	2	8	3
Unspecified	23	22	46	27	69	25
Other	5	5	3	2	8	3

to diagnosis student needs. An even smaller percentage indicated that they used the assessment to evaluate instruction. Although teachers' assessment may look at a range of important student characteristics—achievement, social development, aptitude, higher thinking skills, personality—these teachers were unquestionably more concerned with achievement than any other characteristics. This may relate to both the importance of this characteristic for these teachers and to the relative ease in documenting these assessments because they usually involve specific tests.

These teachers showed that they relied on their own observations to conduct a majority of assessments. These ranged from evaluating oral reading, writing, and map making to art activities and group interactions. Teacher-developed objective tests were the most likely paper and pencil assessments to be described, while text-embedded were least likely to be discussed in the journal entries. Finally most teachers said they recorded assessment results in the gradebook; fewer teachers noted that they provided other kinds of feedback, either written or verbal, to students.

This section gave an overview of teachers' journal assessments, noting the purposes, characteristics, strategies, dimensions and records discussed. Teachers' journals also contained rich descriptive information about their experiences in conducting these assessments. The next section describes teachers' perceptions about this aspect of their assessment experiences.

Teachers' Criticism of Their Assessments

The journal entries were analyzed in search of evaluative comments on how well assessments worked and how they might be improved in the future. The teachers interpreted the directions freely and frequently wrote incomplete descriptions thereby leaving questions about the classroom assessment environment unanswered. Enough information was gathered from teachers' responses, however, to draw the conclusion that teachers are able to criticize assessment processes and outcomes.

They were willing and able to point out the weaknesses in their assessment process. In contrast, they were less skilled in providing any indepth analysis of those weaknesses. If an assessment worked, teachers often voiced pride or enthusiasm, but they seldom pinpointed factors which contributed to success. When an assessment did not work, teachers tended to relate it to instructional issues or problems more often then they did to the adequacy of the assessment.

However, from time to time, teachers did express concern that exercises failed to test the students' knowledge of the unit in question, noting that there was an overemphasis on recall-level questions. This observation most often was made about district or textbook publisher tests. Their own tests, or tests of their colleagues, were criticized for their excessive wordiness or ambiguity in questions. The need for better planning prior to test construction was often noted.

Both elementary and secondary teachers spoke forcefully regarding standardized or district testing practices. This was one arena where they were not reticent to point out problems and where they were direct in addressing not only the limitations of the tests but the uselessness of standardized test results. Generally, for these teachers, standardized tests failed to provide needed diagnostic information. The tests seemed unrelated to instructional goals in that the content of the tests did not match what they were teaching or what they were expected to teach. Teachers noted that there are too few items and the tests do not assess critical thinking.

Elementary teachers recognized that some students have difficulty in following directions on the answer sheets, suggesting the need for more test taking practice. Others found the vocabulary too hard and unrelated to the instructional goals of their classroom.

We noted a significant number of teachers who used observational or performance assessments regularly in their classes. Secondary teachers who taught business, physical education, science, art, and home economics used performance assessments often and were most likely to have developed more structured rating scales. They suggested that they needed to improve the criteria or sharpen the rating scale in order to differentiate student performance more carefully.

The elementary teachers rarely used rating scales or checklists but often noted how much more important observation was than objective testing in assisting the instructional process. They made frequent use of mental notes. But a few admitted that the reliability of mental records and snap judgments was highly questionable.

Grades and grading are a continual, nagging problem for secondary teachers but were rarely mentioned as a concern by elementary teachers. Secondary teachers struggled constantly with fairness in grading practices, especially as it related to the need to account for social behavior, effort, and attitude. Physical education teachers often wondered how to devise appropriate ways of assessing responsibility, cooperation, and effort. Several teachers noted their frustrations with motivating students to complete assignments or take particular assessments seriously when those efforts were not graded.

SUMMARY OF THE TWO SELF-REPORT STUDIES

Stability and Change in Assessment Procedures

We found four interesting changes in assessment procedures as grade changes. First, the purpose for assessment varies with grade. Elementary assessment tends to be formative, secondary summative. Second, the higher the grade level, the greater the tendency for teachers to report using their own assessments rather than published tests. Third, teachers' concern about assessment quality increases with grade level. And fourth, teachers' attention to specific quality control procedures increases slightly with grade level. Thus, grade level appears to be an important variable in understanding classroom assessment. Elementary, junior high, and high school environments differ in fundamental ways.

The increased use of teacher-developed tests at higher grade levels might reflect the teachers' need to tailor tests to cover unique classroom objectives at higher levels. The reason for increased concern about assessment across grade levels may relate to the increased importance placed on grades as a measure of student progress and success as grade level increases. And increased attention to quality control may reflect greater concern with accurately judging and grading students: clearly grades take on more importance as students advance in the school system, and can influence future decisions of students. These and other speculations deserve further consideration in future research.

Assessment procedures also differ as a function of school subject. This is to be expected and our data support this notion. When teaching math and science, teachers tend to rely more heavily on paper and pencil tests than they do when teaching writing and speaking. Speaking and writing instruction tends to include more performance assessments. Regardless, concerns about improving test quality and use tend to remain quite constant across subject.

We also have evidence that each teacher tends to be relatively consistent in the assessment methods they use. They do not vary their testing methods as the purpose for assessment varies. As these teachers describe their levels of use of various modes of assessment, only a handful report that they anticipate using or were preparing to use a new type of assessment in the future. These teachers are not exploring new assessment approaches.

Teachers' Concerns About Assessment Quality

At least three-quarters of the 228 teachers queried in the survey study expressed some concern about the assessments they used. Further, over half of the respondents indicated concern about each of the four assessment methods. Journal entries also reflected interest in and concern about quality. Even when teachers reported being relatively comfortable with their use of a given form of assessment, they were not reluctant to express a desire to improve their use of that form and the manner in which they used the results it produced. In addition, teachers frequently reported concern about their ability to effectively integrate assessment given the time constraints imposed by the classroom. Overall, teachers' responses in these studies indicated concern about assessment quality and frustration at the lack of time available to deal more adequately with the problem.

But even more paradoxical and potentially troubling is that although teachers are obviously concerned and many want to improve, at the same time, as cited above, these teachers do not appear to be in the process of changing in ways that will improve their assessment methods. Clearly, many are concerned, but appear to lack the opportunity, time, means, or motivation to revise their assessment approaches.

Teachers' responses to the assessment practices questionnaire and their journal entries provide valuable information about their preferences for assessment methods. In their questionnaire responses they indicate what they perceive to be their strengths and weaknesses in applying the methods they select. Journal entries also reflect teachers' self-perceptions and, additionally, provide descriptions of actual practice from which some additional inferences can be made about the adequacy of their assessment practice. In order to validate teachers' reports and to deepen our understanding of how assessment "works" in the context of daily instruction, our logical next step was a series of direct observations in classrooms.

CHAPTER 4

Initial Observations of Classrooms

Teachers' questionnaire and journal responses about their assessment practices indicate grounds for concern about the adequacy of their practices. Teacher journal data amplified the questionnaire responses, however both methods fail to provide a rich enough understanding of assessment practices to form a basis for developing training which will meet the need for improved knowledge and practice so strongly articulated by those teachers.

We also wished to discern what discrepancies, if any, exist between the assessment methods teachers report using and the methods they actually use. The only viable strategy for validating the questionnaire and journal data and to prepare fuller descriptions of actual classroom practices would be to directly observe teachers in their role as assessors.

Further, teachers' survey responses and journal entries suggested that assessment is both a discrete activity and an integrated activity. Discrete, easily identifiable instances of assessment would be students completing assignments, doing boardwork, and taking tests or teachers grading, conducting oral questioning, and checking student performance against their expectations. But it is also an activity that is an intergral part of the instructional stream.

Thus, to validate and enrich our understanding of assessment as a practice, we went directly into the classroom, observing the daily process of four teachers in three sixth-grade classrooms.

METHODOLOGY

Participant-Observation

While some of the dimensions of classroom assessment practice were known to us from our own and others' research, it was not yet clear to us how assessment "worked" in the course of a teacher and students' class day. In order not to prejudge or prematurely define the nature, extent, or effect of classroom assessment, we elected to conduct these initial classroom studies using the methodology of participant-observation research.

Participant observation has been widely and successfully applied to educational research, but had not previously been used for study of classroom assessment practices. It is a method uniquely appropriate for capturing a broad range of practices such as our questionnaire and journal data suggested teachers attempt to use. Most especially, participant observation would enable us to study assessment practices which are interactive in nature, such as oral questioning and teacher feedback to students.

Key Areas of Inquiry

We anticipated that data would emerge that would assist us in answering four key questions:

- What are the purposes served by classroom assessment? Which purposes do these teachers rely on most frequently?
- What are the various student characteristics measured? Which are measured most often? Most extensively?
- What are the assessment strategies used? Which are used most?

  Types of assessments

  Key dimensions upon which these may vary (e.g., planned versus spontaneous; structured versus informal; identified versus not identified as a test; important versus not important to teacher or students)
- What is the form of the assessment record? What feedback is given?

As participant observers, we did not enter the classroom with a structured set of questions or any preliminary restrictions as to what would constitute relevant data. Rather, we observed and participated in the classrooms, taking notes on all the activities that took place, allowing the content, structure, and impact of assessment practice to emerge from the accumulation of teacher and student interactions witnessed and assessment documents interpreted in the context of these ongoing interactions.

Three Diverse Environments

We elected to observe sixth grade for three reasons: First, this is a grade level in which teachers tend to rely on all forms of assessment, including the observation-based methods that dominate the early grades and the paper and pencil instruments of junior high and high school. Second, teachers are beginning to shoot for more complex achievement targets as students are readied for junior high. And third, these more diverse tools and targets still drive instruction in a self-contained classroom, making observation more manageable. No attempt is made to argue representativeness for these three sixth-grade classrooms. They were selected to represent three contrasting environments. Classrooms are (pseudonyms) as follows:

Carol's Class
Carol is in her first year back in the classroom after multiyear absence and is teaching one of six sixth grades in the central public elementary school of a small industrial community. She has twenty-seven students in a self-contained classroom.

Ann's Class
Ann's is one of two sixth grades in a suburban elementary school where she has been teaching for several years. She has twenty-six students in a semicontained classroom. Students are ability-grouped for reading and math with the students in her colleague's class and the teaching shared.

Clint and Brenda's Class
Clint and Brenda are a stable teaching team who conduct the only sixth grade in a nonsectarian private school's elementary division. They have forty-two students whom they instruct as a whole group for some subjects and who are ability or heterogeneously grouped for

others. The school provides narrative assessment reports, rather than grades.

The three classrooms were observed during the final quarter of the school year.

Conduct of the Studies

After conducting pilot observations to develop parallel descriptions, note-taking forms, and other standardization techniques, researchers met with their principal and sixth-grade teacher(s) to inform them in very broad terms of the intent of the study. The specific interest in assessment was not revealed at that time.

Each researcher then established a routine of visiting in the classroom, spending at least twenty days with the teacher and students. Usually, a visit lasted a full day, so that all subjects could be observed. All days of the week were covered to assure that weekly routines were observed and recorded. We came to know the students in the classes and were able to follow the student-teacher interactions across the weeks, developing a sense of the teachers' approach to each individual, as well as to the class as a group.

Over the course of the time spent in the sixth-grade classrooms, researchers became an unremarkable, even useful part of the classroom routine. While we sometimes sat quietly in corners observing instruction and regularly read assignments and analyzed grade books and other records, at other times we functioned as teacher's aides, leading small group work sessions or providing one-on-one tutoring assistance. We also joined faculty and students as they went to lunch and sat in on parent-teacher conferences.

Informal, spontaneous interviews with teachers and students took place throughout the observation period. When interesting interactions took place, or the teacher's practice was not completely clear, the researcher briefly queried the teacher at the first opportunity. At the end of the observation period, the researcher and teacher(s) met for an extended interview, where key observations and tentative conclusions were presented for corroboration and discussion.

Each participant observer study was separately prepared as a narrative report (Stiggins et al. 1985), before findings were compared across the three classrooms. The rich descriptions of the three classrooms were then used as a basis for developing a structured instrument for profiling classroom assessment environments. The paragraphs below offer illustrative highlights from these descriptions.

PURPOSES FOR ASSESSMENTS

A key area of inquiry was the purposes to which assessment is put in these classrooms. Teacher reports in the survey and the journals had indicated that assessment plays a broad range of roles, including diagnosing individual and group needs, sizing up students, grouping and placement, assigning grades, feedback to students, parents, and school managers, control and motivation, communication of expectations, instructional decision making, and preparing students for later assessments. The following paragraphs highlight key assessment purposes that were observed.

We originally planned to look for purpose choice and frequency. The classroom observations enabled us to address several additional questions about assessment purpose: Which purposes are these teachers' assessments intended to fulfill? Is the intended purpose met with the assessment as applied? How well do the teachers use the information available to them from the assessments they undertake? How do purposes interact? How is assessment practice shaped by school policy?

Grading

Two of the three classrooms we observed required that assessments be reported out in the form of grades. This purpose dominates all assessment practice in the two classrooms. Indeed, 25 to 30 percent of available instructional time is spent on assessment in these sixth grades, much of it directed toward grade assignment.

In both Carol's and Ann's classes the most salient purpose for assessment—from both teachers' and students' point of view—is assignment of grades. In Carol's classroom, subject periods regularly begin with grading of homework papers exchanged among students. In-class assignments are also exchanged and graded.

Nearly every sample of written work is transformed into a grade. This amounts to eight to ten samples—assignments, tests, classwork—each day. They are assigned points and are recorded for later averaging into grades. Through this constant grade-assignment activity, assessment is also used to control and motivate students. Grading is used to secure attention and effort.

Similarly, grading is a salient activity in Ann's class. Indeed, she prefaces most activities with a "this will be graded" admonition. Students also frequently ask whether an assignment will be graded and, if it is not, they treat the work as unimportant. Grades also provide the primary basis for feedback to students, although Ann provided considerable oral feedback during question periods.

Clint and Brenda's private school classroom presents a stark contrast, since no grading takes place. They accomplish the same purposes through alternative forms of recording and feedback. Their students and parents receive twice-yearly multipage narrative reports in place of report cards. They take great pains and spend much class time communicating their expectations and providing feedback to the group and to individuals. Written and oral assessments are constant, performance is recorded, and all are returned with statements about accomplishment in addition to many having point scores.

Communicating Expectations

All forms of assessment are used to communicate expectations for achievement and behavior. Carol, for example, communicates her achievement expectations and expectations for levels of cognitive operation through her assessments. This is most obvious in the continual focus on grading of homework and classwork and her regular testing program, but also evident in her question-and-answer strategies and the feedback given to good and poor responses. Clearly, Carol's students learn their achievement targets from her assessments, not from the lists of instructional objectives she hands out.

Clint and Brenda communicate their achievement and behavioral expectations almost constantly. When assignments are set, they are discussed at some length; on major projects expectations are repeated at least daily. Then, as students start to work on assignments (homework is begun in class), they circulate checking that all have understood.

Diagnosis

All four teachers regularly use assessments diagnostically: for ability-grouping, for referral to gifted and remedial programs, for grade retention and promotion, and, in the case of Clint and Brenda, decisions about which students to admit and expell.

Carol uses homework to diagnose which students are having difficulty with the assignment. As a daily routine in each class period, immediately after homework or test papers have been handed in and students are busy on the next day's assignment, she scans the grades, identifies those who had problems, and gathers them in a back room for special help. Diagnosis of group needs is far less frequent in her classroom. Special circumstances like students' failure to learn under a substitute teacher cause her to recycle instruction, but the pace of required material prohibits reteaching. Carol focuses on responding to the most needy individual while the group goes ahead.

Ann makes use of her question-and-answer sessions to diagnose individuals. She sets questions at differing levels of difficulty, so that her expectations for each student can be evaluated. She carefully monitors students as they work on practice problems and makes judgements based on the questions they ask about the work. Occasionally she will select students for special help sessions, but at other times expects them to come forward with problems. For group diagnosis she makes use of pretests, for example a pretest that enabled her to decide that a math chapter could be skipped.

Although Ann was aware of several students with potential learning problems, she chose to manage these problems through regular group instruction. One student who performed poorly on assignments and tests despite fluent reading ability and strong oral performance in class was consistently praised for his efforts and reprimanded for incomplete assignments. His continued poor performance indicated that a more individualized diagnosis of his particular problems was warranted.

Both individual and group diagnosis is readily observed in Clint and Brenda's classroom. The team meets daily to evaluate the success of the instruction and decide when to move the class forward and when to repeat instruction, as well as identifying students in need of individual help. Using their observations of students' performance in class, their written assignments, and information from one-on-one work, plans are developed for the class and for specific students.

For the group, reteaching or moving on is discussed and, when necessary, exercise sets are developed and additional assignments set. One particularly clear example was the institution of spelling as a focus of instruction. Concern that the class as a whole was not focusing sufficiently on correctness of spelling in their essays led to a week-long series of spelling bees. This was the first spelling instruction the sixth graders had received all year. For individuals, Clint and Brenda set additional exercises, plan tutoring sessions, and agree upon exemptions from specific assignments.

Sizing Up

Each of these teachers described "sizing up" assessments that they conduct at the beginning of the school year, in order to get a quick fix on the class as a whole and the capabilities of individuals. These are assessments of their own devising and each reports that they are good bases for judgement and that these early conclusions are by and large borne out as the year progresses. Ann has developed her own exercises and uses them to group, refer, and establish expectations for her students.

In Carol's school a standardized placement test is used, but she does not rely on it for anything more than guidance. She modifies the results indicated by the standardized test based on her own observations and exercises and sometimes based on parent preferences.

Clint and Brenda have also devised a set of sizing up activities for the beginning of the school year, including a math test covering both fifth and sixth-grade material and an interview of a fellow student that provides information on students' written and oral language skills, as well as their confidence and ability to interact with fellow students. Only after they have conducted their own sizing up assesesments do they consult the students' standardized test scores from the previous spring, for "confirmation." On the basis of their sizing up assessments Brenda and Clint group their students.

Controlling and Motivating

All these teachers use assessment as a controlling and motivating strategy. Grading is a primary tool for motivating and controlling students in Carol's and Ann's classes. Students respond positively. If an assignment is not to be graded, they take the work lightly and are more off-task. These teachers also use explicit rewards for work completion, such as time to do activities individuals enjoy. Ann motivates students to prepare for and work hard on tests by stressing their importance, conducting practice tests, and outlining the specifics how the test will be structured and what it will cover.

Brenda and Clint rely less on assessment for control, but do make use of it. Work completion is underscored by a wall display of students' status and students who have been off-task in class and have uncompleted work may be required to stay in during recess or after school. They also structure their assessments to motivate. For example, they do not regularly teach spelling and the students loathe it. When they decided that it was necessary to teach it, they conducted the instruction as team spelling bees. Math bees are also common.

Feedback to Students

Each of these teachers provides regular feedback to students, orally and in writing. In all their classes objective assignments are point scored.

Feedback about negative behavior is generally handled privately and sensitively. Ann does demonstratively single students out and place them in special chairs with their backs to the class when their behavior is otherwise uncontrollable.

Each also welcomes and encourages small group or individual work where more feedback is supplied. Carol gives encouraging feedback in her small group sessions. Ann sometimes indentifies students for one-on-one and is receptive when students seek her comments. Brenda and Clint regularly work one-on-one with students as well.

For Ann and Carol, grades remain the primary way in which

feedback is communicated, both to students and to parents. The dominance of grading in these classes has been described above. Ann provides each feedback on progress at midterm by giving each student a print-out of their point and grade standing; it also indicates which assignments are outstanding.

Ann offers frequent oral feedback on in-class performance, praising good efforts and occasionally encouraging some who err with comments such as "good try." However, positive feedback tends to be oriented toward proficient students. For quieter or less academically able students there are generally few verbal rewards and less opportunity to feel successful. Ann's responses in class, like her feedback on written papers, are almost purely in terms of right and wrong/correct and incorrect. Even feedback to students on their behavior tends to be couched in these terms.

Carol uses group praise extensively. She also consistently praises correct answers in recitation. She also uses specific rewards for the completion of major pieces of work, for example, taking successful students on a trip to a video parlor/fast-food restaurant. Generally, the basis for positive feedback lies in work completion, not work quality.

Brenda and Clint offer regular, immediate feedback during instruction, equally distributed to those who are correct and incorrect, strong and weak. Feedback is positive, for example, "you can do better," "we know this is hard for you, but you're making progress," or "now you're showing what you can do." All written assignments are returned with comments and, for assignments such as math problems, scores. On their narrative reports they describe their expectations for the individual and detail their assessment of the student in terms that are highly consistent with classroom feedback. Assignment completion lists are prominently posted on the wall and students regularly consult the listings and then seek out a teacher to secure to make arrangements for completing overdue assignments.

Feedback to Parents

Reports to parents of Carol and Ann's students are, like in-class feedback, focused on grades. In Ann's district scores are reported out to parents on a midterm computer printout which details possible numbers of points, their child's points and grade cutoffs. Ann further annotates the report with her indication of whether the student is above, at, or below average in achievement. In addition, regular report cards are sent out at end of term, with grades computed on a percentage scale. The school had recently adopted this computer reporting system, in part to attempt to minimize parents' grade complaints.

In Carol's district computerized grade reporting forms are also used. However, to supplement grades, she is provided with a list of 100 comments about personal and social behavior and attitude that she can select by bubbling in a selection code so the computer can print that comment on the report card. Carol uses these comment options, but is not satisfied with how they communicate her assessments of the students.

Written feedback to parents of Clint and Brenda's students includes twice-yearly narrative reports, occasionally required parent review of homework, occasional written notes, and a class newsletter. Parent conferences are held as well.

Relation of Assessment to Instruction

As the paragraphs above illustrate, assessment is inextricably tied to instruction in all three classrooms. Both Carol and Ann occasionally use assessment information to identify material to reteach; Clint and Brenda do this on a routine basis. The latter teachers regularly use assessment information to evaluate instruction. Carol and Ann rarely exploited these opportunities.

However, assessment is tightly coupled with instruction in all three classrooms. For example, Carol would pose a series of oral questions to underline each key point in her texts and occasionally would give students practice tests, stating at the conclusion of the exercise that this would not be graded but was a "learning experience." She made daily use of in-class correction of homework as a strategy for reviewing the material, as well as diagnosing the group and assessing for grading purposes.

Various assessment purposes are easily observed as integral parts of Clint and Brenda's instructional process. For example, diagnosis of individuals took place during math instruction. In a group recently introduced to the concept of volume, Clint was inconsistent about correcting students who stated answers in terms of "square" instead of "cubic". Queried about the variance, he stated, "I know the kids. Sometimes it's just sloppiness or carelessness, but they know the concept [so I don't correct]. In some of the others they just don't have it yet [so I stop and correct]."

STUDENT CHARACTERISTICS ASSESSED

Although differences in emphasis clearly emerge when the three classrooms are compared, the four teachers all assess students' achievement (both mastery of material and cognitive reasoning skills), ability, and personal and social development. In the two public school classrooms achievement is the primary basis for recorded assessments. In the private school behavioral characteristics are equally, or more, important. Judgements about ability and observations of behavioral characteristics factor into all the teachers' evaluations of students' achievement.

Achievement

Mastery of content is regularly assessed in these classrooms. Students are constantly monitored—through written assignments, tests and oral questioning in Carol's and Ann's classes; through written assignments, oral performance, and one-on-one sessions in Brenda and Clint's class.

Carol's assessments of content mastery are typical. Without question, her assessments measure how much students know and how well they are able to use their knowledge. In math students are called upon to apply what they have learned to solve problems. In science all levels of reasoning skills are required. In computers students are called upon to perform and show progress in computer operations. In language arts students perform in two distinct ways, but only one becomes an assessment: They write daily in their journals, but these are never formally evaluated. Day-to-day language arts instruction focuses on aspects such as spelling and capitalization rules, which are consistently graded.

All four teachers are concerned that higher order thinking

skills are acquired by their students. Carol's oral questioning ranges over all skill levels with the exception of evaluation, however text-based assignments and tests she regularly used failed to match this broad range in some subjects. Ann, too, integrates some higher order skills into her own assessments, but relied on text-based tests that primarily elicited recall. In Clint and Brenda's class recall is almost never assessed; questions and assignments were focussed at higher levels. In one instance they decided to use a text-based assessment as an assignment, specifically because it consisted of multiple-choice and true-false recall questions and "they should be exposed to that."

Ability

All four teachers articulated (and were seen to alter their assessments and their instruction on the basis of) differentiated expectations for individual students. For both Carol and Ann, their perception of individual students' ability is used to decide between two grades, when the student lies on the borderline. (Less-able students get the benefit of the doubt.) The teachers judge ability largely on the basis of students' quickness and ease in grasping new concepts and the level of students' standards for their own performance.

The most formal assessment of ability is conducted through their sizing up assessments at the beginning of the year, but the teachers regularly amend this initial assessment as they observe student performance. Sizing up is based on teacher-devised assessments and they tend to disregard information from standardized measures.

All four teachers' decisions about grouping are made on the basis of their ability judgements and each regroups students based on revised assessments of ability. However, referral for special services, especially remedial services, may entail bringing in a diagnostician who administers additional assessments.

While all four teachers make regular use of assessments of student aptitude, all are reluctant to discuss their students in ability terms. Clint and Brenda appear to be especially sensitive on this issue, preferring to call their homogeneous grouping "experience grouping." None of the teachers uses ability references in conversations with students and all are guarded in using such descriptions when communicating with parents and school managers.

Personal and Social Characteristics

All four teachers closely monitor student behavior. For Carol, Clint, and Brenda behavior assessments are part of the records provided to parents (see above). While Ann's district reporting system precluded use of nonachievement factors in grading, student behaviors clearly affect how she manages and motivates her class.

Carol has some sanction for assessing behavior that is established by the comments section on her reporting form. She wishes there were more opportunity to assess these characteristics. In actual practice, she communicates her behavioral expectations clearly to her students and monitors compliance with the established rules. She monitors social development in terms of peer relations, group work, temperament, and activities during nonclass and one-on-one time. She draws inferences about personality, adding confidence, anxiety, self-concept and sense of humor to the traits observed. These assessments are crucial to the effective functioning of her classroom.

Clint and Brenda attempt to place an emphasis on assessment of behavior that is equal to the priority they place on achievement assessment. They state that, "About half our job is making citizens of them." They evaluate their teaching success in terms of changes in students' everyday behavior.

This priority influences their daily assessment practice. Oral feedback on personal and social skills is fully as common as feedback on academic performance. Assignments of academic work are sometimes second in importance to opportunities for personal growth. For example, the newly elected class president took the intiative to come to Clint to argue that he could not both complete a major lanaguage arts assignment and organize the class' performance for an upcoming assembly. He was granted a waiver from the assignment. Clint's basis for the decision was that the boy was correct about the value of the organizing experience and that he was able, for the first time, to articulate what his own learning priorities were.

TABLE 4.1
CLINT AND BRENDA'S NARRATIVE ASSESSMENT REPORTS

	Number of Comments	
	Achievement	Personal/Social Skills
Reading	174	51
Language arts	275	66
Math	169	112

Their narrative final reports on students clearly indicate what characteristics they choose to assess. Table 4.1 summarizes a content analysis of their comments.

In reading and writing, where Brenda and Clint make a great many very specific comments on individual skills contributing to content mastery, achievement-related comments outnumber social and personal behavior comments. Yet the latter constitute 20 to 30 percent of the comments. In math, where specific subskills are fewer, personal and social behavior comments approach the number of achievement-related comments. In observed classroom assessment, the proportion of personal and social behavior comments is higher, almost half of the feedback, in all three subject areas.

The narrative reports accurately reflect Brenda and Clint's classroom assessment practice, which inextricibly interweaves achievement and personal growth. An example of their assessment of one student's writing progress will illustrate:

> As Ulrich has matured, writing and self-expression became easier. . . . His style is clear, direct, and often peppered with humorous wit. We enjoy reading what Ulrich composes and respect the obvious growths he has made this year. He shows better organization of thought, more cohesion, neater penmanship, and a broader understanding of basic grammar requirements. Ulrich is not the best of spellers but is quick to seek help and can even be cajoled into using a dictionary. His exuberance doesn't include proofreading, but when he slows down a bit, he has the potential for catching many of his own errors. . . . He feels rightly proud of his progress.

While, due to school policy, only Clint and Brenda develop written evaluations uniting their achievement and behavioral assessments, Carol and Ann use much the same mix of student characteristics when they describe their students in evaluative terms.

ASSESSMENT METHODS

Students in these three classrooms are assessed in a wide variety of ways including tests, homework assignments, in-class work, oral questions, and performance on class presentations and development of visual and written products. The teachers' choices of assessment methods create the basic ecology of their classroom, setting the pace and rhythm, forming students' expectations of their role, and establishing the fundamental nature of the interaction that takes place. Carol's class will illustrate.

The daily rhythm Carol sets for each subject period is parallel: initiated with ten or so minutes of homework correction, then carried through with oral questioning, ending with seat work and small group sessions for those whose homework scores were low. This rhythm has its crescendos at regular intervals on weekly or unit test days.

Carol's classroom can also be characterized in terms of the roles set for students: for example, she relies heavily on their active participation in the diagnostic process, expecting them to assess themselves and come to her when they need more or special help. While she selects some students for her small group sessions, any student who feels weak is free to join, and many do.

Carol's choices of assessment methods and the ways she applies them establish the nature of student-teacher interaction. Student-student relations are influenced as well. Analysis of her oral questioning pattern, for example, reveals that volunteering is positively rewarded, so able students are eager to engage her attention. It is also clear from observation that she does not encourage endless questioning about the management, as opposed to content, of assignments, so students seek these clarifications from her individually, if not turning to peers. Most importantly, Carol's never-absent grading emphasis influences all interaction, even when it is not the immediate topic of discussion.

The other two classrooms could be similarly sketched, each illustrating how the applications of different methods of assessment structure key aspects of the classroom ecology.

Selection of Methods

Choices of assessment method obviously derive in part from the teachers' assessment purposes. For example, Carol and Ann must develop bases for assigning grades, so they gravitate toward ready solutions such as objectively scorable assignments and tests. All four teachers have placement responsibilities, so each has developed a sizing up procedure.

However, other factors, including student characteristics to be assessed and teachers' training and experience, profoundly influence the decisions. Clint and Brenda's assessment methods are affected by their priority on student personal and social growth. They create performance assessments, often group assessments, that challenge students socially and personally, but which minimize individual competition and comparision. These assessments also provide oppportunities for academically less able students to demonstrate other strengths, an ideal to which they are philosophically committed.

None of these teachers has had any formal training in classroom assessment. It appears that experienced teachers have developed their repetoire of assessments over years in the classroom. New teachers have less flexibility, as Carol exemplifies. She uses text-embedded assignments and tests, even though she has some doubts about their appropriateness, because, as a newly returned teacher, her preparation load is too heavy to permit her to devise her own measures.

The following paragraphs briefly describe how key assessment methods are applied in these sixth-grade classrooms.

Paper and Pencil Tests

Tests are a regular part of the classroom assessment activity in Carol and Ann's classes, but are absent from Clint and Brenda's assessment scheme. Both Carol and Ann rely on unit tests that are tied to textbooks. Tests are generally multiple-choice, true-false, and short-answer. In Carol's class tests are approached rather routinely, but Ann carries out a thorough review before each test, describing exactly the kinds of questions that will be on it. The tests contrast with Ann's and especially Carol's oral questioning: they require recall almost exclusively, while both teachers solicit higher order thinking in recitation.

All four teachers do administer standardized achievement tests, as required by their district or school. Of the three, Ann appears to place the most importance on these assessments in her interactions with her students and apparently regards the results as an indirect evaluation of her work. She was visibly pleased with the high number of her students who scored high enough for accelerated math placement. Clint and Brenda try hard to mitigate the stress that their students experience from this unaccustomed exercise by downgrading its importance, but the seventh grade placement exam was so anxiety-provoking that two students could not complete it. Carol takes little regard of the results.

Written Homework and Classwork

Written assignments and assignments of products are the backbone of the assessment structure in all three classrooms. Since they do not test, Clint and Brenda must rely upon assignments, augmented by performance, as the basis for their assessments. They collect, comment upon and/or score, and record written assignments in math and language arts several times weekly. They use dittoed workbook sheets or teacher-developed exercises in math and language arts. Science assignments are usually larger scale, combining written work and performance. In writing class, major essays are due every few weeks, with smaller compositions approximately weekly.

Brenda and Clint communicate their expectations orally, but very clearly. Students who ask questions that clarify the assigment receive very positive feedback. The completion status of all assignments is posted on the classroom wall. After a certain number of incompletes have accumulated, the student must meet with one of the teachers to negotiate how the work is to be caught up. At these meetings alternative strategies are often worked out, since Clint and Brenda regard the process of taking responsiblity to be as important as any single piece of the work. Students are encouraged to redo work that they are not pleased with and many do.

In Ann's class, assignments are almost daily in very subject. They consititute a source of information for her recorded grades that is at least equivalent to her tests. For example, in the report that went out during the observation period, 71 percent of the 2,100 possible points came from assignments. Most of her assignments, like all of Carol's, are taken from the curriculum materials. In both classes the assignments, like the tests, tended to focus on recall to a far greater extent than the teachers did in their oral questioning during instruction. The importance of assignments is heavily underlined by Ann's and Carol's practice of having students correct each other's papers, then asking students to read their scores aloud for recording.

Oral Questioning

Recitation is a prominent instructional strategy in all three classrooms. Carol takes some oral questions out of her text materials, but also adds her own, most of which require higher-order thinking. While recitiation does not factor directly into the grading scheme, she relies on oral questioning for diagnosis and for controlling and motivating the students, as well as for instructing.

Carol has worked out a questioning pattern that apparently enables her to diagnose and control her class, but may not equally motivate all students. She asks questions at the rate of thirty to forty for each class period, or about 200 per day. Tracking the student targets of questions, we found that Carol differs from the frequently reported pattern of addressing questions primarily to the center of the room: she focuses twice as often on those on the far left and right. She also relies on volunteers 90 percent of the time and those volunteers answer 80 percent of the questions correctly, as contrasted with less than 30 percent correct for nonvolunteers. Thus, some students get fewer opportunities to perform and less eager students may not be required to be fully attentive.

Ann also uses oral questioning extensively. A review of responses to her questions revealed that most students eagerly volunteer to answer questions; most volunteers answer correctly; few students are called on; nonvolunteers are less likely to answer correctly; and, interestingly, students who volunteer and participate actively are far more likely to receive praise for correct responses than are other students. Again, as in Carol's class, some students are able to slip by without attending to discussion.

Clint and Brenda also conduct recitation, though far less frequently. Their questions are almost exclusively of a higher order nature. During recitation they ask for volunteers, then, when the class starts on seat work, seek out nonvolunteers to inquire why they are not involved in discussion and provide necessary help. They use oral questioning for group, as well as individual diagnosis, and often reteach based on students' reponses. Willingness to participate in recitation is often listed among positive comments on students' narrative evaluations.

Performance Assessment

Clint and Brenda rely heavily on performance assessment. While paper and pencil assessments and oral questioning clearly dominate Carol's and Ann's classes, both also conduct performance assessments.

Carol requires writing assessments, book reports, science products, and, in computer class, keyboarding. Students also produce maps and art products. And, their behavior is observed and assessed, albeit informally.

What is most striking about Carol's performance assessments is the range of clarity with which performance expectations or standards are communicated to the students. In computers it is always quite clear and the book report assignment is fully thought out and articulated. However, the intent and expectations for keeping a journal are far less clear, and these products are never collected for assessment. When grading products such as maps, she appeared not to have appropriate strategies for evaluating the full scope of the work, relying instead on easily countable features such as the accuracy of labelling on a map. When such reversion to objective, correct/incorrect criteria was not possible, she did not grade the product, avoiding the use of subjective judgment.

Ann exhibited similar reluctance to tackle subjective assessment of performance, especially assignment of grades to products. Her assessment of writing, for example, focuses on issues of grammar, punctuation, and spelling, rather than concept or composition.

Clint and Brenda have developed their skills in assessment of performance and have well-established strategies for communicating expectations, recordkeeping and feeding back to students. Their comments on written compositions address all levels, from points of grammar to voice, structure, semantic devices, and concept. They file a duplicate copy of these responses on major assessments and record their comments on smaller writing assignments in a ledger book.

Reading is taught orally by Clint and Brenda, i.e., entirely through performance in small groups. After each session the group instructor makes a record of each student's performance on a matrix that calls for pluses, minuses and comments on accomplishments in mechanics such as phrasing, scanning, and sounding out words; on several comprehension skills; and on behavior such as effort. These records become key information for the narrative final reports on each student.

Clint and Brenda also require art products in many subjects and oral recitation of poems and reports. All oral recitations are assessed in terms of content and quality of performance and students receive multidimensional written evaluations.

Grading Methods

Both Carol and Ann depend upon point systems for assigning grades. Since they grade almost entirely on the basis of objective correct/incorrect items, the conversion to grades is fairly straightforward. However, they contrast in their use of the point totals.

Carol assigns a grade on the scale of 90 percent is an A, 80 percent a B, 70 percent a C, 60 percent a D, and less an F to each assessment. All these pregraded assessments, large and small, assignment and test, are equally weighted for averaging to determine end-of-term grades.

Ann maintains running point totals throughout the term, then converts these totals into grades on a similar percentage scale. She does put a grade indication in each returned paper, so students can monitor their progress. On one occasion, when students had unexpected difficulty on a test, Ann modified her grading scheme and graded that particular test on a curve, so that higher grades could be assigned.

Again, Clint and Brenda assign no grades.

Students' View of Assessment

During the course of the observations, we frequently discussed with individual students how they perceived the assessment process. Both academically strong and weak students regard their assessment environment as basically fair. They attribute success to hard work, although not all weak and inattentive students take responsibility for their poor performance. Most do not question the teacher's practices or judgements. An exception is that academically weak students comment that they do not like having to read their grades aloud in Carol and Ann's classes.

We also discovered that most students are acute interpreters and some are clever consumers of their assessment environment. Strong students in Ann's and Carol's classes always had their hands up to volunteer, a practice that both teachers reward, both orally and in making borderline grade decisions. Weak students were seen to try desperately (usually unsuccessfully) to get the teacher's attention when they did know an answer.

Students in all three classes demonstrated precise knowledge of how long and under what circumstances they could delay or revise assignments. Particularly in Brenda and Clint's class, but also with Ann and Carol, students were able to negotiate one-on-one about their work. In talking with the researchers they were able to articulate how the grading system works, how assignments are assessed, and the relative importance of individual pieces of work.

Students also make active decisions about how to operate within the assessment environment. For example, in Carol's class students well knew that they could redo work, but few chose to do so. They stated that they didn't have time to repeat and keep up with the new work, a reflection of the relentless pace of the classroom progress. Brenda and Clint's students were aware of their standing opportunity to redo work and some chose to take advantage, often by negotiating some lessening of other assignments in subjects where their performance was stronger.

In Carol's class we observed that some weaker students consistently tried to keep their lack of understanding hidden. Some just didn't want others to know; some stated that they didn't want to slow down the whole class.

As has been noted above, all these teachers rely on students' capability as self-assessors. They expect and encourage them to decide when they need extra attention. Clint and Brenda always set the students the task of evaluating sixth grade and their accomplishments as a major writing assignment toward the end of the year. These essays provided an opportunity to examine the students' perceptions more closely.

The students' self-evaluations mirror the assessment environment their teachers have established. Like their teachers, they focus their achievement statements on specific skills, such as vocabulary, oral phrasing, or fractions. They reflect the balance of academic and personal growth their teachers seek. When the self-evaluations are compared with the teachers' final reports (see Table 4.1), strong parallels emerge. Overall, two-thirds of students' comments are directed to achievement and one-third to personal and social skills, similar to the teachers' narrative reports. In the seventeen essays that have sufficient detail to permit one-on-one comparison with the teachers' narratives, there are only two substantive discrepancies: one student reports lower self-esteem than her teachers perceive and a second is less satisfied with her academic progress. Otherwise, students' and teachers' assessment of accomplishment are highly congruent, as are their choices of what academic and personal progress to address.

To further probe students' perceptions, we requested that each teacher set as a writing assessment a letter to an imaginary fifth grader that explains how to succeed in sixth grade. The essays demonstrate that students are perceptive and sensitive participants in assessment. Table 4.2 shows in order of frequency the strategies that were so commonly mentioned as to constitute class consensus on how to succeed in their particular classroom environment.

The leading comments are directed to assessment practices or relate directly to characteristics that are assessed. The students are able to articulate key aspects of these three environments. All cite their teachers' concern with completion and punctuality. Ann's students have picked up her stress on the seriousness of testing. All note that behavior is important and their reports document the contrast between Ann and Carol's emphasis on attentiveness and focus on the teacher-student interaction as opposed to Clint and Brenda's greater stress on the quality of teacher-student and

TABLE 4.2
LEADING STRATEGIES FOR HOW TO SUCCEED
IN SIXTH GRADE

Carol	Ann	Brenda and Clint
Complete homework on time	Complete work on time	Establish a good relationship with teachers
Listen, don't talk, follow directions	Try hard, listen, behave in class	Complete homework
	Study notes and past assignments for tests	Be nice, kind, polite
		Be punctual

student-student interactions. Clint and Brenda's students put first priority on establishing a good relationship with the teacher. Note that in none of the classrooms does quality of work appear among the common descriptors.

The assessment researchers generally concur with the students' reports in each case. The students have articulated key points about their teachers' assessment priorities and the ecology of their classroom environment. Assessment, then, plays a defining role in the students' experience of schooling.

SUMMARY AND CONCLUSION

We found these three assessment environments to be far richer and more dimensional than we ever could have expected. Space limitations permit only a glimpse of the many and varied assessment events we saw. We are unable to convey here in enough detail the many and varied roles we saw assessment playing in these classrooms or the profound impacts they had on students and teachers.

We began by exploring purposes for assessment. We found many. In this case, the contrasts between the two public school classrooms and the private classroom were stark. We examined student characteristics assessed and found teachers gathering far more than data on student achievement. We collected observation on assessment methods used and found much variation both in the methods these teachers rely on and the quality of their application of those methods. And we explored forms and uses of feedback and and found that, while grades and grading dominate, they are by no means the only forms of communication used to share results.

In short, we found rich similarities and differences across these three settings. The next question was, how do these classrooms compare to the others that comprise our schools. But first we had to establish a standard way to describe classroom assessment environments so they could be compared. In the next chapter, we describe how we accomplished this.

CHAPTER 5

Profile of Classroom Assessment Environments

Our initial observations in the three sixth-grade classrooms led to narrative descriptions of classroom assessment environments of surprising complexity. However, while the specific attributes of each environment varied widely from the other two, there did emerge from the complexity and variation a pattern of environmental dimensions that appeared to permit a coherent description of each classroom.

To test the utility of framework of key dimensions, another series of field studies was conducted, this time at the high school level. These observations were guided by a profiling instrument that allowed the observer to describe each dimension of the assessment environment in a particular classroom in terms of a continuum along which classrooms might be expected to vary.

Researchers visited eight high school classrooms, two each in mathematics, science, social studies, and language arts, using observations, interviews, and document analyses conducted over several weeks to test the significance of constructive features included in the initial assessment-environment profile. As the studies unfolded, researchers met regularly to discuss emerging findings and plan subsequent observations to confirm or deny the meaning and relevance of specific elements in the emerging profile framework.

Once more, as in the sixth-grade studies, detailed narrative notes of classroom activities were taken. But in this case, observations were guided and made more focused by reference to the significant domains identified in the first set of studies. Ongoing classroom visits enabled us to seek out specific information shown significant in other classrooms. Similarly, teacher and student interviews were both open-ended and structured to solicit missing data known to be significant to a comprehensive profile. Documents—textbooks, assignments, grade books, student records—were analyzed to extract data corresponding to and complementing the various assessments observed.

As a result of this interactive process of observation and discussion, researchers were able to articulate a complete framework for profiling the assessment environment in any classroom. The profile is structured around eight key factors:

- Assessment purposes
- Assessment methodologies, as each is applied to assessing achievement, affect, and ability
- Criteria used in selecting the assessment method
- Quality of assessments
- Feedback
- The teacher as assessor: background, time expenditure and personal/professional characteristics
- The teacher's perception of the students
- The assessment-policy environment

Each factor contains several specific assessment dimensions within it. The complete framework of factors and dimensions is described in this chapter. Then Chapters 6 and 7 apply the framework to the various high school classroom environments studied.

To describe the environment in any particular classroom, there are three key questions one must ask about any assessment dimension in that environment. These questions probe whether the teacher is *informed* about that dimension or attribute of an assessment environment, how *relevant* the dimension is for the particular environment being profiled, and whether there is evidence that the dimension is in fact considered or *used* in the classroom.

ASSESSMENT PURPOSES

In the course of our observations, we were able to establish nine different roles assessment can play in the classroom. The actual purposes used varied from classroom to classroom and from teacher to teacher. Thus, one key factor in the description of the assessment environment of any particular classroom is the identification of the purposes served by assessment in that context. In analyzing each potential purpose for or use of assessment in any given classroom, again, one can ask whether:

• the teacher is informed about that use,
• how relevant that use is for this particular classroom, and
• whether the teacher in fact uses assessment in that way.

The list of possible purposes includes:

Diagnosing Needs of Individual Students

In this case, the teacher's task is to identify the strengths and weaknesses in the educational attainments of individual students. To determine if a particular teacher is informed about this use of assessment, one might ask:

• Is the teacher aware of individual differences among students?
• Can the teacher specify ways to conduct such diagnoses?
• Has the teacher developed tools and systems for diagnosing?

To determine the relevance of diagnosing student needs in any particular classroom, one might ask:

• Is the achievement target amenable to individualization?
• Does the student load realistically allow for individualization?
• Does the teacher think diagnosis is a relevant instructional use of assessment?

Finally, to ascertain the utility of a particular assessment purpose in a given classroom, one can ask if the teacher in fact uses assessment results to individualize instruction to some extent, such as by working with individual students one-on-one or through grouping students with like needs.

Diagnosing Group Needs

This part of the teacher's assessment task is to detect the common instuctional needs (i.e., strengths and weaknesses) of a class or group of students, so an efficient instructional treatment can be planned for all. To determine the status of this use of assessment in any particular classroom, one might again ask how well informed the teacher is about it:

- Can the teacher specify ways to detect group needs?
- Can the teacher specify such needs?

To ascertain the relevance of this use of assessment, one might ask if group diagnosis fits into the classroom in question and if the teacher perceives its value in that context. Then, to determine if assessment is used in this way, one might seek evidence of such tracking of group needs.

Assigning Grades

The decision to be made by the teacher in this case is what grade to report on a report card as feedback on student performance to students and parents. The teacher who is well informed about sound grading practices:

- understands and has carefully considered the alternative factors that can be factored into the student's grade, and
- has developed a sound philosophy about those potential ingredients and their weighting in that teacher's grading system.

In addition, as with the other purposes for assessment, one can ask about the relevance of grades in a particular classroom, and whether the teacher values and assigns grades.

Identifying Students for Special Services

The general question in this case is whether the teacher uses classroom assessment to select students for placement into advanced or remedial programs. To ascertain the teacher's level of information about this use, one might ask if the teacher is aware of relevant selection policies and/or can specify criteria to be used to select assessments. The issues of the relevance and actual use of assessment in this way depend on whether the teacher is in fact called upon to make or contribute to these types of selection decisions.

Controlling Student Behavior

The use of assessment in this case is not to inform a decision; rather, it is to motivate students to behave in particular ways. The teacher might use assessment or the threat of assessment to encourage studying or to control the patterns of social behavior among students in the class, for example. To determine if the teacher is aware of and informed about this use of assessment, one might ask:

- Can the teacher specify reasons for using assessment in this way?
- Can the teacher specify strategies for the effective use of assessment as a motivator?

The issue of relevance centers on whether it makes sense to use assessment in this way in this particular classroom and whether the teacher values this use of assessment. Then the final issue is whether assessment is used as a behavior management or control mechanism.

Evaluating Instruction

Does the teacher use classroom assessment as a means of documenting the success or failure of a particular instructional program or treatment? In this case, the assessment is not as much an evaluation of the student as it is an evaluation of the teacher and the teaching. A thorough profile of the purposes of assessment in a particular classroom includes an analysis of whether the teacher evaluates his or her own instruction. Here is the profile of questions to be addressed:

- Is the teacher aware of the potential value of and informed about methods of evaluation? Can the teacher describe basic instructional-evaluation strategies?
- Is it relevant to evaluate instructional treatments in this context? Does the teacher value this use of assessment?
- Is there evidence that such evaluations are in fact conducted?
- Is there evidence that instruction is influenced by such evaluation?

Communicating Achievement Expectations

Students come to understand the achievement expectations of their teachers in part by looking for patterns in the assessments used by those teachers. Once those patterns are determined, students can predict the form and focus of future assessments, can prepare accordingly, and can maximize their chances of success.

The classroom assessment task for teachers is to use assessment effectively to focus student attention on the important outcomes of instruction. Teachers are informed about this use of assessment if they can cite alternative means of communicating achievement expectations, including assessment. This use of assessment is relevant if it communicates the achievement target to students in a particular classroom and the teacher values assessment as a vehicle for doing so. Under these circumstances, one can seek documentary evidence that the target message is sent via assessment and read by students using this medium.

Assessment as a Teaching Strategy

Teachers have the option of using assessment either as a means of estimating the status of student learning for decision making or as a way of teaching important concepts or skills to students. For example, they might use practice tests to teach test taking skills. Or they might actually involve students in the assessment process, such as by making them evaluators of each other's work, as a means of helping students internalize achievement expectations—thus helping them to become better performers. The informed teacher can:

- cite advantages and limitations of this use of assessment, and
- specify strategies of using assessment as a teaching aid.

Then, as with the other uses of assessment, one can ask whether it is relevant to use assessment in this way in any particular classroom and whether there is evidence that assessments are used to teach.

Relative Importance of Various Uses of Assessment

In describing the assessment environment in any given classroom, one can employ information on the teacher's level of awareness about alternative assessment purposes, assessment practices, and assessment values to determine the relative importance of the various uses for that teacher. The resulting patterns of assessment uses will vary from teacher to teacher and from classroom to classroom. It may also be possible to identify an ideal environmental profile against which to gauge the appropriateness of the profile of assessment use in any particular classroom.

METHODS USED TO ASSESS ACHIEVEMENT

The teachers we observed used a wide variety of assessment methods to determine various different forms of achievement of their students. Both achievement targets and methods used to assess them varied greatly among teachers. Targets fell into four categories: content, thinking, behaviors and products. Methods fell into three categories: paper and pencil assessments, performance assessments (based on observation and judgment), and personal communication with the student. Therefore, another step in the process of profiling the assessment environment in any particular classroom is describing the targets and assessment methods used. Across environments, teachers varied according to how clear they were about targets, how well informed they were about each assessment option, how relevant methods were for any particular classroom context and the extent to which various methods were used.

Nature of the Achievement Target

Before outlining the assessment methods dimension of a classroom assessment environment, we must outline variation observed among teachers in the goals and objectives, or achievement targets, they set for their students. These expectations varied greatly across teachers, across classrooms and even across subjects within the same classroom. As the target varied, so did the nature of the assessment methodology teachers selected to reflect those targets in their assessments of student achievement.

Four specific types of targets were observed:

- subject matter content knowledge to be mastered,
- higher order thinking skills to be demonstrated,
- specific behaviors to be demonstrated, and
- products to be created that possessed specific attributes.

These were not necessarily mutually exclusive, tending to blend together on occasion.

Any particular classroom assessment environment can be profiled in part in terms of the extent to which it aims at any of these targets (i.e., the extent to which the assessment of any particular target is relevant), how clearly the target is articulated, and whether the teacher in fact assesses the relevant targets effectively.

Paper and Pencil Assessments

Four specific types of paper and pencil assessment instruments were identified:

- teacher-developed tests and quizzes,
- text-embedded tests and quizzes,
- homework and seatwork assignments, and
- standardized tests.

Each type might take any of a variety of forms, including multiple-choice, true-false, matching, fill-in, and/or essay.

Queries as to the extent to which the teacher is informed about the development and/or use of any of these options might take these forms:

- Does the teacher understand the attributes of a sound assessment and can the teacher apply those attributes to new or previously developed tests?
- Can the teacher design (i.e., plan) sound assessments?
- Can the teacher construct sound assessment exercises?
- Can the teacher interpret test results accurately?

To ascertain the relevance of any particular types of assessment to a given classroom, one might ask if the material covered is amenable to assessment via the method in question. In addition, one might ask if previously developed assessment instruments are available to cover material taught. And finally, one might determine if the teacher sees value in that type of assessment in her or his context.

Then, to conclude this phase of the profile, documentary evidence might be collected on the extent to which each method of assessment is in fact used in any particular classroom.

Performance Assessment

These are assessment methods that rely on teachers' observations and professional judgments as the means of evaluation of student achievement. Teachers might observe behaviors as students demonstrate them and evaluate their appropriateness. Or they might observe products created by students to determine the presence or absence of specific attributes. We observed many examples of such assessments in classrooms. And so, another relevant dimension of a classroom assessment environment reflects the teacher's use of this option.

Questions as to how well-informed the teacher is about this option, how relevant it is for any particular classroom, and the actual extent of its use are much like those identified for paper and pencil assessments: Does the teacher understand the attributes of a sound performance assessment? Can the teacher identify student characteristics effectively assessed in this way? Can the teacher design and develop such assessments? Are intended achievement outcomes reflected in the form of behaviors and/or products, rather than, or in addition to, correct answers to test questions? Does the teacher value this type of assessment? Does the teacher use this type of assessment?

Personal Communication

We observed teachers gathering information about student achievement through personal communication with the student. This form of assessment also took many forms: evaluating student answers to questions posed during instruction, discussions, conversations and/or interviews with students, and conversations with others about students. Thus, it clearly represents a dimension of the assessment environment that varies across classrooms.

Teachers might vary in how well informed they are about the use of personal communication as assessment. One might ask if the teacher is aware of the attributes of a sound assessment that rely on this information-gathering strategy and whether they know how to apply those standards appropriately. One might ask if the context (intended outcomes, student/teacher ratio, etc.) allow for the application of this assessment method. And one might document the extent and nature of its use in any particular classroom.

Other Methodological Issues

In addition to these three basic forms of assessment and their many variations, we uncovered other dimensions of achievement assessment methodology that can vary across classrooms. For instance, one might add to the profile how well informed the teacher is about it, how relevant it is to use, and how often teachers in fact use group (cooperative)-assessment tactics, peer assessments, student self-assessments, and/or tactics to control for cheating on assessments.

METHODS OF ASSESSING AFFECT

Classroom assessment environments also vary in terms of the extent and nature of the measurement of affective and social characteristics of students. Teachers vary, for example, on the traits they value and therefore assess and try to develop. They differ on the clarity of their understanding of these traits and in the extent of their awareness of the need to gather dependable information on them. In addition, they differ in the methods they use to gather affective information. We observed several different assessment methods in use, including observations of student behavior, questionnaires, interviews and discussions with students and others, and referring to past student records. As with the alternative methods of assessing achievement, teachers vary in their level of information about each method, how relevant or useful each option is in their context, and the extent to which they actually rely on each method to gather useful information.

Observation

Teachers can and often do draw inferences about students' affective traits based on their observations of and judgments about student behavior. They observe both the behavior patterns of individual students and the interaction behaviors of groups of students. For instance, they might draw an inference about a student's attitude by observing social behavior with classmates, or they may infer level of motivation from the pace or amount of work completed. One can ascertain how well informed a teacher is about this use of this form of assessment by asking:

- Can the teacher provide clear definitions of such traits that translate into explicit performance expectations?
- Does the teacher understand and know how to apply the principles of sound sampling of student performance in assessing these traits?
- Does the teacher know how to apply strategies for developing and conducting sound performance assessments of affective and social outcomes of instruction?

The relevance of assessing affect by means of observation depends on whether evidence of the presence or absence of any particular trait can be dependably inferred from observable behavior and whether the teacher regards such assessment as useful. In addition, of course, one can document the extent to which any particular teacher does observe and evaluate affect.

Questionnaires

Teachers can also rely on paper and pencil questionnaires to assess various affective characteristics. Teachers vary in the extent to which they are prepared to do so, how useful they feel such data collection practices are, and the extent to which they use questionnaires. Those who are prepared know the principles of sound questionnaire design and know both the strengths and limitations of such instruments. Teachers will regard questionnaires as relevant and useful to the extent that the traits they wish to assess are translated into questions to be asked of and answered by students.

Personal Contacts with Students

Teachers can supplement observational data and questionnaire data with information gathered through direct one-on-one personal interaction with the student, whether by means of interview or more casual conversation. Teachers vary in the degree of their preparedness to assess effectively in this way, the extent to which they regard such assessment as relevant and useful, and the extent to which they actually assess in this way.

Opinions of Others

Teachers also gather data on affective characteristics through personal contacts with people other than the student. They might conduct discussions, for example, with other students, parents, other teachers, guidance counselors, or school psychologists. The relevant dimensions of a classroom assessment environment are teacher knowledge of, values about, and use of this data source.

ASSESSMENT OF STUDENT INTELLIGENCE, ABILITY, OR APTITUDE

Classroom assessment environments differ in the manner and extent to which they acknowledge and/or accommodate differences in student "intelligence" or ability to learn. Teachers vary, for example, in their understanding of this concept and in the definitions they ascribe to it. They also differ in the amount of importance they attach to it as a factor in student learning. Some think it is critical and check records carefully so they know student intelligence test scores, while others prefer not to know. And finally teachers differ in the extent to which they accommodate differences in what they perceive to be the aptitude or ability level of their students as they actually plan and conduct instruction.

CRITERIA FOR SELECTING ASSESSMENT METHODS

Teachers vary in the criteria they employ when deciding which assessment method they will use to, for example, measure student achievement. Several key factors to consider are listed and defined below. As with other assessment environment ingredients, teachers differ in the level of information they have about each potential selection criterion, how much value they place on it and how often they actually apply it.

- Match to target—assessment method can be made to reflect the intended outcome of instruction (e.g., a paper and pencil test of math problem solving, a performance assessment of speaking skill)
- Adequate sample—assessment method supplies sufficient sample of performance given amount of assessment time and resources available
- Interference controlled—method permits elimination of extraneous factors that can cause misassessment, such as rater bias; inadequate reading or other communication skills on the part of the respondent; cheating; or personality factors that can mask true achievement

- Results fit purpose—various decisions require differing forms of assessment scores or results; assessment method produces proper form
- Economy of use—amount of time and/or effort required to develop, administer, score and report

Teachers vary in their understanding of these and in the relative importance they attach to each.

QUALITY OF ASSESSMENTS

Classrooms vary in the quality of the assessments developed and used there. Since teachers vary in their understanding of quality control criteria, they also vary in their proficiency in applying those criteria. Regardless of their form, whether paper and pencil, performance assessment, or personal communication, classroom assessments can be evaluated in terms of their quality using the selection criteria listed in the previous section.

For example, we can list several specific quality control standards against which to check the quality of paper and pencil tests, including match of the test to content and thinking taught, use of proper item format for intended outcome, items clearly written, etc. Similar standards are available for performance assessments: clear, written performance criteria, match of method to intended outcome, thoughtful exercises yield an appropriate sample of performance, etc. The quality of assessments in classrooms vary on these and other attributes of sound assessments.

COMMUNICATION OF FEEDBACK ON
ASSESSMENT RESULTS

Classroom assessment environments vary with regard to several salient features of the feedback on assessment results delivered to students. Two forms of feedback are relevant: oral and nonverbal feedback and written feedback. The profile of feedback patterns can vary in terms of its proportional distribution to students of various types:

- academically strong versus weak students,
- students who are correct in their responses versus those who are not,
- male versus female students, and
- students with various racial/ethnic and socioeconomic backgrounds.

Further, specific characteristics of the feedback itself can vary in terms of the proportion that is:

- oral versus nonverbal versus written,
- positive versus negative,
- public versus private,
- fair versus unfair,
- focused on achievement versus other factors,
- germane versus irrelevant,
- immediate versus delayed, and
- delivered within versus outside of class.

Another dimension of the feedback profile of a classroom assessment environment is the nature of feedback delivered to parents. This can vary in its frequency and in terms of the proportion that is: grades on report cards, written comments, and direct personal communication.

TEACHER CHARACTERISTICS

Teachers bring various critical attributes to the classroom that feed into the development and maintenance of the assessment environment in that classroom. Among those attributes are background preparation in assessment, a plan or set of values for how to spend their time, a set of personal traits, and a set of perceptions of the students with whom they work. All of these contribute to the profile of a classroom assessment environment.

Teacher Background

Teachers vary, for example, in their assessment backgrounds, i.e., where they acquired the assessment wisdom reflected in their current assessment practices. Alternative sources of knowledge of assessment methodology include preservice or graduate teacher training programs, inservice training programs, ideas and suggestions of colleagues, readings in the professional literature, guidelines that accompany textbooks or curriculum materials, and/or wisdom derived through years of experience. The origin may be related to the assessment values and practices manifested in classroom practice.

Teacher Use of Time

Teachers vary in the amount of professional time they spend involved in assessment in relation to the amount of time spent involved in other teaching activities, such as planning instruction, teaching one-on-one, teaching whole groups, or managing student behavior. In addition, we found variation in how teachers spend their assessment time, whether:

- reviewing and selecting predeveloped assessments,
- developing or revising their own assessments,
- administering assessments,
- scoring assessments,
- recording results,
- providing feedback, or
- evaluating the quality of their assessments.

The profile of a classroom assessment environment depicts the allocation of a teacher's time across these activities.

Personal Traits of the Teacher

We were able to identify a series of personal characteristics that both vary among teachers and seem to be related to the assessment environment. For instance, teachers can be profiled in terms of their:

- perception of their role in the classroom, whether maker and teacher of curriculum or provider of curriculum developed by others,

- professional expectations of self, from little to a great deal,
- structure needs, from unstructured to highly structured,
- definition of high quality performance on the part of students, from demanding correctness to evaluating degrees of quality,
- reliance on stereotypic views of students, ranging from never to frequent,
- attention to exceptional students, from no attention given to a great deal,
- sense of performance norms or expectations, from no sense to clear sense,
- orientation to risk taking or experimentation in the classroom, from no risks to frequent risks,
- orientation to cheating, ranging from no concern to great concern,
- values placed on promptness of work completion,
- preferred interpersonal environment surrounding assessment, whether cooperative or competitive,
- basis for interpreting assessment results, whether norm-referenced or criterion-referenced,
- attributions of reasons for student success or failure, ranging from totally due to teacher to totally due to the student, and
- values regarding grading practices, varying in terms of weight given to achievement, ability, or affective and social characteristics.

Teachers bring many important personal characteristics to the classroom environment. Clearly, these influence the nature and quality of assessment there.

Teacher Perceptions of Students

Based on our observations, we have concluded that classroom assessments are interpersonal activities with significant antecedents in the teachers' perceptions of various attributes of their students. That is, teachers appear to select assessment methods in part on the basis of their evaluations of a variety of characteristics of their students. Those perceptions can be solicited from teachers and can be included in the assessment environment profile.

Several such student characteristics are listed below. Any particular classroom assessment environment can be profiled in terms of whether the teacher regards the students to be high or low on the continuum of that trait, whether variation in that trait across students is recognized, and whether the teacher accommodates that variation in instruction. Perceived student traits that may affect assessment practices include:

- ability to learn,
- willingness to learn,
- rate of achievement,
- level of personal responsibility,
- study skills,
- social skills,
- willingness to perform,
- feedback needs,
- self-assessment skills,
- sense of fairness of assessments used,
- amount of test anxiety, and
- parental pressure to achieve.

ASSESSMENT POLICY

School districts, buildings, and departments often establish assessment policies that govern or constrain assessment practices and procedures. Classroom assessment environments vary in the extent to which they are covered by such policies, whether teachers are familiar with and understand the implications of those policies and, most importantly, whether teachers allow their assessment practices to be influenced by these policies. Relevant policies might focus on:

- required curriculum content and skills that must be taught and assessed in the classroom,

- the assessment practices to be used in district and classroom assessment programs,
- procedures for providing feedback or results, such as report card grading policies,
- homework requirements,
- teacher evaluation procedures, or
- issues governing selection of students for special programs.

SUMMARY

Obviously, classroom assessment environments vary on many counts. They are multidimensional, dynamic entities that reflect attributes of the larger educational and social context within which they exist, attributes of the teacher who sets up the environment, and attributes of the students who function within it.

In this chapter we have identified and described literally dozens of variables that can serve as the basis of the profile of any particular classroom assessment environment. These are listed in a profiling instrument form in Appendix B. Key variables include assessment purposes served, assessment methods used, criteria used to select from among available methods, the actual quality of assessments used, the nature and quality of feedback provided in the classroom, teacher characteristics, and policies that govern assessment.

In the next two chapters, we illustrate the richness of description that can be achieved by applying this framework to the realities of assessment in a variety of classrooms. We reveal how the process of observing classrooms, interviewing teachers, and studying assessment documents can produce the data needed to profile and compare various assessment environments. It may be that additional applications of the descriptive framework in a broader range of contexts will reveal that we can generate an "ideal" profile for certain types of classrooms. Only time and more research will tell.

But for now, our major point is that the profile reveals how much teachers need to know about assessment to establish and manage their own effectively functioning assessment environment. Read the following high school social-studies classroom profile description and the subsequent comparisons of profiles across classrooms with a sense of their implications for teachers, teacher-training programs, instructional leadership responsibilities, and assessment policy.

CHAPTER 6

Applying the Assessment Environment Profile

We used the framework to profile the assessment environments in great detail in eight high school classrooms.* Our goal was not only to record each element in the profile, detailing the complexity of classrooms, but also to be able to describe in rich detail how the various elements come together to create a total environment.

Space limitations will not permit the description of all eight high school classroom assessment environments in this volume. Therefore, to demonstrate the precision of the description that can be obtained using the framework, we present in full the profile of a sophomore history class taught by Mr. Smith (a pseudonym). And then, to show the sensitivity of the framework to variations in students, content, and the use of assessment, we compare the history class profile to that of a senior accelerated economics class taught by the same teacher.

Both classroom assessment environments were profiled by the same researcher. Based on several days of observation, as well as interviews with the teacher and students and the analysis of assessment documents, the researcher used the rating scales provided in the profile instrument to map specific elements of each environment. Then explanatory comments are added to fill-in detail about each.

---

*The observation and recording scheme used to profile these classrooms is reproduced in its entirety in Appendix B.

PROFILE OF A HISTORY CLASS

I. ASSESSMENT PURPOSES

A. Diagosing individual student needs

Uninformed _ X _ _ _	Well-informed*
Irrelevant _ X _ _ _	Relevant
Not used _ X _ _ _	Used frequently

B. Diagnosing group needs

Uninformed _ X _ _ _	Well-informed
Irrelevant _ X _ _ _	Relevant
Not used _ X _ _ _	Used frequently

Comments: (Parts A and B). Diagnosis cannot have a major influence on this teacher's work, since the entire year's activity is closely blocked out in advance. Each chapter's homework, tests, makeups, lectures, films, and speakers are designated in full detail in an individual file which Mr. Smith has meticulously compiled. Since this is not the first year with the text, these plans have been used before to the teacher's satisfaction. Little adjustment is therefore made based on ongoing diagnosis. And the class cohorts are, in the teacher's estimation, quite similar from year to year and from one individual class to another.

What diagnosis of students, individual and group that is performed, is done primarily through a fall sizing up task and through review assignments that precede each test. In the fall, Mr. Smith "gives a few exercises" that enable him to tell what skills the students are bringing to the class. Typically, these consist of a map-reading task, a note-taking exercise, and a few direct questions. Results are not taken too seriously, since he finds that "there is consistency from group to group each fall."

---

*Each researcher charged with profiling understood that each point—each rating scale represents a point in a continuum anchored at both ends by polar adjectives, with outer points representing extremes and midpoints representing a balance between the anchors. For example, the terms *very* and *somewhat* serve to modify the adjectives in this illustration. All raters were trained to complete profile ratings according to standard procedures.

Pretest review exercises could function as a diagnostic instrument, but that is not their purpose. They are due the day of the test, so they do not affect test content or pretest class emphases. Their only diagnostic function is as a check, if the test results are generally bad, as to where the students might be falling down.

C. Assigning grades

Uninformed	_	X	_	_	_ Well-informed
Irrelevant	_	_	_	X	_ Relevant
Not used	_	_	_	_	X Used frequently

Comments: (Part C). All written work is graded. With the exception of two or three more artistic products (e.g., a drawing of a Civil War combatant) assigned during the year, grades are derived directly from written assignments and tests. Assignments receive points and their due dates are set—all work for a unit or chapter must be submitted before the test over that material. Work not submitted on time is assessed as a zero. Tests are point-graded and all points placed on a curve, then grades assigned to show the general distribution of about 15 percent As, 20 percent Bs, 50 percent Cs, 10 percent Ds, and 5 percent Fs.

Some assessments are not taken into consideration in grading. The limited oral questioning that does occur is not recorded, and is used as a check of on-task behavior. Mr. Smith is strict about not bringing such information into his grading practice, regarding it as part of instruction, not part of assessment. There is more that he wants students to know than is on the assignments and tests. Classroom observations give him an index of whether individuals or the group are getting just the minimum, i.e., the material assessed in writing, or if they are learning more than that. But this information does not affect instruction or assessment.

D. Grouping for instruction within class

Uninformed	_	X	_	_	_ Well-informed
Irrelevant	X	_	_	_	_ Relevant
Not used	X	_	_	_	_ Used frequently

E. Identifying students for special services

                Uninformed _ X _ _ _ Well-informed
                Irrelevant _ _ _ X _ Relevant
                Not used _ _ X _ _ Used frequently

Comments: (Part E). At this school teachers can and do make recommendations for special service placements, e.g., in and out of accelerated classes. Mr. Smith has more than once recommended a student for removal from his accelerated groups, having ascertained that "they are unable to follow the structure" of the seminar-like course. He judges this through a demonstrated inability to keep informed about current events as they pertain to the class when asked to perform orally.

F. Motivating and controlling students

                Uninformed _ X _ _ _ Well-informed
                Irrelevant _ _ X _ _ Relevant
                Not used _ _ _ X _ Used frequently

Comments: (Part F). Tests are clearly regarded by the teacher as motivational tools, assuring that the material is studied. Review assignments serve the purpose of forcing the students to go back over the chapter or unit in preparation for the test. All assigments function for this purpose, evidenced by their deadline date of the day of the relevant test.

Assessment is used indirectly to control students in the classroom. While there is little use of oral questioning of the unruly to keep students on task, Mr. Smith hands out homework assignments at the beginning of class and students who choose not to be attentive are kept busy and quiet working on their assignment. It does not appear that they must be secretive about this, just quiet and not annoying to others.

G. Evaluating instruction

                Uninformed _ X _ _ _ Well-informed
                Irrelevant _ X _ _ _ Relevant
                Not used _ X _ _ _ Used frequently

Comments: (Part G). Generally, as described in I.A–B., above, instruction is preplanned and largely lecture, not subject to alteration due to diagnosis of individual or group needs. Repetition and review are either part of the general preplan or not done.

H. Communicating achievement expectations
        Uninformed _ _ X _ _ Well-informed
        Irrelevant _ _ _ _ X Relevant
        Not used _ _ _ _ X Used frequently

Comments: (Part H). The frequent written assignments and tests are the measure of Mr. Smith's achievement expectations. He makes it clear that the students are being held responsible for a certain body of material and that assuring this learning is the purpose of the assessments.

I. Communicating affective expectations
        Uninformed _ X _ _ _ Well-informed
        Irrelevant X _ _ _ _ Relevant
        Not used _ X _ _ _ Used frequently

Comments: (Part I). While turning back tests and assignments, Mr. Smith makes affective comments, during observation only negative comments. For example, he might say to a student that his or her score (apparently a low score) reflects the level of attention that the student has been giving the class. The habitually tardy also get such negative comments when their papers are returned.

J. Providing test-taking experience
        Uninformed _ X _ _ _ Well-informed
        Irrelevant X _ _ _ _ Relevant
        Not used X _ _ _ _ Used frequently

K. Accountability Uninformed _ _ _ _ X Well-informed
                Irrelevant _ X _ _ _ Relevant
                Not used _ X _ _ _ Used frequently

Comments: (Part K). Mr. Smith places great value on his personal professionalism and sees himself as free to operate however he wishes, provided he meets professional standards and contractual obligations. He rarely has grade complaints. (See the description of the social studies department's discussion of policy for Law Day, Section VIII, below.)

L. Instructional strategy

Uninformed _ _ X _ _ Well-informed
Irrelevant _ X _ _ _ Relevant
Not used _ X _ _ _ Used frequently

M. Relative importance of purposes

Given "100 importance points" to distribute across the purposes listed below, how would you distribute those points to reflect the relative importance of the decisions listed?

Diagnosing individual needs	2
Diagnosing group needs	2
Assigning grades	60
Grouping for instruction	0
Identifying students for special services	2
Controlling and motivating	20
Evaluating instruction	1
Communicating achievement expectations	10
Communicating affective expectations	3
	100 points

II. ASSESSMENT METHODOLOGY

Testing takes place at the end of each chapter and each three-chapter unit. Since a chapter is covered in a week, each Friday is a test day. Quizzes are not given. Tests are point-graded and placed on a curve. The curve is based on an at least 50 percent correct score for a passing (C) grade. Usually, the teacher reports, there are more A and B grades than D and F grades. Test grades and assignment scores are summed by some method not made clear in response to our queries to make up a final grade that is reported as a zero to four point scale.

Along with the weekly tests, assignments form the core of assessment. There are assignments "practically every day," all written for submission and point grading. A "basic assignment" is "reading text and answering questions in writing." Before each test there is a "summmary" task that serves as a review. These may be submitted as responses to questions the teacher sets or an outline chronology. Assignments are to be turned in the following day, but will be credited if turned in any time prior to the test on the material they pertain to. Students have the right to request a rewrite, if they turn their work in long enough before the test to have the rewrite completed.

Tests are fill-in, multiple-choice, setting events in chronological order, matching sets, and short essays each with a value of five points. Make-up tests are all short essay. Quizzes are not given.

A. Assessment of Achievement

  1. Teacher-developed paper and pencil tests and quizzes
                Uninformed __ __ X __ __ Well-informed
                Inappropriate __ __ __ __ X Appropriate
                Not used __ __ __ __ X Used frequently

  2. Text-embedded paper and pencil tests and quizzes
                Uninformed __ __ X __ __ Well-informed
                Inappropriate __ X __ __ __ Appropriate
                Not used __ X __ __ __ Used frequently

Comments: (Parts 1 and 2). Mr. Smith develops his own tests and quizzes. He states that the tests that accompany the text are too "rote," that they measure only recall and that that is not his goal. Occasionally he will "borrow" one of the "good" questions from the text. However, analysis of the test questions developed by the teacher indicate that his tests, too, are basically recall exercises. (See II.A.13, below.)

3. Performance assessments

Uninformed _ X _ _ _ Well-informed
Inappropriate X _ _ _ _ Appropriate
Not used X _ _ _ _ Used frequently

Comments: (Part 3). Performance is not regularly solicited, much less assessed. History is basically a lecture course, with regular written assignments. Map-reading tasks and the two or three "art assignments" given during the year would constitute the only examples which we could observe or discover through interview. The "art assignments," of which the drawing of a civil war soldier or other period character is an example, were letter graded based on "effort," "interest taken," and "accuracy," although these terms were not further defined upon questioning. They counted as regular assignments.

4. Oral questioning strategies

Uninformed X _ _ _ _ Well-informed
Inappropriate _ X _ _ _ Appropriate
Not used _ X _ _ _ Used frequently

Comments: (Part 4). Little oral questioning is used, rather Mr. Smith lectures on selected points within the assigned text material that he expanded on in great depth. In a 40-minute class, the number of questions asked averaged less than two per period; some periods none were put to the class. Most were inferential— could they draw some conclusion or speculation from what he had just presented—and all were responded to by volunteers.

5. Standardized tests

Uninformed _ _ X _ _ Well-informed
Inappropriate X _ _ _ _ Appropriate
Not used X _ _ _ _ Used frequently

Comments: (Part 5). There will be a social studies minimum competency tests from the state soon; the social studies staff at this school is not in favor. However, they are working to prepare questions and general scope of the test drafts, in order to shape it, if possible.

6. Group assessment methods
   Uninformed _ X _ _ _ Well-informed
   Inappropriate X _ _ _ _ Appropriate
   Not used X _ _ _ _ Used frequently

7. Opinions of other teachers
   Uninformed _ _ X _ _ Well-informed
   Inappropriate _ _ X _ _ Appropriate
   Not used _ _ X _ _ Used frequently

Comments: (Part 7). This teacher shares opinions about individual students freely with his colleagues, although he does not feel that such information influences his own view. He does take recommendations from colleagues into consideration when evaluating for placement in accelerated classes.

8. Assessment of reasoning skills
   Uninformed _ X _ _ _ Well-informed
   Inappropriate _ _ _ _ X Appropriate
   Not used _ X _ _ _ Used frequently

9. Regular assignments
   Uninformed _ _ _ X _ Well-informed
   Inappropriate _ _ _ _ X Appropriate
   Not used _ _ _ _ X Used frequently

Comments: (Part 9). Assignments are set almost daily. They are point-graded and point totals are letter graded at the end of the marking period. Most assignments are short-answer questions to be answered, although map completion is also frequent. These map assignments are basically replications of maps in the text.

Editorial cartoons are also given out with questions to be answered about them. Much of this daily work is from materials accompanying the text. Almost all of it is recall work. One of the students reflected on the class work, noting that "it's always the same" and, in fact, that observation seems accurate.

10. Student peer rating

                       Uninformed X _ _ _ _ Well-informed
                  Inappropriate X _ _ _ _ Appropriate
                      Not used X _ _ _ _ Used frequently

11. Student self ratings

                       Uninformed X _ _ _ _ Well-informed
                  Inappropriate X _ _ _ _ Appropriate
                      Not used X _ _ _ _ Used frequently

12. Proportion of all assessments for all purposes that are of various types

	History
Teacher-developed paper-and-pencil tests	60
Text-embedded paper and pencil tests	5
Performance assessments	0
Oral questions	2
Standardized tests	0
Opinions of other teachers	0
Regular assignments	33
Group assessments	0
Student peer ratings	0
Student self ratings	0
	100%

13. Cognitive levels of questions posed in:

	Assignments*	Study and Discussion Questions		Oral Questions†	Tests and Quizzes	
		Text-Emb.	Teach. Devl.		Actual	Make-up
Recall	70%	74%	100%	—	99%	70%
Analysis	—	6%	—	—	—	—
Comparison	20%	2%	—	—	—	30%
Inference	—	4%	—	100%	1%	—
Evaluation	10%	14%	—	—	—	—

*Both text-embedded and teacher-developed.
†N here is extremely small; little oral questioning occurs.

14. Dealing with cheating

Uninformed _ X _ _ _ Well-informed
Inappropriate _ X _ _ _ Appropriate
Not used _ _ X _ _ Used frequently

Comments: (Part 14). Make-up tests are always different from the regular test. They require short essays, rather than objective answers, so they cannot be copied from another student who has taken the test. During tests Mr. Smith constantly monitors the room, walking around and watching the students, occasionally asking someone to move further from neighbors.

B. Assessment of Affect
Value of this factor for this teacher
Unimportant X _ _ _ _ Important

Comments: (Part B). Generally, Mr. Smith distances himself from any consideration of affective variables in his assessments. He is careful to assign points and/or grades to written or presentation work. He admits no other factors in his grading process. There is no hint of extra credit work or raising of grades for students on the basis of willingness to rewrite their assignments—the second point result is simply substituted for the first attempt.

1. Observing individual students

              Uninformed _ X _ _ _ Well-informed
             Inappropriate _ X _ _ _ Appropriate
               Not used _ X _ _ _ Used frequently

Comments: (Part 1). Very little attention is paid—Mr. Smith lectures, using the same lecture regardless of the attentiveness, skills, etc., of the students. The single example that suggests attention to affective factors of individual students is the creation of the alternative review schema for those students who complained that they just couldn't get the facts straight. Mr. Smith felt they had weak study skills and this matrix format would assist them. The alternative assignment is assessed as equally sufficient work.

2. Observing group interactions

              Uninformed X _ _ _ _ Well-informed
             Inappropriate X _ _ _ _ Appropriate
               Not used X _ _ _ _ Used frequently

3. Using questionnaires

              Uninformed X _ _ _ _ Well-informed
             Inappropriate X _ _ _ _ Appropriate
               Not used X _ _ _ _ Used frequently

4. Using interviews (formal and informal)

              Uninformed _ X _ _ _ Well-informed
             Inappropriate X _ _ _ _ Appropriate
               Not used X _ _ _ _ Used frequently

Comments: (Part 4). Mr. Smith does not spend a great deal of time one-on-one with his students. He readily answers questions before and after class, but few students seek him out, nor does he encourage this. He thinks they should go to counselors with general academic or personal problems.

5. Opinions of other teachers

              Uninformed _ _ X _ _ Well-informed
             Inappropriate _ _ X _ _ Appropriate
               Not used _ X _ _ _ Used frequently

6. Opinions of other students

Uninformed _ _ X _ _ Well-informed

Inappropriate X _ _ _ _ Appropriate

Not used X _ _ _ _ Used frequently

7. Opinions of parents

Uninformed _ X _ _ _ Well-informed

Inappropriate X _ _ _ _ Appropriate

Not used X _ _ _ _ Used frequently

Comments: (Part 7). In this school most parents are actively involved in their children's education, are attentive to homework, push their children to achieve. This teacher does not seek out parents' opinions, nor does he regard them as important for any decision he makes.

8. Past student records

Uninformed _ X _ _ _ Well-informed

Inappropriate X _ _ _ _ Appropriate

Not used X _ _ _ _ Used frequently

Comments: (Part 8). The teacher does not report any reference to past student records.

9. Checklist of affective characteristics measured (considered):
   (none measured)

__	Seriousness of purpose	*Code:*
__	Motivation and effort	F = formal assessment
__	Attitude	conducted
__	Learning style	I = informal assessment
__	Interests	conducted
__	Values	= Not measured
__	Preferences	
__	Academic self-concept	
__	Locus of control	
__	Anxiety	
__	Maturity	
__	Social skills	
__	Study skills	
__	Other (specify: _____)	

10. Relative importance of affective assessment methods:

Observing individual students	70
Observing group interactions	0
Using questionnaires	0
Using interviews (formal and informal)	0
Opinions of other teachers	30
Opinions of other students	0
Opinions of parents	0
Past student records	0
	100%

Note: Very low overall use.

C. Assessment of Ability

1. Value of this factor for the teacher

Unimportant _ X _ _ _ Important

Comments: Teacher's Definition: General cognitive skills that enable a student to comprehend the intent of an assignment or reading and to interpret it in order to complete it successfully.

Measurement of Ability		
	Measured formally	__
	Measured informally	__
	Not measured	X

Ingredients considered in assessment of ability, if measured:

FACTOR(S) INCLUDED IN ASSESSMENT	MEASURED HOW?

Comments: Mr. Smith tries to assess purely on the basis of achievement (and is confident he succeeds). This means learning a body of knowledge and becoming able to learn from nontextual materials such as maps, historic photos, and cartoons.

2. Check decisions influenced by results (i.e., change with varying levels of ability).

__ Instructional objectives
__ Instructional strategies
__ Grouping for instruction (within class)
__ Methods for measuring achievement
__ Grading standards
X̲ Students selected for special services (accelerated courses)
__ Other (specify: _____)

D. Text Assessments

Checklist of assessment components provided with text

Available	Used	
X̲	___	Oral questions for class use
X̲	X̲	Homework assignments
X̲	___	General-assessment guidelines for teachers
X̲	*	Paper-and-pencil tests
___	___	Performance assessments
X̲	___	Scoring guidelines
___	___	Quality-control guidelines
___	___	Other (specify: _____)

*Occasional questions selected for integrating into teacher-developed tests.

III. CRITERIA FOR SELECTING ASSESSMENT METHODS

A. Results fit purpose

Uninformed _ X̲ _ _ _ Well-informed
Unimportant _ _ _ _ X̲ Important
Not used _ _ _ _ X̲ Used frequently

B. Method matches material taught

$$\begin{array}{llllll}\text{Uninformed} & X & \_ & \_ & \_ & \_ & \text{Well-informed}\\ \text{Unimportant} & \_ & \_ & \_ & \_ & X & \text{Important}\\ \text{Not used} & \_ & \_ & \_ & \_ & X & \text{Used frequently}\end{array}$$

Comments: (Parts A and B). Generally, his test recall qu :stions do ascertain if the students have studied the material. Commenting on a revised review assignment option he developed at students' request, he said he was glad he'd designed this alternative, since, "Their scores improved and that, of course, is my goal." Certainly recall questioning suits the pedagogy of lecture about factual matters.

C. Ease of development

$$\begin{array}{llllll}\text{Uninformed} & \_ & \_ & X & \_ & \_ & \text{Well-informed}\\ \text{Unimportant} & \_ & \_ & X & \_ & \_ & \text{Important}\\ \text{Not used} & \_ & \_ & \_ & X & \_ & \text{Used frequently}\end{array}$$

D. Ease of scoring

$$\begin{array}{llllll}\text{Uninformed} & \_ & X & \_ & \_ & \_ & \text{Well-informed}\\ \text{Unimportant} & \_ & X & \_ & \_ & \_ & \text{Important}\\ \text{Not used} & \_ & \_ & \_ & X & \_ & \text{Used frequently}\end{array}$$

E. Origin of assessment

$$\begin{array}{llllll}\text{Uninformed} & \_ & \_ & X & \_ & \_ & \text{Well-informed}\\ \text{Unimportant} & \_ & \_ & \_ & X & \_ & \text{Important}\\ \text{Not used} & \_ & \_ & \_ & X & \_ & \text{Used frequently}\end{array}$$

F. Time required to administer

$$\begin{array}{llllll}\text{Uninformed} & \_ & \_ & X & \_ & \_ & \text{Well-informed}\\ \text{Unimportant} & \_ & \_ & \_ & \_ & X & \text{Important}\\ \text{Not used} & \_ & \_ & \_ & \_ & X & \text{Used frequently}\end{array}$$

Comments: (Parts C through F). These tests are easy to write, though it takes some consideration to be assured that the entire domain is sampled; they are easy to grade; and they can be administered in a class period. Since one day a week is given over to testing, this last is an important factor. Further, time is given to review of the test when it is turned back; up to 20 minutes is spent on going over the questions and putting up the point results and the curve.

Make-up tests are short essay, with specific points assigned to each essay and Mr. Smith can readily state just what information has to be there to get credit, so these, too, are easy to score. He reports that he does correct for bad writing on assignments, sometimes requiring rewrite, but this is not done on tests nor is it factored into scoring.

Mr. Smith draws most of his regular assignments from materials provided with the text and develops his own tests. It is important to him that the tests not be known to the students, suggesting that origin of the test is a factor.

G. Degree of objectivity

Uninformed X _ _ _ _ Well-informed
Unimportant _ _ _ _ X Important
Not used _ _ _ _ X Used frequently

Comments: (Part G). This is a most important factor. Although he has a well-planned, highly quantifiable grading strategy and tests that are predominantly objective (multiple choice, reorder, matching, fill in the blank), he worries that he is "too subjective." His comments on this subject indicate that he feels the best way to correct for this is to assess often, but that may not be sufficient.

H. Applicability to measuring thinking skills

Uninformed X _ _ _ _ Well-informed
Unimportant _ _ _ _ X Important
Not used _ _ _ _ X Used frequently

Comments: (Part H). This is an important consideration. Mr. Smith eschews use of the text-embedded tests because they are "too recall." His tests, he says, sample all levels of skills. Analysis of these teacher-developed tests, however, indicates that almost all of his questions, like those in the text, are recall. Thus, Mr. Smith is not able to correctly apply an assessment principle that he himself regards as critical.

I. Effective control of cheating

Uninformed __ __ X __ __ Well-informed
Unimportant __ __ X __ __ Important
Not used __ __ __ X __ Used frequently

Comments: (Part I). Cheating is handled through use of a different test for make-up. It is short essay, rather than objective questions, so papers cannot be borrowed. There does not seem to be any concern on the part of this teacher that assignment work is shared. Indeed, he comments that some of the students who ask for the alternative review assignment work them up together. The assignment work must be completed to get credit and, he feels, students must comprehend it in order to do well on the tests. That is sufficient monitoring.

J. Relative importance of criteria

Results fit purpose	10
Method matches material taught	10
Ease of development	5
Ease of scoring	15
Origin of assessment	5
Time required to administer	15
Degree of objectivity	20
Applicability to measuring thinking skills	10
Effective control of cheating	10
	100%

IV. QUALITY OF ASSESSMENTS

A. Percent of *paper-and-pencil assessments* (teacher-developed or text-embedded) having the following characteristics (need *not* total 100%):

percent	
90	Clear description of assessment specifications
60	Matches content of instruction
80	Matches cognitive levels of instruction
90	Minimizes time required to gather needed information

80	Item format matches desired outcome
90	Items clearly written
90	Items sample domain
95	Scoring procedures planned
0	Scoring criteria written for essays
90	Clear directions
90	High-quality reproduction
90	Test scheduled to minimize distractions

Comments: (Part A). Scoring criteria for essays: All the "essays" on regular tests are short written answers and they are awarded 5 points. Make-up tests consist of longer essays, usually 4 or 5, given 5 points each. Grades for tests are derived from letters or the 4-point scale, so total number of points for the test is irrelevant. The essays are all recall; Mr. Smith "knows what should be there" and assigns points. He marks for style, spelling, etc. on assignments (and sometimes requires a resubmission), but these are not considered on tests.

Match between content and instruction is high in one sense but not in another. Mr. Smith lectures the facts and then asks for facts back on the tests. The assignments are also predominantly factual, especially the review assignments to prepare the students for the tests. There was, however, a marked difference between the content of instructional lectures and the material on assignments and tests. For classroom lecture, Mr. Smith selected certain aspects to describe in detail (e.g., a battle line in World War I) which did not appear on the tests. They cannot be interpreted as focusing on the most important issues, but rather as interesting incidents selected for some other reason. The students appeared to be aware of this, for only those who were interested in the topic paid attention. Thus, with regard to whether the items sampled the domain, yes, they did clearly do so with regard to the text material, although the lectures did not point to that.

Scoring procedures were fully planned and articulated to the students. The placement of the cuts on the curve was generally set at 50 percent of the points for a C, although this went up to nearly 60 percent, if the class scored generally well.

B. Percent of *performance assessments* having the following characteristics: (Performance assessments not used)

Percent

	Clear description of trait to be measured with levels of proficiency articulated
_____	Matches intended outcomes of instruction
	Minimizes time required to gather needed information
_____	Clear performance criteria
_____	Students aware of criteria
_____	Thoughtful exercises yield performance samples
_____	Exercises sample performance domain
_____	Performance rating planned
_____	Results match information needs

C. Percent of *oral questions* having the following characteristics:

Percent

30	Sampling methods cover range of achievement levels of students
10	Strategies involve everyone
95	Teacher waits for response
10	Student's response given supportive reaction
30	Questions match cognitive levels of instruction
0	Written performance records maintained

Comments: (Part C). There was very little oral questioning in these classes; questions averaged less than two a period. All were answered by volunteers; no records were maintained. Questions were inference, i.e., could the student take the presentation the teacher was engaged in one step further. This contrasted with the basically recall written assessment environment and the generally factual content of the lectures.

V. FEEDBACK PROCEDURES

A. For *oral* and *nonverbal* feedback

Percent of feedback delivered to students who are:

Percent
<u> 70 </u> Strong (vs. weak)
<u> 70 </u> Correct (vs. incorrect)
<u> 70 </u> Male (vs. female)

Percent of *oral* or *nonverbal* feedback having the following characteristics:
Percent
<u> 95 </u> Delivered in class (vs. out of class)
<u> 30 </u> Oral (vs. nonverbal)
<u> 90 </u> Public (vs. private)
<u> 50 </u> Positive (vs. negative)
<u> 90 </u> Fair (vs. unfair)
<u> 10 </u> Focused on achievement (vs. affect)
<u> 90 </u> Germane (vs. irrelevant)
<u> 90 </u> Immediate (vs. delayed)

Comments: (Part A). Mr. Smith varies his tone of voice and his facial expression little. There is almost no eye contact with the class. Even admonishments to misbehaving students are very controlled. Indeed, in the few cases in which such control actions were necessary, he quietly moved up to the offender, without even being noticed, and spoke in a quiet manner, yet conveyed strong approbation, even barely controlled anger. Such actions had a strong effect on the individual and the class. The class was generally quiet and, if many were not tracking the lecture, they were quiet and under control. Students responses to questions rarely evoked verbal comment or even nonverbal comment.

B. For *written* feedback to students

Percent of feedback delivered to students who are:
Percent
<u> 50 </u> Strong (vs. weak)
<u> 50 </u> Correct (vs. incorrect)
<u> 50 </u> Male (vs. female)

Percent of *written* feedback having the following characteristics:

Percent

20	Comment (vs. symbol)
40	Positive (vs. negative)
90	Fair (vs. unfair)
95	Focused on achievement (vs. affect)
90	Germane (vs. irrelevant)

Uses samples of performance as feedback

Never __ X __ __ __ Frequently

Uses public-achievement chart as feedback

Never __ X __ __ __ Frequently

Comments: (Part B). Some students' assignments got written comments, especially in the "essay"/short-answer sections, where language problems were noted. The written feedback was minimal, but certainly appropriate where used.

C. Feedback to parents   Minimal X __ __ __ __ Frequently

Relative use of different media:

99	Grades
0	Written comments
1	Consultations
100%	

Comments: (Part C). If there are problems, he follows the school policy for written parent contact, but does not see them unless they come in to meet with the counselor and request his presence.

VI. DESCRIPTION OF TEACHER AND ASSESSMENT

A. Teacher's background

1. Teacher experience, number of years:

21	Overall
21	At grade level
21	In school
21	With content

2. Relative contributions of various sources to teacher's knowledge of assessment methodology

Percent

10	Teacher preparation training
0	Inservice training
10	Ideas and suggestions of colleagues
2	Professional literature
2	Teacher's guide to textbooks
76	Own experience in classroom
100%	

Comments: (Part A). This teacher would like more training in assessment and evaluation.

B. Teacher's expenditure of time

1. Proportion of time spent in *teaching* activities

Percent

25	Planning
2	Teaching (one on one)
53	Teaching (group)
20	Assessing (see list below)
0	Other (specify: _____)
100%	

2. Proportion of time spent in *assessment* activities (paper-and-pencil, performance assessment, oral assignments)

Percent

10	Reviewing and selecting assessments
30	Developing own assessments
18	Administering

_35_	Scoring and recording
_5_	Providing feedback
_2_	Evaluating quality
100%	

Comments: (Part B). 1. Here I have construed "teaching activities" to exclude time spent in and out of class on noninstructionally related activities, such as reading announcements.

2. Note that assessments are developed before the term starts and all work is fully laid out. Assignments usually are not developed by the teacher, but drawn from text materials; some tests and many assignments are used from year to year.

The following addresses how students' time is spent, at least their in-class time (for which we have data). In these classes time usage breaks down as follows:

Instruction	60%	(Lecture is 90% of this; at most oral questioning 10%)
Assessment	35%	(One day a week is testing, i.e., 20% of all class time; tests and grading are reviewed in class; assignments are not discussed in detail)
Other	5%	(Little class time is used for other purposes)

C. Teacher characteristics

			Servant of policy delivering
Role in the classroom	Curriculum maker and presenter	X __ __ __ __	required content
Expectations of professional self	Expects little	__ __ __ __ X	Expects a great deal
Structure needs	Rigid	X __ __ __ __	Flexible
View of high-quality performance	Correctness demanded	X __ __ __ __	Degree of quality eval.
Stereotypic view of students	None	__ X __ __ __	Expressed often

Attends to exceptional student	Never	__ __ X __ __	Frequently
Sense of performance norms	Unclear	__ __ __ __ X	Very clear
Orientation to experimentation	No risks	__ __ X __ __	Risk taker
Orientation to cheating	No concern	__ __ X __ __	Major concern
Amount of cheating	None	__ __ X __ __	A great deal
Value of promptness; importance of timely work completion	Unimportant	__ __ __ __ X	Important

Interpersonal environment of the classroom regarding assessment:

Cooperative	None	__ X __ __ __	Frequent
Competitive	None	__ __ __ X __	Frequent

Attributions for reasons of student success/failure:

Percent
 70 Due to student
 30 Due to teacher
100%

Basis for grading students:

Percent
  5 Sense of ability
 95 Demonstrated achievement
100%

Interpretation of assessment:

Percent
 50 Norm-referenced
 50 Criterion-referenced
100%

Comments: (Part C). Mr. Smith highly values his autonomy as a professional in charge of his own classroom. His comments on his and his colleagues' opposition to testing standards indicate this.

He sees it as his responsiblity to communicate the base content of the subject matter and how he does it is his decision. At the same time, he regards it as his basic public charge to instill a fundamental set of information about these social studies topics in his students. High school, he says, is the last chance to make informed citizens and social studies teachers must do this.

Mr. Smith expects students to become part of the classroom process, following the regular pattern of the weeks, knowing what is expected of them, and taking responsibility for themselves. He does not try to make overtures to students to motivate them, nor seek to know why they do not perform. This self-responsibility or maturity factor appears to be an important part of what he tries to teach albeit not explicitly. Students' failure to learn becomes their own choice. Notably, he is open to amending assessment, if students bring their difficulties to him, as he did when a group requested a different review assignment in history.

He is committed to assessing on the basis of achievement, but, in fact, takes in some affective and ability variables as well.

The curve system used for grading is partially criterion referenced, i.e., 50 percent is always the minimum required for passing.

VII. TEACHER'S PERCEPTIONS OF STUDENT CHARACTERISTICS

A. Ability to learn

$$Low \_ \_ X \_ \_ High$$
$$No\ variation \_ \_ \_ X \_ Great\ deal$$
$$Variation\ ignored\ X \_ \_ \_ \_ Addressed$$

B. Willingness to learn

$$Low \_ \_ X \_ \_ High$$
$$No\ variation \_ \_ \_ \_ X\ Great\ deal$$
$$Variation\ ignored\ X \_ \_ \_ \_ Addressed$$

C. Rate of achievement

$$Low \_ \_ X \_ \_ High$$
$$Decreasing \_ \_ X \_ \_ Increasing$$
$$No\ variation \_ \_ \_ \_ X\ Great\ deal$$
$$Variation\ ignored\ X \_ \_ \_ \_ Addressed$$

D. Maturity

Irresponsible __ __ X __ __ Responsible
No variation __ __ __ __ X Great deal
Variation ignored X __ __ __ __ Addressed

E. Study skills

Undeveloped __ __ X __ __ Developed
No variation __ __ X __ __ Great deal
Variation ignored __ X __ __ __ Addressed

F. Social skills

Undeveloped __ __ X __ __ Developed
No variation __ __ __ X __ Great deal
Variation ignored X __ __ __ __ Addressed

G. Willingness to perform

Reticent __ __ X __ __ Willing
No variation __ __ __ X __ Great deal
Variation ignored X __ __ __ __ Addressed

H. Feedback needs

Weak __ X __ __ __ Strong
No variation __ __ X __ __ Great deal
Variation ignored X __ __ __ __ Addressed

I. Self-assessment skills

Undeveloped __ X __ __ __ Developed
No variation __ __ X __ __ Great deal
Variation ignored X __ __ __ __ Addressed

J. Sense of fairness

Unclear __ __ X __ __ Clear
No variation __ X __ __ __ Great deal
Variation ignored X __ __ __ __ Addressed

K. Reaction to testing

Tranquil __ __ X __ __ Anxious
No variation __ __ X __ __ Great deal
Variation ignored X __ __ __ __ Addressed

L. Parental expectations

Unclear _ _ _ X _ Clear
Low _ _ _ _ X High
Unimportant _ _ X _ _ Important
No variation _ X _ _ _ Great deal
Variation ignored X _ _ _ _ Addressed

Comments: (Part VII). Mr. Smith generally regards most of these factors as either irrelevant or things that he should avoid attending to. His general approach appears to be to refuse to cater to student insecurities, variation, etc., in order to motivate them to rise above these things and take responsibility for learning the material of the course. His students get little feedback, but he feels he gives significant feedback.

His definition of success is measured overtly only in achievement terms: the students demonstrate that they have mastered a specified set of material. He has fairly and accurately evaluated and reported their progress. And, though not expressed to them, he looks for the students to grow in ability and motivation to do independent work.

VIII. ORIGINS OF POLICY

These policies impinge on the classroom:
Testing
State: Minimum competency test in preparation, not yet used.

Department: The department is working cooperatively to prepare a position statement for input to the state wide competency test; it has as its policy that individual teachers should decide their own requirements—"We fought long and hard for academic freedom," says the subject teacher.

Reporting (and Grading)
District: District requires grade reporting four times for nine-week periods. They do not require that a specific grade be tied to some specific percent. District also provides a "comments report," computer form with 20 affective and achievement comments to select from.

School: Recommends that 50% be a passing mark minimum on any test.

Homework
School: Teachers must send work home for any student who falls behind, then contact counselor, and, at third stage, request meeting with parents, student and counselor.

District: District policy is that schools must set up some procedure for consultation with parents by fifth or sixth week of a grading period in which a student is not completing sufficient work to expect to pass.

Class Size
District: There are "guidelines" but the union has not yet succeeded in setting contractual limits.

Selection for Special Programs and Recognition
District: Establishes criteria for accelerated and skills emphasis students and places primary responsibility on counselors.

School: Counselors select students for special programs, but teachers can make recommendations and expect that their recommendations will probably be followed. Teachers can dismiss unqualified students from their accelerated track classes, if they cannot or will not do the work.

Departmental: The department staff selects all students for special recognition through vote at its weekly meeting.

Attendance
District: Policies are generally set by the district.

School: Absence, lateness rules are set by the school and teachers are expected to adhere to them. Some teachers serve as hall monitors to intervene directly with tardy students.

Content to be Taught
State: Approves a list of acceptable texts to be selected from by the districts.

District: Approves a list of texts to be selected among by the schools.

Department: Entire staff reviews and selects by vote among the offered texts. Teachers may deviate from the text, but may not use a different text.

Discipline
District/School: All discipline procedures are specified by the district and applied to building conditions by the school administra-

tion. Building policy on what constitutes an excused or unexcused absense is firm.

Department: By consensus the department arrives at methods by which to assure that activities out of school which they authorize are categorized as excused absences.

SUMMARY OF PROFILE FINDINGS

This assessment profile provides insight into one teacher's assessment practices and instructional philosophy. In these history classes, the primary purposes of assessment are grading and motivating: motivating students to learn a body of material through assignment of grades on daily assignments and weekly tests. The assessment practices form a core structure in the classroom routine and consume a third of available class time.

This teacher takes his assessment work as an important part of his professional responsibility, although it is routinized and expedient testing models are followed. All tests are teacher-developed. Assignments are carefully selected when adopted or adapted from text and materials provided with the text. While he voices concerns that his assessment methodology may be "too subjective," there are virtually no assessments that require judgment on his part, since both tests and assignments are written exercises that require short-answer, multiple-choice, and other objective techniques almost exclusively. Affective variables and ability judgments play little part.

Assessment matches instruction in level of thinking skill required, i.e., factual information is presented and recall is measured. But test content derives from the reading assignments, not from the elaborations that make up the lectures. Thus, student off-task behavior is common in class and not a detriment to achieving high grades.

Feedback to students is communicated largely through grades. Variations among students are disregarded insofar as possible, in an apparent attempt to achieve evenhandedness through assessment of students based only on the evidence of their mastery of the material as indicated in their written work. All students are regarded as competent to meet course mastery requirements, although they may evidence lack of motivation. The teacher holds himself accountable for assuring that students learn a core of information about history that they will need for adult life. Assessment serves the purpose of demonstrating, to himself and others, that this obligation is being met.

ACCELERATED ECONOMICS: A CONTRASTING ASSESSMENT ENVIRONMENT

Comparison of this same teacher's senior accelerated economics classes demonstrates the sensitivity of the assessment profile for uncovering assessment practices, philosophies, and training needs. The following information is exerpted from analysis of a formed assessment profile of Mr. Smith's economics serminar. In sharp contrast to the sophomore history courses, in which daily written assignments and weekly objective tests are a set routine, senior economics students are assessed on the basis of both written tests and oral performance activities.

Written work for the semester includes just four unit tests and a final exam, all objective in format much like history. But, fully half the grade is based on oral reporting of assigned topical material. Students are grouped for developing and presenting these reports, but are graded individually, using criteria of factual correctness and completeness and also affective factors such as speaking clearly, confidence, and ability to think on their feet and respond to questions. Grading of these reports takes place simultaneously with the presentation, with Mr. Smith stating that it is clear to him if "it's all there" (A), a "small amount missed" (B), or "a lot missed" (C). Students are distributed on a curve, but the lowest possible grade is C for an accelerated class. Also unlike history students, economics students must pay careful attention to classroom presentation, since test questions are in part selected out of students' oral reports.

Mr. Smith's goal for history students is to master a set of material presented through readings and lecture. But in accelerated economics it is not content that matters, but the ability "to understand the structure of the course." Students who do not comprehend the expectations in this less directed environment are dropped from the seminar.

Questions to students in economics range across all thinking skill levels, contrasting with the purely inferential questioning posed in history. Tests, however, are still largely recall. Economics students are perceived to all be motivated, skilled, and mature. Those who are not are dropped to standard economics. Analysis of class time on different tasks also reveals the interesting observation that in economics, but not in history, instruction and assessment are overlapping activities. About one-fifth of the class time is spent in presentation by the teacher and three-fourths is consumed by the oral reports, assessments which also constitute the primary mode of instruction.

Thus, a different sense of the task, as well as a different perception of the students, leads a teacher to create two very different assessment environments. The assessment profile reports the similarities and differences between the two environments in a way that leads directly to identification of the assessment difficulties for this particular teacher. The weaknesses may find different articulation, but can be seen to derive from the same specific set of skills needed. Consider the following.

Diagnosis and Evaluating Instruction

In neither class are these two important purposes for assessment applied.

Match of Content in Instruction, Assessments and Materials

In each of the classes two of the three are matched and one fails to match. In history, the tests are derived from text materials, but lecture material is not tested. Students do not pay attention in class. In economics, text material is not tested, rather questions are derived from student oral reports and teacher instruction. Economics students do not read the text assignments, but they do attend class.

Thinking Skills

In history, lectures and tests are almost exclusively recall, while some assignments may be at other levels. In economics, tests are recall, while questions to oral report groups are at all thinking skill levels. Further, the teacher's confidence in his ability to state questions at higher levels is not borne out by his practice.

Assessments Based on Teacher Judgment

While Mr. Smith reported that he worries that his tests are "too subjective," his testing is, in fact, almost entirely objective questioning of recall. On the other hand, in his one key practice of performance assessment, he is confident that his unwritten standards for evaluating economics oral reports are valid and reliable. Yet, these evaluations are not only highly subjective, they compound achievement and affective variables.

Grading Practices

Both history and economics are curve-graded, with a preset distribution of grades. In history, point accumulations for each grading period from assignments are converted to curve-based grades and, once again, curved at the end of the year. Letter grades, derived from points, are averaged to compute final letter grades.

CONCLUSION

Thus, these profiles serve to identify possible assessment difficulties of an individual teacher. These kinds of insights emerged from the profiles of all teachers studied.

While we do not intend to provide such detail about all, we do use the following chapter to compare and contrast some of the most interesting features of the eight high school classrooms studied. The result is a clear sense of the diversity of assessment environments to be found in schools.

CHAPTER 7

Similarities and Differences in Assessment Environments

The profile of a history classroom detailed in the preceding chapter offers a rich description of one assessment environment. This chapter explores the differences and similarities among the eight high school environments to which that same profile was applied, analyzing the data across classrooms and subject areas in terms of the key factors in the profile: assessment purposes, assessment methods, criteria for method selection, assessment quality, feedback procedures, teacher characteristics affecting assessment, teacher perceptions of students, and policy issues. Recall that the classes studied included two each in math, science, social studies and language arts. Complementary conclusions from our initial, less-structured sixth-grade classroom studies (described in Chapter 4) supplement the high school findings described below. This chapter illustrates the capability of the profiling instrument to capture the essential components that characterize diverse assessment environments.

Some of the particulars of assessment practice reported and some of the conclusions drawn represent only initial inferences on our part as to the broader nature of classroom assessment environments. Our conclusions on the ways in which classroom assessment patterns change across various subject areas await verification by other researchers and in other classroom contexts.

Still these studies, though limited in number, indicate that the profiling instrument can and does identify factors and address issues that complete description of a classroom assessment environment must encompass. While we cannot assert with confidence what classroom assessment environments generally look like, we do proport to understand what is required to develop a description of an environment. Collecting a representative sample of assessment profiles using this instrument will thus enable us to develop appropriate and sufficient training and intervention, confident that we will meet teachers' pressing needs.

ASSESSMENT PURPOSES ACROSS CLASSROOMS

Several patterns emerge in these eight teachers' assessment purposes. They use assessment most commonly to assign grades and communicate achievement expectations. Teachers are generally explicit in communicating grade expectations. As examples, some use written grading policies, sample problems and reviews, written assessment tasks, and even practice tests to give students a sense of what is important to know.

The grading of academic achievement dominates almost all environments, despite the fact that teachers dislike grading. Several teachers believe grading to be a bureaucratic requirement that is counterproductive to their goals for teaching, while others devise elaborate and time consuming assessing and recording schemes to resolve concerns about fairness, objectivity, and accountability. All keep records on student performance for the purpose of compiling the final grade or report. There is considerable variation in how elaborate these records are and how much and what types of information are collected to determine grades.

Measurement for grading purposes is almost completely criterion-referenced in the sense of the use of percent cutoff scores. However, objectives and criteria for performance are often somewhat vague. Cutoff scores for grades vary greatly; although some are fixed by policy. Teachers vary in their consistency in applying cutoff scores. It is common to merge point methods with curve grading. Teachers offer students opportunity for repetition of an assessment or extra work for grade improvement both in sixth grade and high school classes.

Affective and personality factors, such as motivation, effort, or a teacher's sense of a student's capabilities, influence grades in most classes. Further, teachers demonstrate considerable discretion in compiling information for the purpose of determining grades. Grades serve to send many different messages to students, only some of which relate to achievement. Teachers often use their grading authority to communicate both affective and academic expectations to students. They are not often challenged to explain a grade to either students, parents or administrators nor are they likely to check out the effects of grades upon students.

Among the subject areas, mathematics assessment is most limited to assessment of achievement alone. The high school social studies and science teachers share the mathematicians' concern about the "objectivity" of their grading schemes. However, the latter subject area specialists appear to be more judgmental in execution of grading than the math teachers, both in applying their achievement criteria and in taking nonachievement factors into account in some classes. By contrast, the language arts teachers regarded their subject matter as "subjective" and freely admitted that they incorporated judgement about achievement and affective traits into their grading of assessments.

Most high school teachers are not to be responsible for assessment for the purposes of grouping, selecting for special services, and providing test-taking experiences. Role differentiation in the secondary school influences these assessment purposes. Sixth-grade teachers bear a wider range of assessment-related responsibilities, for example, grouping within their own and with cognate-grade classes. But, even at these lower grades, students are often "tracked" or channeled by guidance counselors and, once placed, the teachers generally treat the entire class as a group.

There is considerable variation across teachers in assessment for the purposes of diagnosing, controlling and motivating, evaluating instruction, communicating affective expectations, accountability, and using assessment as an instructional strategy. Diagnosing is based on information from oral questions, review of homework and individual conferences. Diagnosis is more commonly conducted through assessment in the sixth grades than in the high schools and instruction is more frequently altered in response to information on student mastery gained through assessments in the lower grades.

At the beginning of the school year all the sixth-grade teachers administer assessments designed to size up their students. Both high school social studies teachers and one of the language arts teachers also assigned an essay-writing exercise as a sizing-up assessment.

While assessment is less used as an instructional strategy in high school than in sixth grade, some high school teachers use it as a basic instructional technique. Essay writing in language arts is a good example. Much class time, in both sixth-grade and high school classes, is devoted to correcting or going over results of homework assignments, thus combining students' doing the work of correcting each other's papers, ascertaining mastery of the material, and amplifying and extending instruction in response to the results.

VARIATIONS IN ASSESSMENT METHODOLOGY

Assessment of Achievement

Across the eight high school classrooms, teachers spend about a quarter of the available time on assessment-related activities. Class time devoted to assessment is even greater in the sixth grades, where assessment ranks in time consumed just behind whole-group instruction.

Across the subjects, methods commonly used to measure achievement on an ongoing basis across subjects include daily written assignments, paper and pencil tests, and oral questions used as assessments. Oral questioning is a primary instructional and assessment method in some of these classrooms. Reliance on oral questioning appears to vary with the teacher, not with the subject. It often serves the purpose of controlling and motivating, as well as measuring achievement and affective variables, such as interest. This group of teachers tends not to rely on standardized tests, group assessments, opinions of other teachers, or student-peer assessments. A great deal of variation is seen across teachers in their reliance on performance assessments, student self-assessments, and text-embedded tests—varying from no reliance to nearly total reliance on these methods for certain assessment purposes.

- *Performance assessments,* i.e., measures based on observation and judgment, are used to measure achievement in high school language arts, science, and social studies, but not in math. Performance is the dominant assessment method in one of the sixth grades, but was used to some extent in the other two also.

- *Student self-assessment* varies across teachers. Some teachers leave it up to their students to let them know if they are having difficulty. It is much more common at the lower-grade level.

- *Text-embedded assessment* use varies as a function of the availability of such assessments. Those who use texts that have accompanying assignments and tests use them to varying degrees, while those who do not have them available obviously do not use them. Textbooks more often serve as a source of daily assignments than of test questions. These teachers tend to want to develop their own tests.

Most of these teachers are concerned that their assessments measure higher order thinking skills. Generally, they felt that they were doing this successfully, although analysis of assessments, particularly tests, did not always bear out this confidence. Thinking skills assessed varied greatly by subject at both grade levels.

These teachers sometimes use assessment methods without sufficient understanding of how to use them well. For example, it is not uncommon for teachers to espouse teaching higher order thinking skills, and, in some classes, integrating a range of skill levels into their oral questions and assignments, only to require recall of facts and information on tests, unaware of the discrepancy. The result is invalid assessment.

Further, teachers who relied on performance assessment methodology almost universally did so without explicit performance criteria (i.e., a clear set of standards against which to compare student performance). When this occurs, the danger of invalid and unreliable assessment is great. In other cases, teachers reported judging group activities or projects as a basis for individual student performance, unaware of the complexities of sorting out differential contributions of group members to overall project success. And, finally, oral questioning during class, while used most often as instructional rather than as assessment devices, is conducted with virtually no written recordkeeping systems, but integrated holistically into individual student assessments.

On the positive side of achievement assessment, most of these teachers develop their own paper and pencil tests and tests usually reflect the content they emphasize in class. Further, the paper and pencil tests tend to be of fair technical quality (clear items, appropriate formats, sufficient samples, etc.). In addition, some movement was noted away from objective tests and toward performance and other assessments when outcomes warrant it. Finally, as a group, they mostly assess actual, demonstrated classroom achievement, specifically defined, rather than basing assessment on defined concepts of student ability.

Assessment of Affect

Affective assessments contribute greatly to the diversity among classroom assessment environments. These measures focus predominantly on the students' seriousness of purpose, level of apparent effort and attitude (positive or negative feeling about the teacher and/or the subject). Teachers measure these factors by observing the rate and quality of student work and through interpersonal contact with the student. Results influence student grades and teacher expectations of students.

At the sixth-grade level, affective characteristics are, in these teachers' views, part and parcel of their assessment responsibilities. Some teachers are required to offer comments, largely affective, from an established list as part of the grade report. In the nongrading sixth grade, affective comments make up about a third of the evaluative essay that is provided to parents; these two teachers concur that "making citizens" is their most important charge.

In high school, assessment of affect is not so overt a part of the scope of assessment, but it is never entirely absent. Factors such as punctuality, attentiveness, and effort tend to be weighed in high school, as in the sixth grade. Most affective assessments are performed on the basis of observation of individuals and group interaction. Affective factors are most important to the language arts teachers, who readily admit to relying upon them. Some other teachers make decisions, such as permitting extra-credit work, based on their judgements of affect, but fail to see that these are factors affecting their grading schemes. None of these teachers has stated criteria for affective assessment. Only a few make the use of affective judgments known to their students.

Within the affective dimension of classroom assessment, one issues emerge as worthy of further consideration when thinking of teacher training needs. We must explore the dangers of linking affective assessment to the school reward system, such as when teachers grade students in part based on the student's level of motivation or attitude.

There appears to be a stereotypic personality type among high school students which teachers respond to favorably. These are the students who *appear* attentive and aggressive during class and who therefore receive higher grades than others, not because they have learned more of the material but because they have learned to act like they are learning more. The implicit message communicated to these students seems to be, "You don't have to learn as much if you *look like* you're trying." Some students may be more prepared culturally to read these messages and fit this stereotype than others. This may lead to race, ethnic and sex bias in assessment and grading systems. Profile data on teachers' perceptions of students appear to confirm this is an area for concern.

The reward system of classroom assessment environments also appears to operate on the assumption that a simple relationship holds between grades and student motivation. These teachers appear to assume that if students know a grade is linked to some particular behavior (e.g., studying for a test), then they will behave accordingly to obtain the reward. But, in fact, it appears that the actual behavior/reward relationship is far more complex than this. For good students, i.e., those with a record of high achievement, that simple relationship probably holds: they will work to get another rewarding A. But, this does not hold true for students whose experience has been one of failure, not success. These are the students in the lower end of the distribution of achievement. Many teachers cling to the premise that grades serve to motivate these students to learn despite more test evidence that for many this simply is not the case. For many, grades are a punishment—a constant public reminder of failure—not a reward. Working hard seems to have produced only failure in the past, so why bother. Once a student loses grades as a reward, teachers have lost their only motivating tool and the motivation to continue to study is gone and eventually so is the student. Curve-based grading systems favored by a few teachers assure that a portion of the class will always experience that grading leads to failure.

Assessment of Ability

Ability is not a well-defined concept for any of these teachers; however, most, and especially elementary teachers, rely upon it for some of their judgments about students. The high school teachers reject the notion of "mathematics ability," although sixth-grade teachers tend to hold some concept of "math aptitude." It appears that ability comes to account for positive student behaviors that surprise the teacher. For example, one of the social studies teachers relied heavily on an ability concept to explain high achievement and strong motivation in students whose parents were uneducated, uninterested, or not native English speakers. On the other hand, lack of ability is not cited by any teacher as a reason for student failure to perform.

Text Assessments

In all subjects and at both grade levels studied, teachers make wide use of text-embedded assessments for homework assignments. In contrast, fewer than half these teachers ever used the paper and pencil tests provided with their texts.

CRITERIA FOR SELECTING ASSESSMENT METHODS

Teachers across high school subject matter areas seem quite consistent in the factors they consider in devising or selecting assessments. Factors typically given careful consideration are: time available for assessment; the match between assessment and instructional objectives, including applicability of assessment to thinking skills and appropriateness for a given purpose; degree of objectivity; and origin of the assessment. Factors considered less frequently include ease of development and scoring and the need to control cheating.

Sixth-grade teachers reflect the same major selection criteria. In addition, peer scoring is a common practice and teachers preferred assessments that facilitated this. Unlike high school, cheating was not considered in selecting assessment methods.

At both grade levels, it is important to recognize that, while these are the criteria considered by teachers, the extent to which they are met varies greatly. For example, as noted above, while teachers intend to measure higher order thinking skills, they are often unsuccessful in doing so. While many strive to remain objective, they fail to understand that vague performance criteria often give rise to unreliable judgments or that it is possible to be both judgmental and objective.

DIFFERENCES IN QUALITY OF ASSESSMENTS

As the above suggests, the quality of the assessments observed varied greatly. Some assessments—typically daily assignments and tests of the paper and pencil variety—were generally sound across subjects. A major exception to this conclusion is the extent to which these assessments measured thinking skills. Examples of good-quality performance assessment were noted, but most suffered from vaguely defined performance criteria and rating procedures. Oral questions were occasionally used as assessment devices, often with no attempt to gather a representative sample of student responses and with no written recordkeeping. In fact, it was generally the case that the teachers observed had spent very little time reflecting on the nature or quality (validity, reliability, and communication value) of their assessments prior to participating in this study.

Within this dimension of the quality of classroom assessments, some important and pervasive attitudes about assessment were noted. First, objective assessment formats tend to be accepted by teachers as dependable just because of their format, regardless of other qualities of the assessment, and are for this reason, preferred as tests. Essay tests and performance assessments, on the other hand, tend to be seen by teachers as subjective and therefore less acceptable merely as a function of format, regardless of other attributes. For this reason, their use is minimized. This is particularly true of high school teachers, some of whom specifically cite accountability requirements as motivating their choice of objective testing.

Students seem less sensitive to this distinction. Whether the test is objective or subjective, students do not question or challenge the teachers' performance criteria or assessment methods. Even in the face of subjective assessments and vague criteria, students seem to unquestioningly accept the teacher's assessment authority. While they may comment among themselves about the apparent lack of fairness of an assessment, they do not query teachers about this.

Other quality control issues worthy of mention include the following:

- As mentioned previously, teachers tended to rely on mental recordkeeping to manage some kinds of performance information, such as responses to oral questions or behavioral indicators of affective traits such as attitude. These teachers remain unaware of the dangers of bias inherent in such recordkeeping methods.

- In addition, some assessments, particularly daily assignments, are often quite short (sometimes two or three exercises). The dependability of grades entered into the gradebook for such assignments must be questioned.

- Further, weighting schemes are popular in establishing grades at the end of grading periods. However, teachers using these schemes are often uninformed and uncertain about how to operationalize their priorities in creating a weighted composite index of student performance.

- Affective assessments are based on various kinds of measures: records of work completion, behavioral observations or personal interactions. To provide sound information, these assessments must be valid and reliable. However, quality control in this arena of assessment often receives little or no attention. Further, questionnaires—a very efficient way to gather affective data—are virtually never used.

COMMUNICATION OF FEEDBACK ON ASSESSMENT RESULTS

The frequency and mode of feedback varies greatly from teacher to teacher, but, generally, feedback is positive, fair, immediate and germane to achievement. Feedback is used as a motivational tool, as well as a report to students on their achievement.

Both in class and in conference, strong students and students with correct answers receive more oral and nonverbal feedback than those who are weak or give incorrect answers. Correct answers tend to elicit some positive response from the teacher, e.g., "ok," "good," but incorrect answers are most frequently simply passed over—the question is asked of someone else or the teacher supplies the answer. Strong students thus get greater feedback because they are more often correct.

Oral feedback to the class is also used to attempt to instill motivation. Discussion of the results of tests or assignments often has an evaluative component and teachers may report their overall assessment of group progress, in addition to going over the correct answers.

In grading, teachers appear generally to be willing to give students the benefit of the doubt. If students have questions or complaints about grades, these are carefully listened to and, if the arguments are persuasive, teachers tend to be flexible. There is little evidence of use of grading for giving punitive feedback to students.

Written feedback practices are distinguished according to grade level, as are practices for providing feedback on grades. Overall, written feedback is regular—most assignments are marked with at least a symbol—and students get feedback in a very timely fashion. In high school classrooms, written feedback tends to be more extensive for the weaker rather than the stronger students thus contrasting with oral-feedback practices. On assignments, wrong answers or overall poor papers are more likely to receive a commment in addition to the grade or point score. Teachers are especially likely to comment when weak students' work is atypical—either better or worse than their usual effort. Most comments are corrective, rather than positive. Such comments are generally fair and focus directly on achievement.

Samples of performance and such public devices as posted achievement displays are little used as feedback mechanisms in high school classes. Feedback on grades tends to be private, rather than public. Student papers are carefully handed back individually and some teachers emphasize verbally that "your grades are your own," so the marks should not be shared with others. Private conferences outside of class time or at the end or beginning of class periods are common. Choice of private over public feedback appears to reflect several teacher concerns: the need to protect students' academic self-confidence; a desire to increase student self-responsibility; teachers' general desire to deemphasize grading; and teachers' need to protect their accountability by minimizing student comparisons and appearance of inequity among grades. These factors may also be involved in teachers' tendency to provide oral feedback to strong and correct students, as noted above.

While oral feedback patterns are very similar in sixth grades and high school classes, written feedback varies. Each of the sixth grades has some public posting of assessment data. These might be blackboard lists of those who have outstanding assignments or displays of student products. Feedback written on papers may be handed out to individuals directly, but sometimes is distributed by one of the students or passed down the rows. Students generally chat about their marks during this process.

TEACHER CHARACTERISTICS

Teacher Background

All of the sixth grade and high school teachers observed during these case studies were seasoned and experienced. The number of years of teaching experience ranged from three to thirty-three years, with nine of the twelve teachers having taught for more than fifteen years. Half of them have spent their entire teaching careers at the same school. All had prior experience in their grades and subject areas.

All twelve teachers report feeling that they received very little useful training in assessment methodology. Their preservice training did not prepare them to address the assessment questions they face daily in the classroom and contributed very little to their knowledge of assessment issues and techniques. Similarly, only two of the twelve teachers have benefited at all from inservice training about assessment. Ideas and suggestions from colleagues (with the exception of the one teaching team) and the teacher's guides of textbooks are seldom used resources, and they do not consult the professional literature on assessment.

By and large, they have developed their own assessment philosophies and practices over the course of years in the classroom. The methods they use to assess and grade their students are the result of years of determining what works for them in the classroom and what they feel comfortable doing. Much can be learned from teachers' experiences and practical classroom applications of assessment techniques. However, as we have seen, teachers may not be aware of the pitfalls or implications of some of their methods, and what appears to be sound assessment is not always done for the right reasons nor always consistently applied or recorded.

Teacher Use of Time

Not surprisingly, teachers spend a considerable amount of their time in assessment-related activities. On average, the high school teachers devote nearly a quarter of their time to assessment. The rest of their time is taken up in group instruction (nearly 40%), one-on-one instruction (15%), and planning (20%). Of the time spent on assessment activities, the biggest block of time (about one-third) is devoted to scoring and recording results. The high school teachers spent about 20 percent of their assessment time developing their own assessments. Administering assessments and providing feedback consume approximately equal amounts of time (20% each). Little time is given to reviewing and selecting assessments (10%) and even less to evaluating the quality of the assessments (5%).

Although the preliminary sixth-grade studies do not provide the detailed analysis of lesson expectations provided by the assessment profile, it is clear that elementary teachers spend even more time on assessment. They use class time for performance assessment and spend lots of class time on assignment scoring and review. As one of the teachers put it, "We spend as much time as we can in direct instruction, but we're *always* assessing."

Personal Traits of the Teacher

These teachers differ widely in their views of themselves and their students and the classroom environments they have created reflect this diversity. Half of the high school teachers work very autonomously, taking full responsibility for developing the curriculum and presenting it and, concomitantly, developing many of their own assessments. The sixth-grade teachers have considerable autonomy over their classrooms and assessment practices also.

Most of the teachers expect a great deal of themselves as professionals. All have a relatively clear sense of performance norms; these are often unwritten, however. Their views of what constitutes high-quality performance vary considerably, ranging across the spectrum from demanding only the correct answer to accepting degrees of quality. As might be expected, similar variation exists in these teachers' needs for structure and in their willingness to experiment.

Most of these teachers, both in high school and in sixth grade, highly value promptness and timely completion of work. The only exception is one language arts teacher and, even though this teacher is very flexible on this point, she still makes note of late papers.

The interpersonal dimensions of the assessment environments created by these teachers also vary considerably and do not follow any patterns related to subject area or grade level. In some classrooms, very little cooperation occurs or is encouraged, in others it is frequent.

Surprisingly, teachers seem relatively unconcerned about cheating. This may be because nearly all of them are interested in teaching the students to be responsible for their own learning. This orientation is reflected in the number of teachers who attribute the lion's share of the responsibility for success or failure to the students themselves. Only one of the twelve would place that responsibility primarily on the teacher.

They enjoy their students as people and most seek some personal contact with them. Most of them, however, operate with some preconceived or stereotypic views of their students. Although one high school teacher articulates stereotypes of individuals, others tend to express these views when thinking of groups of students, but seem able and interested to deal with individual students and their particular needs when time permits. Some teachers are far more willing to attend to individual students than are others.

Stereotypic views can and do influence instruction and assessment in some of these classrooms. The lowered expectations of two teachers may be based on past experience with what students in their schools actually achieve or are willing to achieve, but such expectations may not be fair to individual students in their classrooms this year. Observations such as one high school teacher's explanation that boys who are acting out are "bright" may well have a detrimental effect on boys who don't act out or on girls in general. This teacher clearly gives more attention and feedback to those highly visible boys.

Regarding the grading process, teachers grade almost entirely on the basis of demonstrated achievement. For the social studies and language arts teachers, their sense of the students' ability may enter into the assignment of grades. This is also true for some of the sixth-grade teachers. However, all are unable to articulate clearly what constitutes ability and how to measure it separately from achievement or affective characteristics such as motivation or seriousness of purpose. Students' level of effort is considered by all teachers, particularly in borderline cases. The problems implicit in including ability or effort in the grading process do not seem to be clear to these educators.

Nearly all assessment conducted in these classrooms is considered to be criterion-referenced in the sense that a certain level of performance is expected of all. However, the social studies and language arts teachers and the two teachers in the graded sixth grades, use both norm and criterion referencing. Even when teachers say they are basing everything on a percentage of the total points possible, they often have distributed the points based on the group norm. For example, a language arts teacher reads what she expects will be the top and bottom student papers first to establish a range for distributing the points throughout the set of papers. There is a great need for a clearer understanding of the grading process, what is considered, and how it is considered. Much could be done to help teachers analyze their own practices and assumptions.

In most of these classrooms teachers view instruction and assessment as separate activities. Integration of the two is done haphazardly and rarely to full advantage. Even in the sixth grade, where instruction and assessment seemed to occur simultaneously, only the two teachers in the teamed classroom could articulate how their instruction and assessment are correlated in planning and practice. Most teachers either do not take the time or do not know how to make good use of assessment in presenting instruction, in evaluating it, and in making it more effective and meaningful.

TEACHERS' PERCEPTIONS OF STUDENT CHARACTERISTICS

These twelve teachers have widely varying perceptions of their students' characteristics. Although all feel their students have from moderate to high ability to learn, they rate their willingness to learn, their willingness to perform, and their rate of achievement a little lower. Most, especially high school teachers, see their students as at least somewhat irresponsible. In general, high school teachers think their students' study skills are not as well developed as their social skills, and their self-assessment skills are the least developed of these three characteristics. Students' perceived feedback needs vary across the spectrum from relatively weak to a strong need for feedback. Their sense of fairness and their reactions to testing are also thought to vary considerably.

Each teacher is faced with some (and in many cases a great deal of) variation in these characteristics among his or her particular students. Rate of achievement is the characteristic in which greatest variation is noted. However, teachers' responses to these variations range across the spectrum from ignoring them totally (even though they admit they exist) to addressing them.

Teachers of a particular subject do not necessarily share the same perceptions of their students, nor do they respond in similar ways to the variations among students. One math teacher, for example, recognizes great variation in student traits and therefore dedicates 10 to 20 minutes of each class period to individual students. The second math teacher takes a much narrower view of student motivation and chooses not to address it in his instruction or assessment. The two social studies teachers are aware of variations among their students but differ in the ways they conduct their classrooms. One teacher refuses to acknowledge variations so that his students will rise above those differences, while the second teacher is so attuned to one particular group of students (the boys who act out) that he ignores most other variations among his students. The two language arts teachers tend to be most involved in addressing the variations they perceive among their students.

The high school teachers know surprisingly little about parental expectations, although they think parental expectations are relatively important. Most think parents do not expect much of their children. The extent of parental expectations and parental involvement is related in some teachers' minds to the nature of the community served by the school. An exception is one teacher who makes a special effort to call three parents a night. This teacher is also the sole example of a teacher who takes most of the responsibility for students' success or failure on himself.

As noted in the discussion above about teachers' stereotypic views of students, teachers have well-established (and sometimes erroneous) views of nature and changes in student characteristics over the years. These perceptions have a powerful influence on teachers' expectations for their current students. Teachers may be unaware of the dangers of judging individual students on the basis of apparent "trends."

POLICY AND ASSESSMENT

Policy is an area about which classroom teachers appear to be relatively uninformed and about which they concern themselves very little. Even where district or school assessment and assessment-related policies exist, teachers are largely unaware of them. When they are aware of certain policies, they appear to have the autonomy to ignore them by and large. Teachers very broadly control the conduct of their own classrooms, including assessment aspects.

Grading methodology, frequency of grading, homework assignments, types of questions, etc., are largely ungoverned by policy, regardless of whether school or district policy in fact exists. The only clear requirements appear to be the specified reporting period and the public school requirement to provide letter grades. These the teachers fulfill, albeit in many cases reluctantly. Some teachers feel responsible to have demonstrated records to back up their grade-report decisions, providing extensive markings; others feel no such need, although school policies demand demonstrable bases for grades in class records.

Some of the teachers report that their assessment practices are influenced by consensual practices and agreements developed with their departmental colleagues. In some of these cases departmental practices are in contradiction to established school or district policy.

Departmental level decision making with regard to textbooks governs assessment practices to the extent that they make use of text-embedded assignments and tests. Despite these assessment implications, quality of assessments in the text are rarely a consideration in text adoption. Teachers involved in the selection process neither possess the skills to evaluate tests and assignments, nor recognize the need to secure this information.

In certain areas, teachers are constrained by the roles of guidance counselors. These counselors have a broad mandate to assign students to advanced or remedial tracks and to meet with parents and students. In general, teachers accept counselors' placement decisions and work with the students as best they can. Teachers do this despite the fact that they appear to know little about counselors' knowledge and skills for determining placements across academic subjects, criteria counselors use in making such placements, or the sources and quality of information that they use. However, in at least some schools, teachers can influence or override placements and can intervene directly with students and their parents around academic progress and disciplinary matters. For example, one teacher eschews the school's forms warning of failing grade, choosing instead to make personal telephone calls to the parents. This, he argues, is more congruent with his approach of trying to create motivation by developing confidence and positive attitudes toward school. Teachers vary in their interest in directly dealing with parents, complaints, and student nonclass issues, but they appear to have great leeway to do so, if they choose, regardless of building or district procedure as outlined in policy.

The role of principals as building policy makers in the assessment arena is unclear. In only one case was it clear that a teacher's assessment policy had been affected by his principal's desires—one social studies teacher included what he regarded as higher order thinking questions in his yearly final at his principal's request.

SUMMARY

Classroom assessment environments can and do vary on each of the dimensions in the assessment profile, as even this small sample of sixth grade and high school classrooms has demonstrated. The profile instrument is sensitive to these differences, enabling a comparative analysis of the classrooms to be developed. The multidimensional and scaled structure that has been designed for each of the questions on the profile is essential in pinpointing contrasts and similarities among teachers, subject areas, and grade levels.

Through application of the assessment profile, common areas of teacher strengths and weaknesses have begun to emerge which suggest topics for further research and possible training development needs. These include:

- Assessment is largely used for the narrow purpose of grading; opportunities for such critical activities as instructional improvement including student diagnosis and evaluation of instruction are missed.

- Higher-order thinking skills are not understood and/or not assessed and there is commonly a mismatch in thinking skills level of instruction, assignments, and tests.

- Individual student grades are not always based on valid or reliable data and criterion- and norm-referenced systems are confounded.
- Teachers are unfamiliar with appropriate methods for assessing performance.
- The meaning of objective assessment and valid assessment are confused, leading teachers to regard objective tests as necessarily valid and performance assessments as necessarily less valid.
- Teachers view instruction and assessment as entirely distinct functions and do not know how to integrate instruction and assessment in planning class time.
- Although they wish to base their assessments of students on achievement, teachers often mix affective factors into grading equations as they strive to motivate students.

We believe each of these topics merits further study to amplify our understanding of the realities teachers face and the kind of assessment training they need to meet the challenges posed by assessment. To illustrate the nature of the kinds of higher-resolution studies needed, we turned up the power on our microscope in order to study teachers' grading practices and their assessments of higher order thinking. The results of those studies are presented next.

CHAPTER 8

The Quality of Specific Assessment Practices: Higher Order Thinking Assessment and Grading

Sixth grade and high school assessment case studies reported in the preceding chapters indicate that, while there is broad commonality among teachers in their assessment aspirations, there is great disparity in their abilities to carry out desired assessment functions in ways that produce reliable, valid results and positive reinforcement of student learning. Further study of teachers' practice in assessing students' higher order thinking skills reported in this chapter confirms that teacher confidence exceeds ability to accurately assess higher order skills. And, while we know grading is the primary feedback system in public education and is a leading purpose for classroom assessment, research reported below suggests teachers have difficulty meeting generally accepted guidelines of sound grading practice. Both areas emerge as topics for development of teacher training.

Higher order thinking skills assessment was chosen as a subject of one in-depth investigation due to its importance as a foundation to student achievement, and because of its saliance in the minds and proported saliance in the assessment practices of the teachers in our original profile sample. Tobin (1983) provides a comprehensive picture of the strong relationship between the higher order thinking skills questions of teachers and the subsequent achievement status of their students based on a review of dozens of studies. Our profiles indicated that teachers are aware of thinking-skills research and accept the importance of assessing, as well as instructing, higher order skills and further indicated that most teachers believe they can and do regularly perform this assessment function. Profilers' observations, however, revealed discrepancies between teachers' self-evaluations and the competency of their practice in thinking skills assessment. Confirmation of these discrepancies would indicate both an important training need and strength of the profile in discriminating between reported and actual assessment practice.

Grading was selected as the focus of the second high resolution study because it is the single most important function for assessment, as reported for the profile teachers. It is the most frequently and consistently practiced assessment function, takes up the most class time, and constitutes the most important and direct feedback to students. And, the classroom assessment profile suggested that grading practices, from teachers' methods, from gathering and aggregating to reporting student-performance data, may be questionable from a measurement point of view. The grading study was designed to examine the utility of the profile as a training-need diagnostic instrument, as well as further delineate our knowledge of teachers' grading practices, as the basis for training development.

In the presentation that follows, each study is described in terms of methodology, results, and some interpretation of those results. Then an integrative summary of the two concludes the chapter.

A STUDY OF CLASSROOM ASSESSMENT OF HIGHER ORDER THINKING SKILLS*

The purpose of this study was to describe the extent, nature and quality of teachers' day-to-day classroom assessments of higher-order thinking. Others had addressed teachers assessments of thinking skills in prior research. For instance, Reynolds and Menard (1980) had described teachers' tendencies to disregard several

---

*This is a brief synopsis of research reported in much greater detail in Stiggins, Wikelund, and Griswold (1989).

levels of the Bloom taxonomy of thinking in writing test items. Fleming and Chambers (1983) analyzed nearly 9,000 teacher-developed test items and found over 90 percent assess recall of facts. And Carter (1984) found that teachers experience great difficulty and considerable discomfort writing test items at higher cognitive levels.

However, all of these studies were restricted to the study of paper and pencil objective test item formats and none studied assessments in districts where the teaching of thinking was established as a priority. The study reported below addresses the use of performance assessments and oral questions in addition to paper and pencil tests in the classrooms of a district emphasizing thinking as a valued achievement outcome.

METHODOLOGY

Sample

The sample consisted of thirty-six volunteer teachers distributed equally across the grade-level categories 1–2, 3–4, 5–6, 7–8, 9–10, and 11–12 in a suburban district. All schools and the district had set major long-term goals to teach thinking skills and some inservice training had already begun. Volunteers were told that the study would focus on classroom assessment procedures in general, but explicit mention was made to participating teachers of the focus on higher order thinking skills, in an attempt to control for bias in the study.

The study focused on assessments conducted in four core content areas: mathematics, science, social studies, and language arts. The elementary teachers generally taught a cross-section of subjects while the junior high and high school teachers were specialized.

Data-Collection Methods

Teachers were preinterviewed briefly to gather data on their plans for one instructional day. Student tests and materials underlying the lessons to be observed were obtained for preview at this time. Then each teacher was observed by a trained observer for all class periods during one instructional day. The teachers provided the investigator with samples of paper and pencil assessment instruments used recently. And finally, each teacher was interviewed in-depth shortly after the day of observation.

In preparation, data collection forms were developed, pilot tested and revised by the field staff. Researchers practiced coding questions until a very high degree of proficiency in classifying the thinking skill levels of questions was attained.

The data-collection forms provided space for the researcher to record for each class period during the day:

• background, including the course to be taught, number of students, grade, an estimate of the ability of the students in that class, and class meetings per week;
• instructional information, including goals, new or review material to be covered, and activities planned; and
• any assessment plans for that period.

The classroom observation form structured information on levels of questions so that staff were able to keep a running protocol of oral questioning during the observation day. Each question posed by the teacher was coded as to the level of thinking it reflected, the respondent (whether targeted by the teacher or volunteer), and the correctness of the response. Prior study of assigned materials assured that new versus old information could be distinguished.

A total of 5,221 oral questions were recorded across the thirty-six participating teachers, of which 4,742 could be accurately linked to a specific grade and subject matter area. These were equally distributed across grades, but not subjects. Nearly half of all questions were posed in language arts classes, due only in part to the fact that approximately one-third of the classes (teacher/subject combinations) observed were in language arts. The remainder were equally distributed across the other three subjects.

Teachers provided four to six samples of paper and pencil assessments used recently in their classroom. These included any used on observation day plus others of the teacher's choosing. Since teachers had not yet learned the specific focus of the study at this time, there is no reason to assume that the documents selected were unusual with respect to their focus on thinking skills, however extrapolations from instruments analyzed to all tests used by these teachers or tests used by other teachers are not justified.

A total of 149 assessment documents containing 4,120 individual exercises were analyzed. Of these documents, 38 percent were teacher-developed paper and pencil tests, 30 percent were text-embedded tests, 20 percent were written assignments developed by teachers or selected by teachers out of text materials, 5 percent were standardized tests (developed and used by the district) and the remainder were classified as "other." These were distributed evenly across grade levels. Of the exercises coded, 34 percent were selection-type items, 54 percent were fill-ins, 10 percent were essay and 2 percent required some other type of product as a response.

The distribution of instruments across subjects was uneven. The fewest were collected in social studies (14%), the most in language arts (40%), again, partially an artifact of the great proportion of language arts observed. The remainder were about equally divided between math and science.

These written assessments were then analyzed according to the number and proportion of items that reflected each of the Quellmalz thinking skills (described in the next section). All document analyses were conducted first by the field researcher responsible for that teacher and then were reviewed by a second research team member to assure proper coding. Disagreements were discussed and resolved, sometimes with a third team member. They were rare.

The post-observation interview also followed a prepared protocol. The staff probed the teacher's use of and attitudes about six different types of classroom assessment procedures: teacher-developed paper and pencil tests and quizzes, text-embedded paper and pencil tests and quizzes, written assignments, performance assessments, oral questions, and standardized achievement tests. Teachers described the extent of their use of each of these to measure higher order thinking skills. Further, they provided information about training in thinking skills assessment and instruction, and about their attitudes regarding teaching these skills.

The Thinking Skills Framework

In order to generate data on the classroom assessment of higher order thinking skills that were comparable across teachers, grades, school subjects, and other independent variables, the study focused on the framework of thinking skills outlined by Quellmalz (1985). Five types of thinking are differentiated: recall, analysis, comparison, inference, and evaluation. Each type is described in detail in Table 8.1, along with a note as to its relation to the more commonly used Bloom taxonomy.

This particular framework was selected for a number of reasons. First and most importantly, Quellmalz (1985) makes a compelling argument that these five levels collect all of the elements common to a great many other taxonomic structures of thinking skills. Second, the levels included in the Quellmalz structure are conceptually clear and straightforward, making coding of questions relatively easy. Third, the research staff had developed a teacher training program centered on this taxonomy and therefore was thoroughly familiar with it.

RESULTS

Analysis of Test Questions

Analysis of the items appearing in assessment documents by the type of higher order thinking they require reveals interesting patterns. Table 8.2 presents results by the grades taught by the participating teachers and for the four subject areas, summarized across all grades.

Clearly, the largest percent of items test recall of facts and information (46%). This reliance on recall is strong at all grade levels. Inference is also frequently assessed in these documents (33%). Items requiring analytical thinking were much less commonly used (12%), and comparison and evaluation were hardly assessed at all (9%). One subject area differs distinctly: in mathematics, only 19 percent of the items assess recall, whereas 72 percent of all items tap inference. If we remove math from the grade-level analyses (see Table 8.3), we find an increase in recall (now 55%) and some increase in the percent of analytical items (now 12%). The percent of comparison and evaluation remains unchanged.

TABLE 8.1
SUMMARY OF QUELLMALZ TAXONOMY

Classification	Definition	Illustration
Recall	Most tasks require that students recognize or remember key facts, definitions, character in concepts, rules, and principles. Recall questions require students to repeat verbatim or to paraphrase given information. To recall information, students need most often to rehearse or practice it, and then to associate it with other, related concepts. Verbatim repetition and translation into the student's own words represent acceptable evidence of learning and understanding.	Who was the main character in story?
Analysis	In this operation, students divide a whole into component elements. Generally the part/whole relationships and the cause/effect relationships that characterize knowledge within subject domains are essential components of more complex tasks. The components can be the distinctive characteristics of objects or ideas, or the basic actions of procedures or events.	What are the different story parts?
Comparison	These tasks require students to recognize or explain similarities and differences. Simple comparisons require attention to one or a few very obvious attributes or component processes, while complex comparisons require identification of the differentiation among many attributes or component actions. The separate comparison category emphasizes the distinct infor-	How was the story like the last one?

(*continued*)

TABLE 8.1 (*Continued*)

Classification	Definition	Illustration
	mation processing required when students go beyond breaking the whole into parts in order to compare similarities and differences.	
Inference	Both deductive and inductive reasoning fall into this category. In deductive tasks, students are given a generalization and are required to recognize or explain the evidence that relates to it. Applications of rules and "if then" relationships require inference. In inductive tasks, students are given the evidence or details and are required to come up with the generalization. Hypothesizing, predicting, concluding, and synthesizing all require students to relate and integrate information.	What might be a good title for this story?
Evaluation	These tasks require students to judge quality, credibility, worth, or practicality. Generally we expect students to use established criteria and explain how these criteria are or are not met. The criteria might be established rules of evidence, logic, or shared values. To evaluate, students must assemble and explain the interrelationship of evidence and reasons in support of their conclusion (synthesis). Explanation of criteria for reaching a conclusion is unique to evaluative reasoning.	Is this a good story? Why or why not?

Source: Quellmalz, 1985.

TABLE 8.2
PERCENT OF DOCUMENT ITEMS ASSESSING HIGHER-ORDER THINKING
SKILLS BY LEVEL TESTED, BY GRADE, AND BY SUBJECT AREA
ACROSS GRADES*

Grade	Recall %	Analysis %	Comparison %	Inference %	Evaluation %
			Level of Higher-order Thinking		
1–2	56	12	14	19	0
3–4	41	16	4	34	5
5–6	44	19	4	30	3
7–8	51	7	1	39	2
9–10	42	12	3	39	5
11–12	41	9	4	44	3
Subject (across grades)					
Math	19	0	9	72	0
Science	65	11	5	17	2
Social studies	66	14	5	13	3
Language arts	49	19	5	23	5
TOTAL	46	12	6	33	3

* The grade-by-subject interaction was not explored in this analysis due to the fact that cell frequencies (number of teachers teaching a given subject at a given grade level with an overall n of 36) were very small.

TABLE 8.3
PERCENT OF DOCUMENT ITEMS ASSESSING HIGHER ORDER THINKING SKILLS BY LEVEL TESTED, BY GRADE FOR SCIENCE, SOCIAL STUDIES, AND LANGUAGE ARTS (Math excluded)

Grade	Recall %	Analysis %	Comparison %	Inference %	Evaluation %
			Level of Higher-order Thinking		
1–2	66	18	7	10	0
3–4	43	20	6	20	7
5–6	45	22	5	24	4
7–8	68	10	2	18	2
9–10	53	17	3	20	7
11–12	53	12	5	23	8
TOTAL	55	16	5	19	4

TABLE 8.4
PERCENT OF ORAL QUESTIONS ASSESSING HIGHER ORDER THINKING
SKILLS BY LEVEL TESTED, BY GRADE, AND BY SUBJECT AREA
ACROSS GRADES

			Level of Higher-order Thinking		
Grade	Recall %	Analysis %	Comparison %	Inference %	Evaluation %
1–2	70	5	5	17	4
3–4	51	15	4	25	5
5–6	36	19	5	33	8
7–8	39	35	2	12	12
9–10	48	8	6	25	13
11–12	42	23	2	18	15
Subject (across grades)					
Math	41	26	3	26	3
Science	59	13	8	16	5
Social Studies	48	24	2	16	10
Language Arts	45	17	13	22	13
TOTAL	47	20	4	21	9

Analysis of Oral Questions

Table 8.4 displays the distribution of oral questions by type of thinking required for each of the grade levels observed and for each of the four subject areas summarized across grade level.

Mirroring written documents, nearly half of the questions asked in the classrooms observed assessed recall of facts and information. Unlike tests, oral question skill levels vary by grade. In grades 1 and 2 recall was as high as 70 percent, while in grades 5 and 6 only slightly more than a third of the questions assessed recall. Questions requiring inferential or analytical thinking were also fairly common (21% and 20%, respectively). These three levels of thinking accounted for almost 90 percent of all oral questions. Evaluation and comparison were largely ignored, especially in the elementary grades. The distribution of questions by subject area reveals a parallel pattern.

Math showed the only pronounced differences between oral questions and those of the paper and pencil variety. In the case of oral questions, math was like the subjects, with recall dominating.

COMMENTARY ON RESULTS

Assessment of comparative and evaluative thinking is uncommon, both in written and oral modes. Comparison certainly is not more difficult to assess than other types of thinking and may even be easier to address than some. Evaluation may be viewed as difficult to address because there may be no "right" answer. Teachers must subjectively evaluate answers to evaluation questions using pre-specified criteria. This can be complex.

The teachers' thinking skills assessment patterns were more similar across the full range of grades studied than one might expect. Level of academic development does not seem to influence the nature of questions posed by this group of teachers. The greater emphasis on fostering critical thinking and problem solving urged for middle and high school in the research literature seems absent here. Also, these upper-grade teachers tend to be more specialized in subject area and often develop their own assessment instruments. This would appear to provide a strong foundation for high-quality assessment of higher order thinking. But such assessments are not forthcoming. We speculate that this may be because many teachers lack the building blocks needed to take advantage of this excellent opportunity—that is, many lack a clear and specific thinking framework around which to devise assessments.

At first glance, one might assume it natural that mathematics was so strikingly unique in its emphasis on thinking beyond recall requiring inference in written work. After all, mathematics explicitly focuses on solving problems. However, the other subjects also lend themselves easily to the development of these skills.

Notably, the math teachers emphasized the higher skills only in their written assessments, resulting in a thinking skill level mismatch between oral questions and expectations for written work. An exact match between how one teaches and how one assesses thinking may not be totally necessary or even desirable. For example, as the teacher walks the students through the steps to solve a sample problem, many of the questions asked along the way may require recall of the facts and analysis of the procedures needed to find the ultimate solution. On subsequent written assessment, however, the teacher may simply present the problem and expect a solution. The levels of questions posed in such written assessments, therefore, would be a different order. Presumably this relationship could also hold in the teaching of other subjects. Thus to teach and assess effectively, teachers must not only have a knowledge of how to use different thinking skills objectives, but also when to use them as they vary throughout the instructional sequence.

Effects of Prior Training

The district in which this study was conducted had identified the teaching of thinking skills as a major long-term goal and had initiated some inservice training in this arena. This provided the opportunity to explore the relationship between that training and the assessment practices of the teachers, reported in Table 8.5.

Nearly all teachers in the study had participated in some training (defined as completing at least one workshop) on *teaching* thinking skills. However, participation in workshops on *assessing*

TABLE 8.5
AVERAGE NUMBER AND PERCENT OF QUESTIONS TAPPING
RECALL AND HIGHER ORDER THINKING SKILLS AS A
FUNCTION OF TRAINING

Training in*:	Oral Questions		
	% Recall	% Other	Average Questions Posed
Teaching Thinking			
None (N = 3)	75	25	148
Some (N = 32)	39	61	150
Testing Thinking			
None (N = 13)	60	40	144
Some (N = 22)	39	61	137
	Test Questions		
Teaching Thinking			
None	64	36	63
Some	37	63	116
Testing Thinking			
None	53	47	115
Some	41	59	108

*N = 35 in this analysis because one teacher declined to participate in the postobservation interview and therefore could not be classified as to training status.

thinking skills was not universal, with a third having received no assessment training.

When the percent of all oral and test questions that measured recall versus higher order thinking skills was contrasted as a function of prior training, it emerged that those with training tended to ask a considerably higher proportion of higher order questions than those without training, both orally and in writing. The teachers who lacked training in the teaching and assessing of higher order thinking skills also tended to assess students' thinking less often.

Teacher interview data indicate that, while these teachers believe in the importance of teaching their students to think critically and are confident that thinking can be taught, they are a little less certain about the assessability of thinking skills. Their practice indicates that they, like nearly all the teachers we have studied to date, would benefit from training in this assessment function.

A STUDY OF GRADING PRACTICES*

The purpose of this study was to focus a powerful microscope on the grading practices of a few teachers in order to understand how they determine the report card grades of their students. This study had been preceded by other treatments of grading issues, but few previous studies had probed the actual practices of teachers. Exceptions include studies by Terwilliger (1971) and Kinder and Porwold (1977), both of which have become too dated to provide dependable data on current practices.

Methodology

A sample of introductory measurement textbooks was analyzed to determine what grading practices are recommended by measurement specialists. Then, actual practices of a sample of high school teachers were observed and analyzed in order to determine the degree of congruence between their actual practice and the recommended practices.

Sample. The fifteen teachers were distributed across the core high school subjects: four each in mathematics and language arts, five in science, and two in social studies. All fifteen were volunteers who had a minimum of five years in their subject and grade levels.

Data-Collection Methods. Sample introductory educational measurement texts were examined to identify recommended guidelines for conducting grading practices. We reviewed such texts as Ebel and Frisbie (1986), Gronlund (1985), Hills (1981), and Mehrens

---

*This is a brief synopsis of research reported in much greater detail in Stiggins, Frisbie, and Griswold (1989).

and Lehmann (1984), among others. A total of nineteen specific guidelines were identified covering:

- communicating grading methods to students;
- student characteristics incorporated into grades: achievement, learning ability, attitude, motivation/effort, interest, personality;
- methods of obtaining grades: daily written assignments, written tests, oral questioning, performance assessment;
- amount of grading data gathered;
- quality of grading data;
- consistent policies followed;
- methods of segregating grading components; and
- methods of setting grade cutoff scores: normal distribution, fixed percents, point-total accumulation, deciding borderline cases.

Data on the extent of teacher adherence to each guideline were collected through observation in the classroom, teacher interviews, and examination of documents, including gradebooks, graded assignments and tests, and grading schemes.

Results and Discussion

Fewer than half of the nineteen grading guidelines recommended by textbooks were followed by the teachers studied. First, we will review those that tended to be followed, then those not followed. Possible reasons for teachers' deviation from recommended practice are suggested and the implications for teacher training are drawn.

Following Recommended Measurement Practice. There was an acceptable level of match between high school teachers' grading practice and the standards set by measurement textbook authors on eight of the nineteen standards.

- *Communicating grading methods to students.* It is recommended that students be informed, in advance and in explicit terms, regarding the basis of their grades and the method to be used in determining them, ideally in written form. All teachers reported that they made their expectations and grading practices known to students. Observed depth and clarity of that communication varied; however, practice appears to be congruent with the recommended procedures.

- *Student characteristics incorporated in grades: Attitude.* Since these traits are difficult to define and assess objectively for all students, it is recommended that attitudes not be used for grading purposes. The majority of teachers studied here (13) strive not to consider attitudes. When considered, attitudes are not measured directly or intentionally but inferred from nonsystematic observations of student behavior.

- *Student characteristics incorporated in grading: Interest.* While interest in the subject matter no doubt affects time devoted to study and thus the level of achievement, interest should not be used as a grading variable. Most of the teachers studied recognized that student interest is difficult to define and measure.

- *Student characteristics incorporated in grading: Personality.* Despite the fact that student temperament, disposition, or character influence teacher/student relationships, these are not the traits that schools are primarily intended to develop. Each of the teachers reported strategies they use to control the influence of personality on grade assignment, including rating performance in the blind and involving other teachers in key decisions.

- *Methods of obtaining grading data: Written tests.* It is recommended that paper-pencil tests be used as a primary means of measuring achievement whenever the relevant instructional objectives permit their use. Virtually all teachers regularly used objective and/or essay tests to assess students' attainments.

- *Methods of obtaining grading data: Oral questioning.* Oral questioning during instruction cannot be recommended as providing dependable classroom-achievement measurement for grading since teachers seldom obtain an adequate sample of each student's performance and they are rarely able to sustain sufficient recordkeeping. With just two exceptions, study teachers used oral questioning primarily as an instructional device.

- *Methods of obtaining grading data: Performance assessment.* If they follow certain rules of evidence, teachers can conduct dependable assessments of achievement-related products and student behaviors by observing and subjectively judging the quality of student performance. Almost half of the case study teachers reported using performance measures in such areas as language arts (writing samples), science (lab work), and social-science discussion (group participation charting). Though some of these measures seemed to be based on vague performance criteria and inadequate sampling of performance, their planned use in the grading context is consistent with recommendations.

- *Methods of setting grade cutoff scores: Normal distribution.* In this case, the final frequency distribution of grades is fixed according to a normal curve (thus, grading on the curve). Most experts contend that typical classrooms contain too few students to expect that achievement will be normally distributed within classrooms. Only one teacher used this approach.

Guidelines Not Followed. For eleven of the nineteen standards there was discrepancy between the high school teachers' actual practice and the recommendations in the measurement textbooks.

- *Student characteristics incorporated in grades: Achievement.* It is recommended that achievement—the acquisition of knowledge and skills—be the sole ingredient in determining grades. In practice, all fifteen teachers believed that achievement of instructional objectives should be the primary consideration in grading, however, twelve felt strongly that effort should be considered as well.

- *Student characteristics incorporated in grades: Learning ability.* It is generally recommended that intelligence, cognitive ability, or aptitude not be considered in assigning grades. Grades should indicate how much students have learned rather than an estimate of how much they are capable of learning or how much they have learned in relation to their judged ability level. Study teachers were equally divided in terms of their integration of ability into grading practices. Half used different assessment and grading procedures for students deemed with high ability from those students deemed with low ability. The most able students often were graded solely on their achievement, while the least able were graded on both achievement and effort.

- *Student characteristics incorporated in grades: Motivation and effort.* While effort impacts achievement, measurement specialists held that it not be combined with achievement in an academic grade, and if feedback is provided on this factor, it should be reported separately. However, nearly all study teachers (13 of 15) gave significant weight to effort as a grading variable, as measured in terms of homework completion, extra-credit work performed, and other observations of "appearing to try hard."

- *Methods of obtaining grading data: Daily written assignments.* Daily assignments can serve either of two purposes. They can serve *formative* purposes, providing students with practice and such results are not recommended for inclusion in grades. Assignments can also serve as *summative* assessments, providing evidence of how much of the required material students have learned and such results can be factored into grade computations when interpreted in terms of the amount learned. Nine of the fifteen teachers treated *all* assignments as though they were summative evaluations. Further, most evaluated and kept records of assignments in terms of work completed and not results achieved.

- *Amount of grading data gathered.* It is recommended that enough evidence be gathered over time to allow the teacher to accurately estimate the proportion of required material mastered by each student, typically more than two or three periodic, high-quality assessments for each quarterly grading period. All teachers reported gathering two to six major samples of student work for each grading period. But, performance on daily assignments and a small number of less comprehensive assessments also were recorded as grading data. About half of the teachers did not distinguish data for formative and summative uses and, consequently, *all* evaluation data available were aggregated to determine the final grade.

- *Quality of the grading data.* The key attributes of grading data are: validity (content and taxonomic match between assessment exercises and instructional objectives), reliability (consistency and objectivity), and cost (particularly the time required for development and scoring or rating). It is recommended that achievement data to be factored into the grade be gathered using the most valid and reliable method available, keeping costs reasonable. That means teachers must evaluate the quality of data gathered. Dependability of data (including validity and reliability) was virtually never systematically addressed by these teachers. Assessments fail to reflect the most appropriate cognitive levels of instruction, reliability of scores is rarely estimated, and objectivity checks seldom are made. Quality often is defined in terms of the number of complaints received from students.

- *Consistent policies followed.* Measurement specialists state that district grading policies should be written and distributed to ascribe a common meaning to each of the grade symbols. Half of the study teachers knew of no written district grading policy beyond those that specify the grading symbols to be used, deadlines for completing report cards, and sometimes cutoff scores for letter grades. Many reported that principals (or department chairpersons) often audited their distributions of grades to check the alignment with unwritten expectations for the percent of As, Bs, etc., suggesting the presence of either written or unwritten policies about the expected distribution of grades.

- *Methods of aggregating grading components.* The recommended procedure for norm-referenced approaches is to (a) adjust each component score distribution so that all distributions have equal variability (standard deviations), (b) apply the component weights to the adjusted sets of scores, and (c) add the weighted components to form a composite. The procedure most frequently recommended for criterion-referenced approaches in which components are separately graded is to (a) maintain records for various components in the same score scale, (b) apply the desired weights to the scores, (c) obtain the average of the weighted scores, and (d) convert the numerical average to the most appropriate letter-grade symbol. No study teacher was in compliance with either of the sets of procedures recommended above. Methods used to create the composite index of achievement varied from a subjective guess based on vague symbols and comments in the gradebook to subjective estimation of an average based on a visual scanning of a line of test scores to the use of computer software to do the averaging. In all cases where differential weights were desired, the weighting was accomplished by including differential numbers of exercises or points in the assessment.

- *Methods of setting grade cutoff scores: Fixed percents.* This option equates absolute reference points on an academic achievement average percent scale to points on a letter grade scale. The cutoffs (e.g., 90–100% = A, 80–89% = B, etc.) only have clear meaning when sound assessments allow the teacher to establish a clear link between the grade and the proportion of all required material mastered by each student. Half of the case study teachers used the fixed percent method, but cutoffs usually were chosen arbitrarily and had no clear reference back to the content. Different teachers in the same building sometimes adopted different cutoff scores for the same grade or even used different reporting schemes (e.g., pass/fail versus letter grades) for the same course.

- *Methods of setting grade cutoff scores: Point total accumulation.* This method, in which raw score points are accumulated overtime without converting to percentages and averaging, is not generally recommended because arbitrarily set cutoffs on a total point scale with no clear reference back to a body of material to be learned gives ambiguity to the meaning of the grade. Yet half of the case-study teachers used this approach. All set cutoffs arbitrarily.

- *Deciding on borderline cases.* The textbooks recommend that borderline cases be reviewed and that a final grade be established using whatever additional *achievement* data might be available for that student. However, all teachers reported using subjective nonachievement factors such as effort or attitude to make these decisions, and failed to gather or consider supplementary achievement data in deciding borderline cases.

Possible Reasons for Discrepancies. There are at least three possible reasons why teachers' grading practices may deviate from recommended practices. Recommended practice may represent a matter of opinion rather than an established scientific fact. The philosophical position of teachers and experts may reflect legitimate differences of opinion. To illustrate, the issue of whether or not to factor effort into a student's report card grade is seen by the expert as an assessment matter: Can the teacher define and measure the trait called effort and factor it into the grading equation so as to permit those who see the grade down the road to interpret the effort part of the message contained in that grade? Since such definition, assessment and communication is so difficult to achieve, the experts contend effort is best left out or communicated separately.

But teachers may see the issue from a different point of view.

They value and want to reward seriousness of purpose. Students who care and are on task are easier to manage. Besides, they contend that positive feedback to those who try can help the low achiever gain some rewards. Because grades represent the most powerful of very few feedback options available to them, they use it to encourage trying hard.

Another possible explanation for discrepancies may be that the recommended guidelines fail to take into account the realities of classroom life. For instance, teachers may not have the time or technical statistical expertise to compute end of quarter composite achievement scores according to complicated procedures spelled out in the textbooks.

The third possible explanation is that teachers may simply not be aware of some of the standards of sound-grading practice, because a vast majority have never been trained in relevant, classroom-level assessment and grading practices. For example, many may be unaware of the implications of using the same assessment results from an assignment for both formative (diagnostic) and summative (grading) purposes. These are matters for teacher training.

The path to the reduction of any particular discrepancy between recommended and actual practice, if a reduction is needed at all, will be a function of the reason(s) for the existence of that discrepancy. These paths can only be located when we have a clear sense of the actual practices teachers use. The research reported here begins to provide insight into those practices. More such studies are needed.

SUMMARY OF TWO STUDIES

These two studies were designed to generate a higher-resolution picture of two key aspects of classroom assessment. Through the lenses provided by teacher interviews, classroom observations, and document analysis, a clearer understanding of teachers' practices for higher order thinking skills assessment and for grading has emerged. Each has sharpened the focus of our sense of what it is teachers need to know about assessment in order to effectively manage a classroom assessment environment, as does the whole profile.

Each of the two assessment functions examined here—assessment of higher order thinking skills and grading—is a key to successful instruction. Thinking skills instruction, and therefore assessment, is widely regarded as a critical component of school improvement. Grading is the single most regular and influential feedback activity conducted by classroom teachers. Yet in each of these two assessment functions substantial deficits in the quality of assessment practice have emerged among the study teachers. Teachers have strong motivation to improve their assessment in both areas and both functions appear to be amenable to significant improvement through assessment training. The next chapter takes up the question of assessment training, in these and other areas crucial to improving the practice of classroom teachers.

CHAPTER 9

Implications for Teacher Training

Classroom assessment environments obviously are rich, multidimensional places which contribute much to the quality and impact of instruction. We have conducted a wide-ranging sequence of studies in an attempt to begin to map the key dimensions and capture the richness of these environments. Theorizing that one reason why the measurement community had conducted little research on classroom assessment was its immense complexity, we set out to confront and understand that complexity. Our goal has been to gain insight into the task demands of classroom assessment so we could plan and present to teachers the kind of assessment training that would help them meet those demands. We feel we have succeeded through our task analysis in capturing at least some of the keys to effective classroom assessment. The next step is to translate those results into effective teacher training in assessment. In this chapter, we specify the appropriate content focus of that training, report the results of a study of the current status of teacher training in relation to those content priorities and urge sweeping changes in the teacher training curriculum.

CLASSROOM ASSESSMENT COMPETENCIES FOR TEACHERS

Over the past decades, many have commented on the assessment competencies teachers should possess. Those comments have been based on wisdom derived from many sources. Many have surveyed educator opinion about their assessment training needs (Goslin,

1967; Hills, 1977; and Mayo, 1970), while others have surveyed training programs (Roeder, 1972 and 1973). Still others have synthesized research on school-testing practices and derived generalizations about teacher-training needs in assessment (Natriello, 1987). Some have analyzed flaws in teachers' tests (Fleming and Chambers, 1983; and Carter, 1984), conducted content analyses of measurement textbooks (Goehring, 1973), or examined technical standards for published tests for advice as to appropriate assessment competencies for teachers (Frisbie and Friedman, 1987). Still others have relied on specific philosophical perspectives to argue for specific training priorities (Scates, 1943).

But the essential fact is that these efforts have had no impact on teacher-training priorities or the criteria by which teachers are certified or selected for employment.

Our approach to the identification of the assessment needs of teachers took a different form. It began, as others have, with a review and synthesis of available research on the nature, role, and quality of classroom assessment. Then we turned, as others have, to a survey of teacher opinion about classroom assessment needs. However, at that point we adopted a different research methodology: case studies of classroom assessment environments using participant observer and teacher-journal data-collection procedures. This combination of literature review, survey, and ethnographic research methods allowed us to more effectively zero in on classroom assessment processes.

If the ingredients included in our profile of a classroom assessment environment are in fact as important in the effective management of such an environment, then the profile contains within it the specification of many of the key measurement concepts and skills that teachers need to master to be successful in the classroom. Based on the limited number of classrooms profiled to date, we are unable to argue that we have defined the essence of classroom assessment in the profile. That claim awaits further research relating classroom assessment practices to achievement outcomes. But the fact remains that teachers are in a position to make decisions about each of the dimensions in the profile as they develop their own classroom assessment procedures. They can only make informed decisions if they have mastered the requisite knowledge of sound assessment practices as part of their professional preparation.

Considering the results presented in previous chapters, then, what do teachers need to know about measurement and evaluation and what assessment practices must they master during their professional development? They need to know *why* to assess, *what can go wrong* and how to prevent it, what it means to assess in a *sensitive* way, how to provide effective *feedback*, and how to influence the assessment *policy* around them. These are the assessment competency areas which we suggest should form the basis of teacher training in assessment. All are important; they are not listed in order of priority.

Classroom Uses of Assessment

The well-prepared teacher/assessor understands how the assessment process fits into a wide variety of classroom decision-making contexts and serves as a means of conveying information to students. Such teachers recognize and differentiate among at least twelve different decision contexts they face in the classroom. Teachers assess in order to make *decisions*. They:

- diagnose the strengths and weaknesses of individual students;
- diagnose class or group needs;
- group students for instruction within and/or across classes;
- identify and select students who are in need of special services;
- assign grades on report cards; and
- evaluate the effectiveness of their instructional treatments.

They also use assessment to *teach*. They:

- communicate instructional objectives or achievement expectations;
- communicate social or interpersonal expectations;
- control student behavior and motivation;
- enhance test-taking skills;
- demonstrate personal responsibility for student learning; and
- use the assessment process as a teaching strategy.

Each of these should be integrated into the teachers' professional knowledge base from the perspectives of how it relates to effective instruction, the value of assessment in each context, and the specific kinds of assessment information or results needed to make the decisions involved. This knowledge helps the teacher address the extreme complexity of classroom assessment and give it order.

Providing a Clear and Stable Target

As an overriding theme, classroom assessment training and early experience should establish for teachers the importance of developing a clear and enduring vision of the learning target. Without such a vision, teachers cannot develop sound assessments, design sound instruction to help students hit the target, or help students to see the target or understand the teacher's expectations.

As a result, well-prepared teacher/assessors understand that these targets can take many forms, including a variety of active ingredients. For instance, they might reflect the substantive *subject matter knowledge* students are to master. This content specification often is derived from textbooks or other curricular materials. Effective classroom assessors know that their assessments must include exercises that representatively sample the various elements of that knowledge.

They also know that their achievement targets must reflect a clear vision of the kind(s) of *thinking* they want students to demonstrate. Well-prepared assessors are capable of accurately assessing student performance according to those thinking skill expectations using assessment methods that fit their particular classroom context. Thus, teachers must become familiar with various taxonomies and frameworks of thinking skills. Effective teachers can adopt one framework as a primary focus, pose questions and posit exercises that tap those kinds of thinking, and classify previously written exercises in terms of the kinds of thinking required to complete them.

Well-prepared assessor/teachers also can cast their achievement expectations in terms of (a) specific *behaviors* or performance skills that they want their students to develop and/or (b) *attributes of products* they want their students to be able to create when such criteria are relevant. These performance-assessment criteria form the basis of valid and reliable (i.e., objective) subjective or judgement-based assessments of achievement. Effective teachers have the expertise they need to develop such targets.

Assessment as an Interpersonal Activity

Skilled classroom assessors are keenly aware of the role that academic assessment plays in the interpersonal environment of the classroom. They understand the critical role that interpersonal factors play in the academic assessments they conduct. They know that assessment is never a purely academic or dispassionately scientific process. Rather, it is a process of interpersonal communication with personal effects.

For example, well-prepared teachers are aware of the fact that they are not the only decision makers who use classroom assessment results. Students use assessment results to make very important decisions about themselves and to decide how they fit into the academic and social context of school and beyond. Competent teachers possess a frank and specific understanding of assessment from the students' point of view. They know how to help students develop self-assessment skills and they realize the personal dangers to students of unsound assessment on the part of their teachers.

Tools To Assess Achievement

Appropriately prepared teachers possess a working knowledge of when and how to design, develop, use and value a wide variety of methods for assessing student achievement. At least nine different methods are available for classroom use. Each teacher must understand the advantages and limitations of each assessment method, the common pitfalls to their effective development and use in the classroom, and how to avoid those pitfalls. All methods are important. None should be regarded as more important or useful than another. The judgments as to the utility of the various methods should be made by the teacher over time, in terms of the quality control criteria listed above and the requirements of her or his own context and needs. The available alternatives are these:

- Paper and pencil assessment instruments
  teacher-developed tests and quizzes
  text-embedded tests and quizzes
  homework and seatwork assignments
  standardized tests
- Performance assessments
  observations of and judgments about achievement-related behaviors
  observations of and judgments about achievement-related products
- Personal communication
  answers to instructional questions
  interviews with students
  conversations with students
  intuitions and feelings about students
  comments from others about students

All teachers need to understand each of these as possible sources of data on student achievement.

Tools To Assess Other Traits

Achievement is only one of a variety of student characteristics teachers assess and use in their decision making. If assessment training is restricted to tactics for assessing achievement only, teachers will be inadequately prepared. They should know how to design, develop, use, and value at lease five methods for assessing important affective and social characteristics of their students:

- observing the behavior of individual students;
- observing group interactions;
- using paper and pencil questionnaires;
- conducting personal and group-student interviews; and
- tapping the opinions of others about the traits of students.

Each teacher should know the advantages and limitations of each method, the pitfalls to their appropriate use in the classroom and how to avoid those pitfalls. All methods are equally important. None should be singled out as more valuable. Judgments as to the relative utility of the alternatives should be left to the teacher to be made over time, given classroom experience.

The Meaning of Quality Assessment

Effective teacher/assessors understand and are able to apply those assessment principles that will allow them to produce assessments that are of the highest possible quality, given the realities of the classroom context. Due to the constraints of time and the lack of available technical expertise, teachers cannot be asked to adhere to the same quality control standards as test publishers. Nor should they be taught issues of quality control from the same technical or psychometric perspectives as testing professionals. However, teachers can and should be held accountable for knowing how to *maximize* the quality of their assessments, even if they cannot quantitatively *estimate* that quality.

In other words, they must know how to apply at least four specific assessment-quality criteria. They know that sound assessments:

- Reflect a clear and specific achievement target, detailing:
  - specific substantive subject matter content to be mastered,
  - thinking skills to be demonstrated in the context of that content knowledge,
  - behaviors to be exhibited, and/or
  - products with specific attributes to be created;
- Sample performance in an appropriate manner by:
  - providing a representative sample of all key forms of that performance, and
  - providing a sufficiently large sample to permit confident generalizations to the performance domain assessed;
- Control for those extraneous (nonachievement) factors that can interfere with the accurate assessment of achievement, such as:

quality of exercises,

quality of administration,

quality of scoring, and/or

student traits that can inhibit communication about achievement; and,

• Produce results that the decision maker understands and can use to inform the decision to be made. (Note, therefore, that sound assessments occur in the presence of a clear sense of why they are being conducted.)

Teachers who know how each of these criteria apply to the various types of assessment described below (i.e., paper and pencil, performance and personal communication) are prepared for the realities of the classroom. In actual classroom practice, teachers will weigh these criteria differently in selecting an assessment method for a particular purpose. However, at the outset, all criteria should be considered equally important.

Providing Feedback

The quality of an assessment is only as good as the communication value of the results. Assessments with high-communication value provide results that can be understood and used by the decision maker(s) for whom they are gathered. We already have established that students are high on the list of people who make decisions on the basis of classroom assessment results. If they are to act in their own best interest, they must receive feedback that has high-communication value.

For this reason, well-prepared teacher/assessors understand the advantages and limitations of a variety of forms of feedback, the pitfalls to their effective use in the classroom instruction context, and how to avoid those pitfalls. At least five forms of feedback should be the focus of specific professional preparation for teachers:

• oral and nonverbal feedback;
• feedback in the form of written comments;

- feedback in the form of performance-assessment ratings;
- feedback in the form of test scores; and
- feedback in the form of grades.

Competent classroom assessors master all forms of feedback.

Focus on Assessment Policy

Teachers need to be aware of the role that school, district and even state policy can play in aiding or inhibiting the development of quality classroom assessment procedures. Often, testing and grading policies are written by educators who have little formal background in sound assessment practice. This can lead to the implementation of policies that can have a detrimental influence on the nature and quality of classroom assessment. Teachers need to know how and where to look for pertinent assessment policies, how to evaluate those policies, and how to change policies that fail to promote sound classroom assessment.

OTHER OPINIONS ABOUT ASSESSMENT COMPETENCIES

As we have carried out our research over the past decade, others have become similarly concerned about the measurement training of teachers and have come forth with commentary on the proper focus of that training. For instance, Merwin (1989) holds that beginning teachers should understand the critical importance of the decisions they make in terms of the impact of those decisions on students' lives. This makes assessment a very important dimension of instruction and requires that assessment be of the highest quality, according to Merwin. Therefore, he contends that the beginning teacher should know about: (1) criteria that should be applied when considering the use of information for decision making; (2) techniques for developing, administering, and interpreting the results of classroom tests; (3) procedures for combining information and assigning grades; (4) characteristics of standardized tests and how to interpret the scores they provide; (5) numbers and how they can be used to record and communicate information; and, (6) techniques for manipulating test scores statistically to aid in their interpretation and use.

While we are in general agreement with Merwin, our priorities are somewhat broader. Certainly, his beginning overall context statement about the teacher as decision maker corresponds to our first competency area, which contends that the teacher needs to understand the various decision contexts of the classroom. We understand further that his first entry on criteria for sound assessment refers to the same quality control issues covered in our "meaning of quality" competency. Merwin's second entry and ours both hold that teachers learn to design and develop assessment tools and methods. However, from here on, we see some differences.

For example, our list of assessment tools for teachers appears far more extensive than Merwin's. We do not separate out competencies having to do with standardized tests, the use of numbers, or the manipulation of test scores. While these may be useful at some level, we feel far more compelled on the basis of our results to include other entries left out by Merwin: assessment of higher order thinking skills, assessment of affect, delivery of feedback, understanding the role of assessment in the interpersonal environment of the classroom, and understanding the role of policy in

In another investigation of interest, Frisbie and Friedman (1987) analyzed the *Standards for Educational and Psychological Testing* (1985) in a search for assessment standards that were relevant for classroom assessment and therefore teacher training. The *Standards* provides guidelines for the development and use of sound measurement instruments. They were developed predominately as guidelines for test publishers. But Frisbie and Friedman contend appropriately that at least some of the guidelines can and should also apply to classroom assessments. Through a careful analysis of the standards and their meaning, they were able to identify 90 of the 180 standards as relevant for teachers. Space will not permit the reproduction of the entire Frisbie and Friedman list here. However, suffice it to say that the *Standards* is exhaustive in its treatment of issues related to quality control in assessment (our "meaning of quality"), paper and pencil test design (part of our list of tools), and the statistical manipulation of test data in the service of ensuring proper test development and test use.

Again, as with the Merwin list, while we feel that concepts, relationships and abilities gleaned from the *Standards* are important and are worthy of consideration in planning teacher training in assessment, the results of such an analysis are likely to overlook many keys to effective classroom assessment. For instance, insufficient attention is likely to be given to the wide variety of uses of classroom assessment, measurement of thinking skills, measurement of nonachievement factors, delivery of feedback, and understanding the role of assessment in the academic, motivational, and interpersonal environment of the classroom.

A third study with direct implications for teacher training priorities has been reported by Allal (1988), who studied the classroom assessment grading and promotional decision-making procedures of elementary teachers and found them wanting. Her conclusions regarding training priority fill some of the gaps seen in the Merwin and Frisbie and Friedman lists, in our opinion:

> Although the topics typically dealt with, such as the construction of objective testing instruments, the definition of norm- and criterion-referenced interpretation procedures, are important and should not be neglected, other topics corresponding to major components of teachers' evaluation strategies should be treated in greater detail, both in preservice and inservice training. In particular, with respect to the summative/predictive functions of evaluation linked to the grading and report-card systems of the school system, teachers need explicit training in the following areas:
>
> 1. How to construct simple instruments (checklists, matrices, and charts, coding systems, etc.) for recording qualitative data based on observations and interactions with students.
>
> 2. How to avoid or reduce biases (errors of estimation and judgement) that commonly occur in informal, intuitive assessment procedures.
>
> 3. How to develop and use techniques for combining quantitative and qualitative information drawn from several different sources.
>
> 4. How to conduct discussions with parents and students regarding decisions of promotion and placement (p. 50).

But perhaps the most important statement of assessment competencies for teachers comes from a joint committee for the American Federation of Teachers, the National Council on Measurement in Education and the National Education Association (1990).

Based on a synthesis of all of the preceding studies of the task demands of classroom assessment, including those reported in the previous chapters of this volume, the committee articulated seven professional roles and responsibilities in the practice of classroom assessment for teachers. They contend that teachers should be skilled in:

1. choosing assessment methods appropriate for instructional decisions;
2. developing assessment methods appropriate for instructional decisions;
3. administering, scoring and interpreting results of both externally-produced and teacher-produced assessment methods;
4. using assessment results when making decisions about individual students, planning teaching, developing curriculum, and school improvement;
5. developing valid pupil grading procedures which use pupil assessment;
6. communicating assessment results to students, parents, other lay audiences and other educators; and
7. recognizing unethical, illegal, and otherwise inappropriate assessment methods and uses of assessment information.

IMPLICATIONS FOR TEACHER TRAINING

How do the assessment competencies outlined above compare to assessment training as currently reflected in teacher training programs across the country? Three recent studies, Wolmut (1988), Schafer and Lissitz (1987), and Gullickson and Hopkins (1987), shed light on this issue.

Wolmut recently reviewed teacher certification laws with the intent of analyzing requirements for assessment training. The results of his review are presented in Table 9.1. They reveal specific and relevant statements about assessment training in only nineteen of the fifty states. Wolmut reports that these results are identical to those of a parallel study he conducted 10 years earlier.

TABLE 9.1
STATE TEACHER CERTIFICATION STANDARDS RELATED TO
ASSESSMENT TRAINING

1983	1988

I. States with Specific Content Requirements

AL	Evaluation of teaching/learning	AL	Evaluation of teaching/learning
IN	Educational measurement & evaluation	AZ	Assessment & evaluation
MA	Teacher can use results of various evaluation procedures to stress the effectiveness of instruction (secondary teachers)	IN	Educ. measurement & evaluation
		MA	Use results of various evaluation procedures to stress the effectiveness of instruction (all teachers)
MS	Educational research required for AA, AAA and AAAA certificates	OR	Teaching strategies emphasizing developing of measurable objectives and diagnostic and prescriptive techniques
MO	Tests and measurements		
NV	Counseling and guidance, with emphasis on parent involvement	TN	Measurement and evaluation
OK	Evaluation of learning	VT	Ability to select, use, and interpret formal and informal tests to identify the strengths and weaknesses of individual students
OR	Teaching strategies emphasizing development of measurable objectives and diagnostic and prescriptive techniques		
		WV	Performance assessment measure
TN	Measurement and evaluation	WY	Educational evaluation
WY	Research and educational evaluation		

II. States Requiring a Course on Tests and Measurement

IL	(excluding Chicago)	MO	(Middle/junior high and secondary)
CT			

(continued)

TABLE 9.1 (*Continued*)

1983	1988

III.   States Requiring a Course on Educational Psychology

DE	IL	LA	MD	MI	NJ	NM	OR	SD		CT	DE	DC	IL		LA	MD	MI
WI										NM	(optional)	WI					

IV.   States Listing No Requirement

AK	AR	AZ	CA	CO	FL	GA	HA	ID		AK	AR	CA	CO	FL	GA	HA	ID
IA	KS	KY	ME	MN	MT	NB	NH	NY		IA	KS	KY	ME	MN	MS	MT	NB
NC	ND	OH	OK	PA	RI	SC	TX	UT		NV	NH	NJ	NY	NC	ND	OH	OK
VA	WA	WV								PA	RI	SC	SD	TX	UT	VA	WA

Source: Wolmut, 1988

Based on a survey of the measurement-training practices of 438 of the 707 members of the American Association of Colleges of Teacher Education, or 62 percent of the colleges, Schafer and Lissitz conclude that most teacher training programs do not require a course in educational measurement to graduate and that training programs in educational administration are even weaker in this regard than teacher education programs. Schafer and Lissitz report virtually no difference between their results and results of similar surveys of teacher training in assessment reported by Noll in 1955 and Roeder in 1972.

There are obviously many teachers who receive very little training in measurement. But what of those who do receive training? What do we know of the nature and quality of that training? The answers to these questions can be derived from an analysis of standard measurement textbooks and a discussion of research on teacher and professor perspectives on the relevance of training offered.

Gullickson (1984a) selected a list of key measurement concepts and asked teachers to rank them in terms of their importance in classroom assessment. Then he asked a group of professors who teach measurement courses to rank the same list in terms of the priorities reflected in their courses. With a few exceptions, the rank orders were very different.

In a follow-up study reported in 1987, Gullickson and Hopkins probed more deeply into the nature of measurement instruction. Based on a survey of measurement instructors, the authors are critical of: (a) the timing of measurement training, as it often precedes student teaching, thus robbing students of an appreciation of the complexity of the assessment tasks they face; (b) the practicality of instruction that offers little or no "lab" experience in real-world assessment; (c) the nesting of measurement training in other courses, resulting in superficial training by insufficiently trained faculty; (d) the course content, with its overemphasis on standardized tests and statistics and underemphasis on the qualitative assessment methods with which most instructors feel insecure; (e) the faculty to teach measurement who are inadequately trained in classroom assessment; and (f) the insufficient amount of time given to measurement instruction in the larger context of teacher training. "In sum," they conclude, "it seems apparent that many students, given the substantial constraints imposed on the educational measurement course, will continue to be inadequately prepared for classroom evaluation tasks" (p. 15).

NWREL STUDY OF THE ADEQUACY OF TEACHER TRAINING

While these studies pointed out to us the absence of training for many teachers and the inadequacy of training for many others, they lacked the sharp focus on specific competencies we could obtain given the results of our indepth task analysis of classroom assessment. For this reason, we conducted an investigation of the teacher-training curriculum in the major teacher training institutions of the Pacific Northwest states of Alaska, Hawaii, Idaho, Montana, Oregon, and Washington. Two questions guided the study: Are teachers offered assessment training as part of their undergraduate or graduate preparation? And if so, does that training focus on the competencies outlined earlier in this chapter?

In addition, because several states in the region require candidates to pass the National Teacher Examination (NTE) to be certified, we conducted an analysis of the test specifications and actual items of a sample NTE to determine the depth and nature of the coverage of the candidates professional knowledge in assessment.

Methodology

The analysis of course requirements and content required identification of a sample of teacher-training institutions to be the focus of the study. In each state, institutions were ranked according to the number of degrees awarded to education majors. Starting from the top, colleges were placed in the sample until at least 75 percent of degrees granted in that state were accounted for. This resulted in a list of fourteen institutions across the six states.

College catalogs for each institution were reviewed to determine curriculum requirements and optional offerings. Both baccalaureate and masters degree programs leading to general-elementary and secondary-teaching certification were reviewed to find measurement courses.

Information on the specific content of measurement courses offered was obtained through direct contact with course instructors. Each institution supplied the name of the instructor teaching the course. Each instructor received a brief questionnaire. Questions addressed whether the course was required or optional, what specific topics were covered, what text was used and how the instructor assessed the achievement of his or her student. In those instances where questionnaires were not returned, follow-up telephone calls were made to obtain the needed information. We succeeded in obtaining descriptions of nine measurement courses.

To analyze the NTE, we contacted the Educational Testing Service, publishers of the exam, to obtain a table of test specifications detailing the content covered on the NTE Core Battery and a sample examination. These were analyzed for coverage of assessment-related topics.

Results

Table 9.2 analyzes the content of the courses in terms of the eight essential assessment competencies identified earlier. Only three of

TABLE 9.2
COURSE AND TEXT CONTENT IN RELATION TO
ESSENTIAL COMPETENCIES

	Number of Courses (N = 9)	Comments
I. Essential assessment competencies		
1. Decision making	4	NRT/CRT distinction typically emphasized
2. Meaning of quality		
a. Validity (assessment reflects clear target)	9	Statistical treatment typically emphasized
b. Reliability (sample sufficient, extraneous interference controlled)	9	Statistical treatment typically emphasized
c. Utility of results	1	
3. Tools to assess achievement	7	Major emphasis on standardized tests
a. Paper-and-pencil tests		
b. Performance assessment	3	
c. Personal communication	0	
4. Tools to assess other traits	4	
5. Clear and stable achievement target	4	Stating objectives only
6. Assessment as interpersonal activity	3	Ethics and cultural bias only
7. Providing feedback	1	Grading only
8. Assessment policies	1	
II. Other Topics		
1. History of testing	4	
2. Statistical analysis	4	
3. Item analysis	4	
4. Scaling	2	
5. IQ testing	3	
6. Personality assessment	2	
7. Professional assessment	1	
8. Guidance uses	1	
9. Reference resources for published tests	1	

the nine courses described were required. Part I of the table indicates the percent of the courses which address these competencies in some way. Additionally, Part II of the table lists nine other topics which were addressed in courses, but which were not included among the essential assessment competencies of practicing classroom teachers. The "Comments" column of the table specifies which aspects of the various topics were included in the courses and texts, where topics are known to have been only partially covered.

Decision making, while addressed by four of the courses, received only partial coverage at best. The primary aspect of decision making that was included was the distinction between norm- and criterion-referenced testing, failing to address in detail most of the twelve classroom-level decision-making contexts identified by the NWREL.

The meaning of assessment quality was unevenly covered. The subtopics of assessment reliability and validity were the only two areas of competence that were covered by all courses. However, coverage was shallow and always quantitative, providing more guidelines for estimating quality control factors than practical guidelines for maximizing them in the classroom. Just one of the nine courses addressed the utility of assessment results.

The tools to assess achievement were covered unevenly. While most courses (7 of 9) covered paper and pencil tests and two-thirds of the courses addressed the selection of standardized tests, only three courses provided guidance in the development and use of performance-assessment methodology. Further, the use of personal communication as a means of gathering achievement data was completely ignored. And assignments, instructional questions, group-assessment methods, and use of the opinions of others—all potentially valuable sources of achievement data for teachers—were not found to be covered in any course. The tools to assess traits other than achievement, such as affective characteristics, also were covered in a minority of courses.

Less than half of courses addressed the competency of setting clear and stable achievement targets in assessment terms. And again, even when addressed, the topic was not covered in full; most courses restricted coverage to the importance of stating objectives.

Other possible forms of achievement targets, such as performance rating criteria and use of sample exercises, were not addressed at all as far as we could tell.

Assessment as an interpersonal activity was considered only in three of the nine courses. And, in all cases, the topic was limited to considerations of the ethics of testing and issues of cultural bias. There was no evidence of the treatment of students as assessors or users of assessment results.

Guidelines for providing feedback were presented in only one course. In this case, the only subtopic addressed was grading. Thus, eight out of nine assessment courses failed to prepare teachers to develop sound grading practices or use other forms of classroom assessment feedback.

Issues related to assessment policies were also rarely addressed, finding a place in just one course. Teachers were given no guidelines for evaluating policies in terms of their implication for the quality of classroom assessments.

Courses also pursued content not included among the NWREL essential competencies for the classroom teacher. For instance, four course instructors gave time to the study of the history of testing. Statistical analysis of test scores and statistical item analysis were covered in four of the courses. And quantitative psychometric scaling was taught in two of the courses.

IQ testing was included in three courses. Personality assessment was included somewhat less frequently, but was found in two courses. Professional assessment (certification testing) was addressed in one course.

Other topics that were found in at least one course, were uses of assessments in student guidance and reference resources for published tests.

The assessments used by instructors in these courses may also serve to indicate to teacher trainees what is important to assess and how to assess it. Those methods certainly reflect the values of instructors. In the nine measurement courses analyzed, all but one instructor relied on paper and pencil examinations as their measures of student achievement. Some instructors' assignments required that students apply course concepts in projects or papers. These assignments generally reflected course emphases on more technical aspects of testing. Among these were three courses requiring students to construct a paper and pencil test, two requiring a test-analysis project, and three requiring a statistical analysis project. Research reports and short "problem" papers assigned require that students perform statistical-item analyses or define reliability or validity. One course, by contrast, used assignments that emphasized applications of course concepts to the classroom setting, requiring students to write short responses to simulated problems typical of those that would arise in testing and grading students in the classroom.

An analysis of the coverage of a sample National Teacher Examination battery provided by Educational Testing Services reveals rather shallow, narrow representation of assessment issues. Of the 339 objective test items included in the entire battery, only eleven or 3 percent tested assessment knowledge. This represents 10 percent of the 105-item Professional-Knowledge subtest. Of these eleven items, four dealt with standardized-testing issues, two related to statistical analysis of research data, two addressed issues related to providing feedback, and one each focused on evaluating minority students, use of teacher-made tests and program-evaluation methods.

Effects of Inadequate Training

What are the implications of the mismatch between what teachers need to know about assessment and what they are taught about assessment during teacher training (if they receive such training)? There are many effects on students, teachers and the education community in general. Let us detail some of these.

One major implication of our failure to understand and assist teachers with the task demands of classroom assessment may be the extensive use of unsound measurement procedures in our schools. The result of poor measurement is poor decision making. At the very least, poor decisions mean inefficient instruction, and at worst they can lead to failure to learn and an attendant loss of student motivation to participate in the learning process.

It should be obvious that effective instruction is not possible without effective assessment of student learning. For example, teachers untrained in the appropriate assessment of student achievement will have great difficulty diagnosing students' needs. They will have great difficulty determining the effectiveness of their instruction so that they can adjust to meet those needs. Therefore, one effect of inadequate assessment is that students fail to achieve important learning goals and objectives set for them by their teachers.

But there could be broader effects. To illustrate, consider the case of the student who, as a result of good communication, has attained a clear understanding of what she is to learn in a particular unit. Further, assume that our student has benefited from sound instruction and, with hard work, has met or even exceeded those standards. But, due to inadequate assessment training, the teacher produces a paper and pencil test for the end of this particular unit that fails to adequately test the material the student thinks she is supposed to learn. This might mean the test inadequately samples the content covered, requires thinking skills that fail to match skills taught and/or includes test items that are poorly written. Our student unwittingly is doomed to perform poorly on this test, not because she failed to work hard to meet the objectives so clearly outlined by the teacher, but because the assessment failed to test the intended outcomes. Such failures due to a lack of match between instruction and assessment need happen only a few times, particularly in the early grades, for our student to begin to perceive a sense of futility in studying. If she repeatedly studies the right thing and fails anyway, she is going to lose a sense of control over her own academic well-being, she is going to give up, and having given up, it will be only a matter of time in the face of this kind of failure before she leaves school altogether. Those concerned with causes for high-dropout rate among students these days might look at inadequate assessment as at least a contributor to this serious problem.

Another implication of continuing to ignore classroom assessment will be the continued opinion of laypersons and policymakers that the best or only fair way to measure schooling outcomes is by means of standardized paper and pencil tests. These are sound tests. But they are very limited in scope. These tests do not track anywhere near the full range of outcomes we intend schools to achieve. Yet, they represent the complete focus of our attempts to hold schools accountable. Unless and until we document the validity and reliability of classroom assessments and act to correct any deficiencies uncovered through investigations, we will remain unable to develop a broader set of accountability indicators that reflects the full array of valued targets.

Yet another implication of our failure to address classroom assessment issues is the related use of standardized test scores as the primary index of the effectiveness of school-improvement efforts. Because standardized tests have achieved such a strong reputation as the valued measure of educational outcomes, they continue to be the only criterion variables in currently popular efforts to discover effective teaching practices, despite criticism of these tests as insufficient criteria in this research context (Dunkin and Biddle, 1974; Shulman, 1986). Brophy and Good (1986) have reviewed research on the relationship between teacher behavior and school achievement and again have called for an expansion of our definition of achievement to include more than standardized-test scores. The measurement community will remain unable to respond to this crucial issue until we conduct the research and training needed to help instill confidence in more measures, including teacher-developed classroom assessments.

The final and perhaps most compelling implication of our failure to address teachers' classroom assessment needs will be the continued alienation of teachers from systematic assessment and evaluation processes. If teachers oppose testing, it is because they see it as a large-scale enterprise that fails to address their needs. Many teacher training programs do not require training in assessment because assessment is not *perceived* as relevant to teaching! Until we (1) understand assessment in the teacher's world in terms relevant to the teacher and (2) translate our concepts into those terms, we will remain unable to alter teachers' perceptions of either the validity or the relevance of systematic assessment.

CHANGING TRAINING PRIORITIES

If we are to understand how to change our assessment training priorities, we must first understand why current training fails to provide practitioners with the classroom assessment tools they need. We have argued repeatedly throughout this volume that one cause of the mismatch is a lack of understanding on the part of the measurement community of the demands of the classroom environment stemming from a lack of disciplined inquiry into those demands. As a result, introductory measurement textbooks and courses very often fail to reflect the reality, complexity, and personality of classroom assessment.

We have failed to conduct the much-needed research because we have adhered to the philosophy that measurement is measurement is measurement, regardless of the context within which it takes place. In fact, the science of paper and pencil testing and the quantitative manipulation of scores that has guided our thinking about measurement instruction for teachers is important, but it is far from sufficient. Therefore, one step in changing our training priorities is to revise the content of measurement courses to reflect the differences between large-scale and classroom assessment. The addition of truly relevant and helpful content will help convince teachers and those who set teacher training priorities of the extreme importance of this training. If the content of this training remains unchanged, assessment training will continue to be every bit as unimportant in teacher training as it is today.

If we were to revise course content based on the research results presented herein, major changes would be required in traditional measurement courses. Table 9.3 summarizes those changes. In many cases, the new content priorities would simply build upon traditional, important content. But in other cases, the differences are more pronounced. For instance, we recommend placing a much greater emphasis on the interpersonal role and impact of assessment—a concept rarely covered in traditional measurement courses. In addition, we would add emphasis to the assessment of nonachievement factors in the classroom by providing teachers with training in the design and development of very practical and useable data-collection instruments and procedures.

But perhaps the most fundamental difference between the two approaches is seen in the manner in which issues of assessment quality control are addressed. The traditional approach is to treat these issues in terms of technical definition and quantitative estimation. An alternative is to teach teachers the common pro-

TABLE 9.3
COMPARING TRADITIONAL AND RECOMMENDED CONTENT

Competency Area	Traditional Content	Recommended Content*
Decision making	Uses of assessment covered: diagnosis grouping selection grading evaluating instruction accountability	Traditional content plus other uses: communicating expectation controlling students providing test-taking experience teaching via assessment
Assessment as an interpersonal activity	Generally not addressed	Personal risks of poor and positive effects of sound assessment explored in depth
Providing a clear target	Writing instructional objectives Assessing thinking in terms of Bloom's taxonomy via objective test items	Traditional content plus: developing performance-assessment criteria assessing thinking in terms of various criteria using various assessment modes
Assessment methods: achievement	Paper-and-pencil tests Standardized tests	Traditional content plus: performance assessments assignments oral questions group assessments opinions of others student-record files

(*continued*)

TABLE 9.3 (*Continued*)

Competency Area	Traditional Content	Recommended Content[*]
Assessment methods: other characteristics	Measuring intelligence, attitude, interest and personality (focus on traits)	Substitute for traditional: observations questionnaire use interview use tapping opinions of others student records (focus on methods)
Other topics	Statistical analysis of validity, reliability and item-level data	Not addressed

[*] See Appendix C for recommended background and training materials.

cedural pitfalls to valid and reliable assessment and show them how to design and conduct their assessments so as to avoid those pitfalls. The emphasis is on practical strategies for maximizing quality. Estimation of quality would be secondary.

Finally, given the limited time available for assessment training and the increased content priorities outlined above, we would delete the traditional practice of addressing statistical treatments of test data, such as item analysis, and an indepth treatment of intelligence tests which are of little value to teachers in their classrooms. The point is *not* that these are unimportant. They are important. But we regard them as advanced topics.

As we adjust content, we need to rethink the audiences to whom measurement training is directed. Instead of developing one introductory measurement course for students in many different fields of study, such as psychology, counseling, and education, teachers may be served better by a special course tailored to the unique demands of classroom assessment. Such courses would serve teacher training needs well by giving teachers (in public education and postsecondary education) the assessment tools and skills they need to do their job. Those tools are not the same as the tools and skills needed by psychologists.

In addition, training focused specifically on classroom assessment would serve those who support instruction. For instance, if principals are to be instructional leaders in the true sense of the term, they must be in position to support all key aspects of instruction, including the activity that often takes up a third to half of a teacher's professional time, i.e., assessment. The same is true of resource teachers and other district personnel who play a supporting role for teachers.

And then when the assessment training needs of these practitioners are being addressed, we can turn to the assessment-training needs of policy makers, such as district superintendents, school board members, state legislators and others who act upon assessment results. They too must have a keen understanding of the meaning and limitations of those results if they are to act upon them in an informed manner.

Another critical step in the improvement of assessment training is to acknowledge the fact that the lack of assessment skills in our classrooms cannot be overcome through better teacher-education courses alone. Relevant undergraduate and graduate courses represent part of the answer, but we must also plan to deliver assessment training and technical assistance to those millions of teachers who completed undergraduate and graduate programs that included no assessment training. Only high-quality inservice training can solve this part of the problem. We might allocate both assessment and staff development resources to develop a cadre of classroom assessment specialists who can train and support teachers on a daily basis. The recruitment and training of these specialists, perhaps out of the ranks of teachers, should be a very high priority. We will say more about this in Chapter 10, below.

A Final Comment on Assessment Training

Without question, the most important implications of the research reported in this volume have to do with educator training in assessment. When we compare our portrait of the demands of classroom assessment to the training priorities of teacher education, we see profound and important discrepancies. This does not represent a new insight. We have known of this problem for decades. Yet we have not acted to correct it. We only hope the clarity of our description of the complexity of classroom assessment will make the scope of the mismatch so clear that it can no longer be ignored. Further, we hope our analysis of the complexity of classroom assessment reveals that decisive action can be taken to improve our understanding of and the quality of such assessment.

In Appendix C, we list some of the training resources and support materials available to those who would address these critical teacher-training priorities, whether in preservice or inservice contexts.

CHAPTER 10

Implications for Policy and Research

The results of this analysis of the task demands of classroom assessment also have wide ranging implications for educational policy and the future of measurement research. Policy issues center on curriculum specifications for educator training programs, licensing and certification standards, school district and building staffing patterns, and the allocation of limited assessment resources, among other issues. Research implications center both on the nature of the questions that guide disciplined inquiry on school testing and the research methods used to generate answers to those questions.

POLICY IMPLICATIONS

Training Policy

We can infer from the discussion in the preceding chapter that those who establish training requirements in teacher-education programs must come to terms with the need for relevant assessment training. Such course work needs to find a place in an otherwise full teacher-training curriculum. This becomes critical in those programs currently offering little or no training. Minimum course requirements must include at least a basic course in measurement followed by methods instruction adapting basic principles to particular school subjects and grade levels. Policymakers must face the issue of how to fit this critical component into the full programs.

In addition, a corollary issue in the arena of teacher training policy is what content to include in the assessment courses, when offered. The priority assessment competencies listed in the preceding chapter, or some similar list, need to be rank-ordered in terms of importance so as to prepare the teacher to be effective in the classroom on a day-to-day basis.

Licensing

Another policy implication has to do with teacher and administrator licensing and certification. It is difficult to justify certifying teachers to practice when they have had little or no training in an activity which can consume a third to half of their available professional time. Similarly, it is difficult to conceive of a program designed to certify instructional leaders that overlooks such a critical dimension of instruction as classroom assessment. The growing number of states considering or developing new licensing examinations covering knowledge and application of basic principles of pedagogy need to reconsider test specifications from the perspective of their coverage of essential assessment methodology.

Teacher Evaluation

A third policy implication deals with teacher evaluation and supervision. Often, teacher evaluation procedures require that principals go into classrooms occasionally, observe teacher performance briefly, judge the quality of that performance, and provide feedback to the teacher.

We submit that it is not possible to evaluate teacher performance thoroughly without focusing on the effect of teacher performance on student learning. In addressing this problem, many school districts turn to scores on national, state, or local norm-referenced standardized achievement tests. Their contention is that these scores reflect student achievement, and if the scores go up, then the teacher is doing the job. In fact, this use of norm-referenced standardized achievement test scores to evaluate teacher performance is not defensible from a measurement point of view. These tests are designed to provide broad, shallow coverage of content and to report results on very general, comparative score scales. Therefore, they often fail to test key concepts taught by teachers, while testing other concepts not covered. As such, they simply are too general to document the effect that any particular teacher is having on any particular group of students during any given school year. Further, many factors beyond control of the teacher influence student performance on these tests. Thus it is inappropriate to evaluate teacher performance on the basis of the norm-referenced standardized achievement test scores of their students.

The paradox remains, however, that one of the best indicators of the quality of teaching and teacher performance is student achievement as reflected on assessments that are focused and sensitive enough to reflect classroom content and skill priorities. Day-to-day classroom measures of student achievement can provide this kind of information. But here, once again, we confront the problem of classroom assessment quality. These assessments would represent a viable alternative for teacher evaluation if we could be sure that those assessments were of high quality. In fact, we have already documented the fact that such trust often is not warranted. Therefore, one effect of inadequate assessment training for teachers is that they and their supervisors often are deprived of the precise kind of assessment information that could serve to document whether or not teachers are fulfilling their responsibilities in the classroom. Teacher-evaluation policy needs to be reviewed in light of this issue.

Staffing Policy

A fourth policy implication of these classroom assessment research results is the need to reevaluate the manner in which we staff school districts in order to address assessment needs and issues. Most school districts do not employ a full-time assessment specialist to serve staff needs. In those rare instances when such specialists are present (most often in large school districts), their time is fully consumed satisfying the requirements of large-scale districtwide and federally mandated standardized testing programs. These testing specialists rarely if ever assist teachers with classroom assessment needs.

We urge the creation of a new job title in school districts to fill this gap: the classroom assessment specialist. These new staff members will be translators whose job it will be to know the language and principles of the educational measurement and the language and principles of classroom instruction and to serve as a mediator between the two worlds. They should be clear thinkers, good writers, and excellent trainers. They might come from the ranks of teachers so as to be sensitive to teachers' assessment needs and so they have credibility in the classroom. They might be principals who train to become competent helpers in assessment and whose job is to share that wisdom with their teachers. Or they might be curriculum specialists who are tuned into the unique assessment demands of their area of expertise. Regardless, their responsibility will be to be in the school buildings and classrooms offering training and technical assistance to teachers, principals, students, and parents.

Spending Assessment Dollars

The final, and perhaps the most important policy implication of our research has to do with the division of limited assessment resources between large-scale and classroom assessment. Over the past decade, both the amount and quality of large-scale standardized testing has increased at local, state, national and international levels. The research and development efforts associated with these testing programs exceed a billion dollars a year in the United States. The appropriateness of these expenditures rests on the validity of the implicit assumption that centralized decision making at a policy level informed by centralized testing programs leads to more and better school improvement than does better classroom-level decision making informed by classroom-level assessment. The primacy of this underlying assumption is seen by the fact that we currently spend virtually nothing at local, state, or national levels to ensure the quality of classroom assessments.

We question the validity of this assumption. We believe that teachers' classroom-level instructional decisions based on their own assessments contribute far more to the quality and impact of a student's school experience than do most policy-level decisions. That is not to say that large-scale assessments are unimportant. They are critical. But it is teachers' classroom assessments that students rely on to help them set expectations of themselves, learn what teachers expect, practice hitting valued targets and decide whether to care. And it is classroom assessment results that inform parents—the third important set of decision makers who influence student learning. We suggest that the total domination of limited assessment resources by large-scale testing does not begin to reflect the relative importance of these two levels of assessment in terms of student learning. Assessment resource allocation policies are in urgent need of reexamination.

IMPLICATIONS FOR RESEARCH

We began our studies in the early 1980s with a review of research addressing the nature, role, and quality of classroom assessment. We found the pool of relevant research to be shallow at that time, as had those who explored this issue before us. Our response at that time was to call for more and better research in this important arena.

Now, in the early 1990s, as we complete this first summary of our work to date, Natriello (1987) has published a very current review of recently published research on classroom assessment and concludes as follows:

> Studies of evaluation processes are found to be limited by the lack of descriptive information on actual evaluation practices in schools and classrooms, a concentration on one or two aspects of a multifaceted evaluation process, and the failure to consider the multiple purposes that evaluation systems must serve in schools and classrooms (p. 155).

This commentary suggests, as do our results, that there is much yet to be learned about classroom assessment, if we are to help teachers maximize its quality.

In the course of our studies we have used a wide variety of research methods to try to find data collection and interpretation methods that would allow us to understand the nature, complexity and meaning of the classroom assessment experience from the perspective of the teacher and the student. Those methods have included literature searches, interviews, questionnaires, the use of classroom journals, assessment document analysis, examination of classroom recordkeeping systems, and observations of students and teachers in action. These are not the traditional methods of the measurement researcher, but they have served us well, because they have allowed us to gain the rich description Natriello calls for. If we are to continue to gain new insights into the task demands of classroom assessment, we must continue to explore new research paradigms with new research methods.

We can rely on these diverse research methods to help us generate answers to a very wide range of as yet unaddressed research questions. Just a few of these are listed below, along with some reasons why we believe these are priorities:

- What are the crucial differences in assessment environments as grade level increases and as subject changes within and across grade levels? How do teachers adapt to these differing assessment requirements?

Rationale: If assessment environments vary greatly by grade level and/or school subject, we may need to fine tune teacher training even more precisely to meet their special needs or to provide each teacher with the tools and flexibility to adopt them for special applications.

- How and how well are social and personality characteristics assessed by teachers who are left to their own devices? How do these variables weigh in the various preinstructional, interactive, and postinstructional decisions? What are the effects on students?

Rationale: We know that teachers consider more than just the achievement of students in planning instruction. Beyond that fact, we know little. Student well-being may hinge on these assessments, yet their quality or the appropriateness of their use cannot be assured. The results of this research will inform both training and policy.

- How are teachers' initial impressions of students at the beginning of the school year formed? Are they accurate? How do they change? What are the effects on students?

Rationale: These assessments form the filter through which teachers see and interpret student performance for the rest of the year, according to Airasian (1984). If they are inaccurate, they should not have influence as the resulting bias can do great harm. If they are accurate at the outset but fail to detect changes in key student characteristics, again, the resulting bias can do great harm.

- Teachers plan around activities and content. Does this translate into student evaluation by counting tasks completed? If so, how is this assessment conducted? How is it translated into feedback? What is its effect on student learning?

Rationale: This issue bears directly on the nature and clarity of the expectations teachers hold as valuable for their students. While education agencies at all levels have lists of goals and objectives that articulate the curriculum, the effectiveness of our communication of those standards on the day-to-day decision making is unexplored. The assessment implications of this are profound. Do teachers value and assess the doing or the learning that results from doing?

- What are the specific strategies teachers use to simplify the information-processing requirements of the classroom? What are the implications of each for the reliability and validity of the results?

Rationale: In the face of an erroneous assessment task, the high school teacher facing upwards of 150 students per day, for example, must economize—must be as efficient in assessment as possible. If we can come to understand how such teachers make the task manageable, we can (a) point out those strategies that harm assessment quality, and (b) suggest additional time and energy-saving ideas. Answers to these questions can help focus assessment training.

- What is the assessment process like from the students' perspective? Is it fair? Is it useful? How does it affect learning, academic self-concept, and personal self-concept? How does this differ as grade, subject, and sex/race/social group change?

Rationale: We have yet to study assessment through the eyes of students. Our assessments inform our decisions, we act and students feel the impact of our action. Our assessments inform student decisions about themselves, they act and feel the impact of their actions. Yet, we know so little about what students see and feel about our day-to-day assessments. And we know virtually nothing about the internal workings of the student self assessor.

We can only use assessments to help motivate, study and promote learning if we understand their effects from inside the learner.

In short, more highly focused descriptive studies like those reported in Chapter 8 are needed to begin to fill-in details on our emerging portrait of classroom assessment.

Research on classroom assessment processes must come to have the same level of credibility among measurement researchers as research probing more traditional psychometric topics. Given the expected impact of the two kinds of research on the quality of education, they deserve at least equal research billing. Disciplined inquiry in the classroom assessment should be encouraged as dissertation research. Important, yet manageable research questions abound in this arena for graduate students to address, as demonstrated above. Further, scholarly research in classroom assessment should become a prominant part of the body of measurement research rewarded with tenure at research universities. It is only through this kind of research effort that we will begin to understand the art and science of the kind of assessment that either drives or could drive the high-quality educational system we all desire.

ASSESSMENT AND THE QUALITY OF SCHOOLS

As we reflect on the potential impact on schools of improving the quality of classroom assessment, we must anticipate both benefits and risks. The benefits are quite obvious and very exciting. Sound assessment on a day-to-day basis promises to enhance both the quality and efficiency of instruction. Teachers will gain a clear sense of student needs. Students will gain a clear sense of teacher expectations. Instructional treatments will be evaluated and revised in terms of their impact on achievement measured in terms sensitive to classroom expectations. The result will be greater student learning.

But we would be naive if we didn't anticipate the risks of assessment as well. Sound assessments can reveal dimensions of education that we may not wish to acknowledge. Teachers may find, for example, that students have already mastered what they intended to teach or that students have yet to master prerequisites the teacher assumed had been covered before. In either case, instructional sequences and activities may need to be radically revised in light of classroom assessment results. Are we prepared to adjust to this inconvenience, especially in school contexts where teachers' tasks are defined in terms of completing the textbook or the required curriculum within a fixed time period?

From a different perspective, teachers may find that, upon careful analysis, assessments fail to match their instructional objectives and/or the learning experiences provided for students. As a result, we may find a need to carry out major revisions of classroom assessments. Are we prepared to provide the training, technical assistance and professional time they need to do so?

Or most troubling of all, we may find that sensitive measures of classroom achievement revealing that our instruction is not working—students are not learning what we hoped they would learn. Are we prepared to acknowledge such results and make changes in our methods of teaching?

We have avoided confronting these problems in two specific ways. The first is denial. We have denied that classroom assessment is a relevant educational concern from any perspective. We have not researched it, trained for it, nor set policy to ensure its quality. We have kept assessment and instruction separate from one another and denied that any link could exist between the two. By doing so, we have absolved ourselves of any responsibility for understanding and confronting problems with classroom assessment or high-resolution indicators of outcomes of teaching.

The second avoidance strategy has been large-scale testing. The only logical way we could defend our denial of the importance of classroom assessment was to contend that "we don't need to examine it anyway—we have our standardized tests to ensure sound assessment of those outcomes—at least once a year." Never mind that they don't represent high-resolution assessment; they represent objective, "scientifically" acceptable assessment. They represent our safeguard against mediocrity. And as our fear of mediocrity has increased, our plan of action is to use more and more centralized standardized testing programs. As long as these tests are in place, how can schools go wrong? And if local assessments don't work, we'll institute state assessments. If these don't work, we'll initiate national testing programs. If national assessment doesn't work, we'll try international assessment. Surely one of those will ensure quality education, we hope.

The simple truth is that these avoidance strategies have not ensured the quality of instruction and they never will. We must acknowledge once and for all that the quality of instruction and the amount and nature of student learning is determined in each individual school building and classroom. All teachers must be the best assessor of student learning they can be. All principals must be the best leader of sound classroom assessment they can be. Then and only then can teacher and principal and large-scale and classroom assessment work in harmony to help all students learn. If schools are to be improved, we must move promptly and decisively to make the same investment in the quality of *classroom* assessment that we have in large-scale assessment.

In his comprehensive review of nearly 200 research reports addressing issues related to the impact of classroom assessment of student achievement, Crooks (1988) succinctly states why this form of assessment is so critical to the effective functioning of schools and to student learning. The decisions students make about themselves are the decisions that determine the success of the teaching/learning event and students rely very heavily on classroom assessment results to help them make those critical decisions:

> it [assessment] guides students' judgments about what is important to learn, affects motivation and self-perception of competence, structures their approaches to and timing of personal study . . . consolidates learning and affects the development of enduring learning strategies and skills (Crooks, 1988, p. 467).

Then Crooks relies on available research on the effects of assessment on students to provide a simple vision that might guide our research, development, policy and training in classroom assessment. Sound classroom assessment, he contends:

- emphasizes understanding, transfer of learning to untaught problems or situations, and other thinking skills, relying on assessment tasks that clearly involve more than recognition and recall;

- integrates assessment into instruction using it formatively in the role of assisting students to learn and not just summatively as in grading;
- produces specific feedback that focuses student attention on their progress when that feedback is still clearly relevant;
- relies on cooperation where appropriate to enhance valuable peer and self-evaluation skills;
- reflects carefully tailored standards that are set to be high but attainable in order to maximize motivation;
- provides for consolidation of learning by providing regular opportunities for practice, demonstration of skill and feedback;
- relies on the full range of assessment formats to reflect the diversity of outcomes valued in most classrooms; and
- finds ways to assess all valued outcomes—does not reduce outcomes to those easily measured.

We know the meaning of sound assessment in the classroom. We understand the task demands of sound classroom assessment. We know how to train educators to understand, design, develop, and use sound assessments in the classroom. And we know what kinds of technical assistance teachers need at their disposal to assess in an effective way.

Now we know we must make sound classroom assessment as high a priority as sound large-scale assessment.

APPENDIX A

TEACHER'S SELF-ANALYSIS
OF CLASSROOM ASSESSMENT PROCEDURES

IN (subject): _____

AT (grade level): _____

Richard J. Stiggins, Director
Center for Classroom Assessment
Northwest Regional Educational Laboratory
101 S. W. Main, Suite 500
Portland, Oregon 97204

January 1986
Revision

PLEASE READ VERY CAREFULLY

Reason for the Analysis

This questionnaire has been designed to help you analyze your day-to-day assessments of student achievement. Such an analysis can serve two purposes. First, it can help you analyze and understand classroom assessment as you use it. But more important, it can help us learn more about your assessment needs, so we can plan services to support your testing efforts.

To help you analyze your assessment methods, we have devised a series of probing questions which will require you to think carefully about your testing procedures. This is not a quick questionnaire. It will take about 30 minutes of careful thought on your part. By combining your answers with those of many other teachers, we will be able to reach our goal of understanding the classroom assessment environment more clearly.

The ultimate value of this analysis depends on three key factors: (1) our success in clearly defining differences among several *types of tests,* and (2) your success in clearly focusing on each *different type* of test when answering questions about it and (3) your willingness to provide *reflective, thoughtful* responses. We are interested in learning about your use of and attitudes about six different types of achievement measures:

- the objective paper and pencil tests you develop on your own for use in your classroom
- tests that are embedded in or are provided to you as part of the published text materials you use
- published standardized achievement tests
- oral questioning in the classroom (recitation)
- structured observations and judgments of student behaviors or products, and
- spontaneous observations and judgments you make about student behaviors or products

We are going to ask you a series of questions about your use of and concerns about each of these. PLEASE CAREFULLY STUDY THE DESCRIPTIONS OF THESE TYPES OF ASSESSMENTS PROVIDED BELOW, NOTING THE ESSENTIAL AND UNIQUE CHARACTERISTICS OF EACH.

Types of Assessments

The first assessment category about which we will ask questions is *teacher-developed paper and pencil tests* you develop for your own use in the classroom. This category includes all true-false, multiple-choice, matching, fill-in and short-answer tests and quizzes which YOU DEVELOP to determine if students have mastered the material taught. In the space provided, please provide a *brief* description of a test you developed and used *or* are familiar with. The purpose of this description and the one you provide below is to let us know you understand the meaning of each test type.

The second assessment category about which we will ask questions is *tests embedded or included in the instructional materials,* such as the textbooks you use. These may be found in an instructor's guide or may take the form of questions at the end of chapters in the materials themselves. In the space provided below, please provide a brief description of test exercises you may have taken from text materials *or* are familiar with.

The third type of assessment we are interested in is the *standardized achievement test* battery offered by test publishers, such as the Stanford Achievement Test, Comprehensive Test of Basic

Skills, Metropolitan Achievement Test, and Iowa Test of Basic Skills. This category also covers state-wide or district-wide tests, including norm and criterion referenced tests. Please identify a standardized test you have used or are familiar with.

The fourth type of assessment is the daily question-and-answer process used on a day-to-day basis during instruction to track whether individual students or the class as a group are learning the material. Classroom recitation often provides valuable insights into student growth.

The next two categories include those assessments in which you observe and evaluate actual student behavior and/or products. These are labeled *performance assessment* and include two types of assessment: (1) formal, structured-performance tests, and (2) informal, spontaneous observations of student performance.

Performance assessments are those assessments in which you, the teacher, observe students in the process of doing things (e.g., speaking or oral reading) or examine products created by students (e.g., writing sample or art project). Then, on the basis of your professional judgment, you judge or rate student performance. These are evaluations of student achievement, but they differ from multiple-choice or true-false tests in the types of exercises used, mode of response and scoring procedures, among other things.

Performance assessments take one of two forms. Some are STRUCTURED tests and include: (1) a clearly defined *reason* for assessment; (2) preplanned *exercises* to elicit student responses; (3) a prespecified *response* to be evaluated; and (4) carefully spelled out *scoring* procedures. Here is an illustration:

> In assigning grades to students, a chemistry teacher evaluates each student's ability to successfully set up and conduct two chemistry experiments. Students are observed by the teacher and rated on the set up of the lab equipment, the correctness of procedures carried out, and success in identifying each unknown substance.

Note the four components of this performance assessment:

_____	REASON:	grading
_____	EXERCISE:	scientific experiments
_____	RESPONSE:	conduct lab procedures
_____	RATING:	rate equipment setup, procedures, and results

On the other hand, performance assessments can be much less structured. For example a SPONTANEOUS classroom event may provide a teacher with an informal opportunity to observe and evaluate a student's performance and to judge the student's proficiency:

> In listening to students read orally, a teacher notices that a particular student is having difficulty with a beginning sound. The teacher notes the problem for future remedial work.

In this case, the reason for assessment was not predefined, but is nevertheless very important. The informal assessment was diagnostic and will influence future instruction for that student. The oral-reading activity may not have been structured to be an assessment per se, and the response evaluated was not anticipated. Yet, this activity results in an important SPONTANEOUS performance assessment.

In the questions that follow, you are asked about both the structured and spontaneous performance assessments you use. Please provide a very *brief* example of each type of performance test which you may have used *or* are familiar with.

Structured Performance Assessment:

Exercise:
Response:
Rating:

Spontaneous Performance Assessment:

Exercise:
Response:
Rating:

SPECIAL GUIDELINES FOR COMPLETING YOUR ANALYSIS

1. As you respond to the following questions, please distinguish carefully among these five types of assessments.

2. Many questions ask you to describe attitudes and practices you may not have thought about before. Please *take the time to reflect on these questions before answering.* This analysis is designed to provide in-depth perspectives and may take up to 30 minutes to complete. Please set aside at least that much quiet time to complete it.

3. Our objective is to learn your *actual* assessment activities—*not* your practices as you (or others) think they should be. The self-analysis guide is completed anonymously to encourage you to reflect on and describe assessment *as you really conduct it.*

4. Several questions ask you to estimate the approximate percentage of your tests that have certain characteristics. Precise estimation will be difficult. *Best guesses* will suffice.

5. If any question fails to provide the response option you want, please write in your response.

6. Finally, as you answer these questions reflect *only* on your assessment of student achievement in the subject area and grade you specified on the cover.

    DISREGARD ASSESSMENTS YOU MAY CONDUCT IN OTHER SUBJECTS.

GENERAL INFORMATION

1. How many years have you been a teacher? _____
    This subject? _____

2. Tests can serve many purposes. That is, they can help you make any of a variety of decisions you face in the classroom. Before we ask about tests, however, we would like to better understand the decisions you face.

Listed below are several types of decisions. Please use the scales provided to indicate the relative importance of each of these in your classroom. Remember, describe importance ONLY as it relates to the decisions you make in the subject area and grade you specified on the questionnaire cover.

Diagnosing the strengths and
  weaknesses of individual
  students   important _ _ _ _ _ unimportant

Diagnosing group needs   important _ _ _ _ _ unimportant

Grouping students for
  instruction   important _ _ _ _ _ unimportant

Determining the achievement
  potential of students   important _ _ _ _ _ unimportant

Assigning grades to students important _ _ _ _ _ unimportant

Evaluating instructional unit
  to see if it worked   important _ _ _ _ _ unimportant

Communicating academic
  expectations   important _ _ _ _ _ unimportant

Controlling and motivating
  students   important _ _ _ _ _ unimportant

3. Place a check next to those types of assessment listed below in which you have had formal preservice or inservice, undergraduate, or graduate training:

    _____ Paper and pencil tests

    _____ Curriculum-embedded tests

    _____ Standardized tests

    _____ Oral questioning in the classroom

    _____ Performance assessment—structured

    _____ Performance assessment—spontaneous

4. Place an A next to the *one* source that made the *most impor-*
   tant contribution to your knowledge about how to develop and
   use classroom assessments.

   _____ Undergraduate testing course

   _____ Graduate testing course

   _____ Undergraduate methods course

   _____ Experience as a student

   _____ Information and ideas

   _____ Inservice training

   _____ Trial and error in the classroom

5. Place Bs next to all others that contributed significantly to your
   current practice. Leave those blank that make minimal or no
   contribution.

RELATIVE IMPORTANCE OF ASSESSMENTS

We would now like you to describe the relative importance of each
type of assessment by indicating the weight you give to each in
weighing results and making decisions. Each question below identifies a specific instructional purpose. If a certain type of assessment carries no weight in achieving a given purpose, you should
enter 0 percent next to it. On the other hand, if you rely completely
on one type of assessment for a specific purpose, you should enter
100 percent next to that type. As another example, a response of
20 percent to each of the five indicates equal weight to each in
achieving that purpose. Percentages *for each purpose* should total
100. *Remember:* Best guesses will suffice.

1. When your objective is to *diagnose the strengths and weak-*
   nesses of individual students, what type(s) of assessment do
   you use?

   Your own objective paper and pencil tests   _____%
   Text-embedded tests   _____%
   Oral questioning (recitation)   _____%

Standardized tests   _____%
Structured performance assessments   _____%
Spontaneous performance assessments   _____%
TOTAL   100 %

2. When the purpose is to *diagnose the needs of the class as a group*, what assessments do you rely on?

Your own objective paper and pencil tests   _____%
Text-embedded tests   _____%
Oral questioning (recitation)   _____%
Standardized tests   _____%
Structured performance assessments   _____%
Spontaneous performance assessments   _____%
TOTAL   100 %

3. When your goal is to *group students for instruction,* what type(s) of assessment do you rely on?

Your own objective paper and pencil tests   _____%
Text-embedded tests   _____%
Oral questioning (recitation)   _____%
Standardized tests   _____%
Structured performance assessments   _____%
Spontaneous performance assessments   _____%
TOTAL   100 %

4. When trying to *determine the achievement potential* of your students, how do you assess?

Your own objective paper and pencil tests   _____%
Text-embedded tests   _____%
Oral questioning (recitation)   _____%
Standardized tests   _____%
Structured performance assessments   _____%
Spontaneous performance assessments   _____%
TOTAL   100 %

5. When your purpose is to *assign grades* to students, what type(s) of assessments do you rely on?

Your own objective paper and pencil tests   _____%

Text-embedded tests   _____%
Oral questioning (recitation)   _____%
Standardized tests   _____%
Structured performance assessments   _____%
Spontaneous performance assessments   _____%
                                    TOTAL   100 %

6. When you wish to *evaluate your instruction* to see if it worked, what type(s) of assessment do you use?

Your own objective paper and pencil tests   _____%
Text-embedded tests   _____%
Oral questioning (recitation)   _____%
Standardized tests   _____%
Structured performance assessments   _____%
Spontaneous performance assessments   _____%
                                    TOTAL   100 %

7. When you wish to *communicate academic expectations,* what assessments do you rely on?

Your own objective paper and pencil tests   _____%
Text-embedded tests   _____%
Oral questioning (recitation)   _____%
Standardized tests   _____%
Structured performance assessments   _____%
Spontaneous performance assessments   _____%
                                    TOTAL   100 %

8. When your objective is to *control and motivate students,* what type(s) of assessments do you use?

Your own objective paper and pencil tests   _____%
Text-embedded tests   _____%
Oral questioning (recitation)   _____%
Standardized tests   _____%
Structured performance assessments   _____%
Spontaneous performance assessments   _____%
                                    TOTAL   100 %

USE OF TEACHER-MADE PAPER AND PENCIL
OBJECTIVE TESTS

Focus only on your use of your own tests in the subject and grade specified on the cover in answering these questions:

1. Which of the following *best* describes your current level of use of *objective tests you construct yourself?* Read all statements and check the ONE that best describes you.

    _____ I do not currently use them and do not plan to use them in the future.

    _____ I have decided to start using them in the future, but have not started to do so yet.

    _____ I currently use objective tests I develop myself, but I find them difficult to develop and it takes great effort to use them.

    _____ I use these tests on my own as a regular part of my instruction and do so comfortably.

2. Of the statements listed below, which *one* reflects your *primary concern* about the use of OBJECTIVE TESTS in your classroom. Read all statements, then check the one that concerns you most. If none concerns you, leave all BLANK.

    _____ I am concerned about my *lack of information* about developing and using my own objective paper and pencil tests.

    _____ I am concerned about my *level of training, skill, and experience* in developing and using my own objective paper and pencil tests.

    _____ I am concerned about the *amount of time required* to manage the development and use of such tests.

    _____ I am concerned about *how my students react* when I administer my own objective tests.

    _____ I am concerned about *establishing working relation-*

ships with other teachers to develop and use objective tests.

_____ I am concerned about *making such tests better* and *using them more effectively.*

3. Why is this concern primary for you?

4. Are there other important concerns you have about your use of your own OBJECTIVE TESTS? These may or may not relate to concerns listed above. If you have other concerns, please describe them on the back of this page.

USING TEXT-EMBEDDED TESTS

Now please focus only on your use of tests that accompany texts in answering these questions:

1. Which of the following *best* describes your current level of use of *test items or exercises provided as part of the curriculum materials* prepared by publishers? Check only ONE.

   _____ I do not currently use them and do not plan to do so in the future.

   _____ I have decided to start using them in the future, but have not started to do so yet.

   _____ I currently use text-embedded tests, but I find it difficult to do, requiring great effort to use them.

   _____ I currently use text-embedded tests on my own as a regular part of my instruction and do so comfortably.

2. Of the statements listed below, which *one* reflects your *primary concern* about the use of TEXT-EMBEDDED TESTS in your classroom. Read all statements, then check the one that concerns you most. If none concerns you, leave all BLANK.

   _____ I am concerned about my *lack of information* about text-embedded tests.

   _____ I am concerned about my level of *training, skill and experience* using text-embedded tests.

_____ I am concerned about the *amount of time required* to manage the use of text-embedded tests.

_____ I am concerned about *how my students react* to the use of text-embedded tests.

_____ I am concerned about *establishing working relationships* with other teachers using text-embedded tests.

_____ I am concerned about how I can *use text-embedded tests more effectively*.

3. Why is this concern primary for you?

4. Are there other important concerns you have about your use of TEXT-EMBEDDED TESTS? These may or may not relate to concerns listed above. If you have other concerns, please describe them on the back of this page.

USING STANDARDIZED ACHIEVEMENT TESTS

Please answer these questions about your use of standardized achievement test results in the subject and grade you specified. Remember, this also includes tests used in district and/or statewide testing programs.

1. Which of the following *best* describes your current level of use of standardized achievement tests? Check only ONE.

_____ I do not currently use standardized test results and do not plan to do so in the future.

_____ I have decided to start using such test results in the future, but have not started to do so yet.

_____ I currently use standardized test results, but find them very difficult to use effectively.

_____ I currently use standardized test results on my own as a regular part of my instruction and do so with comfort.

2. Of the statements listed below, which *one* reflects your *primary concern* about the use of STANDARDIZED TESTS in your classroom. Read all statements, then check the one that concerns you most. If none concerns you, leave all BLANK.

_____ I am concerned about my *lack of information* about standardized tests.

_____ I am concerned about my level of *training, skill, and experience* using standardized tests.

_____ I am concerned about the *amount of time required* to manage the use of standardized tests.

_____ I am concerned about *how my students react* to the use of standardized tests.

_____ I am concerned about *establishing working relationships* with other teachers using standardized tests.

_____ I am concerned about how I can *use standardized tests more effectively.*

3. Why is this concern primary for you?

4. Are there other important concerns you have about your use of STANDARDIZED TESTS? These may or may not relate to concerns listed above. If you have other concerns, please describe them on the back of this page.

USING ORAL QUESTIONNING

Please answer these questions about your use of oral questionning in the subject and grade you specified. Remember, this also includes tests used in district and/or state-wide testing programs.

1. Which of the following *best* describes your current level of use of oral questioning? Check only ONE.

_____ I do not currently use oral questioning and do not plan to do so in the future.

_____ I have decided to start using oral questioning in the future, but have not started to do so yet.

_____ I currently use oral questioning, but find it very difficult to use effectively.

_____ I currently use oral questioning on my own as a regular part of my instruction and do so with comfort.

2. Of the statements listed below, which *one* reflects your *primary concern* about the use of ORAL QUESTIONING in your classroom. Read all statements, then check the one that concerns you most. If none concerns you, leave all BLANK.

_____ I am concerned about my *lack of information* about oral questioning.

_____ I am concerned about my level of *training, skill, and experience* using oral questioning.

_____ I am concerned about the *amount of time required* to manage the use of oral questioning.

_____ I am concerned about *how my students react* to the use of oral questioning.

_____ I am concerned about *establishing working relationships* with other teachers using oral questioning.

_____ I am concerned about how I can *use oral questioning more effectively.*

3. Why is this concern primary for you?

4. Are there other important concerns you have about your use of ORAL QUESTIONING? These may or may not relate to concerns listed above. If you have other concerns, please describe them on the back of this page.

USING STRUCTURED PERFORMANCE ASSESSMENTS

Please answer these questions about STRUCTURED-PERFOR-MANCE ASSESSMENTS:

Remember: These are the observations and ratings of performance which you develop and use for a specific reason. They include preselected exercises, a behavioral response and performance ratings.

1. Which of the following best describes your current level of use of structured performance assessments? Check only ONE.

    _____ I do not currently use structured performance assessments and do not plan to do so in the future.

    _____ I have decided to start using structured performance assessments in the future, but have not started to do so yet.

    _____ I currently use structured performance assessments, but find them very difficult to use effectively.

    _____ I currently use structured performance assessments on my own as a regular part of my instruction and do so with comfort.

2. Of the statements listed below, which *one* reflects your *primary concern* about the use of STRUCTURED PERFORMANCE ASSESSMENTS in your classroom. Read all statements, then check the one that concerns you most. If none concerns you, leave all BLANK.

    _____ I am concerned about my *lack of information* about developing and using performance assessments.

    _____ I am concerned about my level of *training, skill, and experience* in developing and using structured performance assessments.

    _____ I am concerned about the *amount of time required* to manage the development and use of such assessments.

_____ I am concerned about *how my students react* when I use structured performance assessments.

_____ I am concerned about *establishing working relationships* with other teachers to develop and use structured performance assessments.

_____ I am concerned about *making such assessments better* and *using them more effectively.*

3. Why is this concern primary for you?

4. Are there other important concerns you have about your use of STRUCTURED PERFORMANCE ASSESSMENTS? These may or may not relate to concerns listed above. If you have other concerns, please describe them on the back of this page.

5. When using structured performance assessments do you:

    A. Clearly define levels of performance from adequate to inadequate?

        _____ Yes, in about what percent of your assessments?

                                  _____%
                                (estimate)

        _____ No

    B. Write down scoring criteria *before* the assessment?

        _____ Yes, in about what percent of your assessments?

                                    _____%

        _____ No

    C. Inform students of scoring criteria *before* the assessment?

        _____ Yes, in about what percent of your assessments?

                                    _____%

        _____ No

D. Plan complete scoring procedures before the assessment?

_____ Yes, in about what percent of your assessments?
_____%

_____ No

E. Observe more than one sample of performance before judging?

_____ Yes, in about what percent of your assessments?
_____%

_____ No

F. Check your performance ratings against other test scores?

_____ Yes, in about what percent of your assessments?
_____%

_____ No

G. Keep records of performance in your memory (in place of written records)?

_____ Yes, in about what percent of your assessments?
_____%

_____ No

H. Rate student performance yourself?

_____ Yes, in about what percent of your assessments?
_____%

_____ No

I. Use students as raters of their own performance?

_____ Yes, in about what percent of your assessments?
_____%

_____ No

J. Use students as raters of each other's performance?

_____ Yes, in about what percent of your assessments?
_____%

_____ No

K. Have a colleague (another teacher) rate the performance of your students?

_____ Yes, in about what percent of your assessments?
_____%

_____ No

L. Compare student performance to a preset standard?

_____ Yes, in about what percent of your assessments?
_____%

_____ No

M. Compare student performance to that of other students (e.g., use a norm group or rank students)?

_____ Yes, in about what percent of your assessments?
_____%

_____ No

USING SPONTANEOUS PERFORMANCE ASSESSMENT OBSERVATIONS

Please answer these questions about SPONTANEOUS-PERFOR-MANCE ASSESSMENTS.

Remember: These are unstructured observations of behavior that occur spontaneously during the day. Though they are unplanned, they still lead to evaluative judgments and ultimately inform your decisions.

1. Which of the following best describes your current level of use of spontaneous performance assessments? Check only ONE.

_____ I do not currently use spontaneous performance assessments and do not plan to do so in the future.

_____ I have decided to start using spontaneous performance assessments in the future, but have not started to do so yet.

_____ I currently use spontaneous performance assessments, but find them very difficult to use effectively.

_____ I currently use spontaneous performance assessments on my own as a regular part of my instruction and do so with comfort.

2. Of the statements listed below, which *one* reflects your *primary concern* about the use of SPONTANEOUS-PERFORMANCE ASSESSMENTS in your classroom. Read all statements, then check the *one* that concerns you most. If none concerns you, leave all BLANK.

_____ I am concerned about my *lack of information* about developing and using spontaneous performance assessments.

_____ I am concerned about my level of *training, skill, and experience* in using spontaneous performance assessments.

_____ I am concerned about the *amount of time required* to manage the use of such assessments.

_____ I am concerned about *how my students react* when I use spontaneous performance assessments.

_____ I am concerned about *establishing working relationships* with other teachers to use spontaneous performance assessments.

_____ I am concerned about *making such assessments better* and *using them more effectively.*

3. Why is this concern primary for you?

4. Are there other important concerns you have about your use of SPONTANEOUS PERFORMANCE ASSESSMENTS? These may or may not relate to concerns listed above. If you have other concerns, please describe them on the back of this page.

APPENDIX B

CLASSROOM ASSESSMENT ENVIRONMENT

Profile Description

Instructions for use: This form is designed for use by an observer conducting a detailed observation and description of a classroom assessment environment. While it is intended primarily for use in research contexts, it also can serve both teachers and administrators observing in classrooms. The effect of such observations will be increased sensitivity on the part of the observer to the key attributes of assessment environments. Observers who review the resulting profile with the participating teacher also can help that teacher become aware of the assessment environment he or she has created.

The observation and description framework contained herein is very long and complex. In that way, it reflects real classroom life. However, users are advised that it is not necessary to generate a complete profile with every use. Rather, parts of the framework can be used to provide focused information on aspects of the assessment environment relevant to particular contexts.

The form (or its parts) is designed to be completed by a "participant observer." That means the user will need to rely on a variety of information gathering strategies to complete it, including observation of teacher and student behaviors, personal communication via interview or discussion with both teachers and students and the analysis of assessment-related documents (tests, quizzes, assignments, etc.).

Information gathered by these means is then transformed by the observer into the subjective ratings that comprise the profile. To maximize the quality of results, before using this form, study the framework description thoroughly (Chapter 5 of this volume) and read the sample profiles presented in Chapters 6 and 7.

Center for Classroom Assessment
Northwest Regional Educational Laboratory
101 S. W. Main, Suite 500
Portland, Oregon 97204

I. ASSESSMENT PURPOSES

A. Diagnosing individual student needs

Uninformed _ _ _ _ _ Well-informed
Irrelevant _ _ _ _ _ Relevant
Not used _ _ _ _ _ Used frequently

B. Diagnosing group needs

Uninformed _ _ _ _ _ Well-informed
Irrelevant _ _ _ _ _ Relevant
Not used _ _ _ _ _ Used frequently

C. Assigning grades

Uninformed _ _ _ _ _ Well-informed
Irrelevant _ _ _ _ _ Relevant
Not used _ _ _ _ _ Used frequently

D. Grouping for instruction within class

Uninformed _ _ _ _ _ Well-informed
Irrelevant _ _ _ _ _ Relevant
Not used _ _ _ _ _ Used frequently

E. Identifying students for special services

          Uninformed _ _ _ _ _ Well-informed

          Irrelevant _ _ _ _ _ Relevant

          Not used _ _ _ _ _ Used frequently

F. Controlling and motivating students

          Uninformed _ _ _ _ _ Well-informed

          Irrelevant _ _ _ _ _ Relevant

          Not used _ _ _ _ _ Used frequently

G. Evaluating instruction

          Uninformed _ _ _ _ _ Well-informed

          Irrelevant _ _ _ _ _ Relevant

          Not used _ _ _ _ _ Used frequently

H. Communicating achievement expectations

          Uninformed _ _ _ _ _ Well-informed

          Irrelevant _ _ _ _ _ Relevant

          Not used _ _ _ _ _ Used frequently

I. Communicating affective expectations

          Uninformed _ _ _ _ _ Well-informed

          Irrelevant _ _ _ _ _ Relevant

          Not used _ _ _ _ _ Used frequently

J. Providing test-taking experience

          Uninformed _ _ _ _ _ Well-informed

          Irrelevant _ _ _ _ _ Relevant

          Not used _ _ _ _ _ Used frequently

K. Accountability

          Uninformed _ _ _ _ _ Informed

          Irrelevant _ _ _ _ _ Relevant

          Not used _ _ _ _ _ Used frequently

L. Assessment as an instructional strategy

          Uninformed _ _ _ _ _ Informed

Irrelevant _ _ _ _ _ Relevant
Not used _ _ _ _ _ Used frequently

M. Relative importance of purposes

Given "100 importance points" to
distribute across the purposes listed below,
how would you distribute those points to
reflect the relative importance of the
decisions listed?

Diagnosing individual
   needs   _____
Diagnosing group needs   _____
Assigning grades   _____
Grouping for instruction   _____
Identifying students for
   special services   _____
Controlling and motivating   _____
Evaluating instruction   _____
Communicating
   achievement expectations   _____
Communicating affective
   expectations   _____
Test-taking experience   _____
                                                  100 points

II. ASSESSMENT METHODOLOGY

A. Assessment of Achievement

1. Teacher-developed paper and pencil tests and quizzes
        Uninformed _ _ _ _ _ Well-informed
    Inappropriate _ _ _ _ _ Appropriate
        Not used _ _ _ _ _ Used frequently

2. Text-embedded paper and pencil tests and quizzes
        Uninformed _ _ _ _ _ Well-informed
    Inappropriate _ _ _ _ _ Appropriate
        Not used _ _ _ _ _ Used frequently

3. Performance assessments

Uninformed _ _ _ _ _ Well-informed
Inappropriate _ _ _ _ _ Appropriate
Not used _ _ _ _ _ Used frequently

4. Oral-questioning strategies

Uninformed _ _ _ _ _ Well-informed
Inappropriate _ _ _ _ _ Appropriate
Not used _ _ _ _ _ Used frequently

5. Standardized tests

Uninformed _ _ _ _ _ Well-informed
Inappropriate _ _ _ _ _ Appropriate
Not used _ _ _ _ _ Used frequently

6. Group-assessment methods

Uninformed _ _ _ _ _ Well-informed
Inappropriate _ _ _ _ _ Appropriate
Not used _ _ _ _ _ Used frequently

7. Opinions of other teachers

Uninformed _ _ _ _ _ Well-informed
Inappropriate _ _ _ _ _ Appropriate
Not used _ _ _ _ _ Used frequently

8. Assessment of reasoning skills

Uninformed _ _ _ _ _ Well-informed
Inappropriate _ _ _ _ _ Appropriate
Not used _ _ _ _ _ Used frequently

9. Regular assignments

Uninformed _ _ _ _ _ Well-informed
Inappropriate _ _ _ _ _ Appropriate
Not used _ _ _ _ _ Used frequently

10. Student peer rating

Uninformed _ _ _ _ _ Well-informed

Inappropriate _ _ _ _ _ Appropriate
Not used _ _ _ _ _ Used frequently

11. Student self ratings

Uninformed _ _ _ _ _ Well-informed
Inappropriate _ _ _ _ _ Appropriate
Not used _ _ _ _ _ Used frequently

12. Proportion of all assessments for all purposes that are of various types

Teacher-developed paper and pencil tests	_____
Text-embedded paper and pencil tests	_____
Performance assessments	_____
Oral questions	_____
Standardized tests	_____
Opinions of other teachers	_____
Regular assignments	_____
Group assessments	_____
Student-peer ratings	_____
Student self-ratings	_____
	100%

13. Cognitive levels of questions posed in:

	Study and Discussion Questions	Oral Questions	Tests and Quizzes
Recall			
Analysis			
Comparison			
Inference			
Evaluation			

14. Dealing with cheating

Uninformed _ _ _ _ _ Well-informed
Inappropriate _ _ _ _ _ Appropriate
Not used _ _ _ _ _ Used frequently

B. Assessment of Affect

Value of this factor for this teacher
        Unimportant _ _ _ _ _ Important

1. Observing individual students
        Uninformed _ _ _ _ _ Well-informed
        Inappropriate _ _ _ _ _ Appropriate
        Not used _ _ _ _ _ Used frequently

2. Observing group interactions
        Uninformed _ _ _ _ _ Well-informed
        Inappropriate _ _ _ _ _ Appropriate
        Not used _ _ _ _ _ Used frequently

3. Using questionnaires
        Uninformed _ _ _ _ _ Well-informed
        Inappropriate _ _ _ _ _ Appropriate
        Not used _ _ _ _ _ Used frequently

4. Using interviews (formal and informal)
        Uninformed _ _ _ _ _ Well-informed
        Inappropriate _ _ _ _ _ Appropriate
        Not used _ _ _ _ _ Used frequently

5. Opinions of other teachers
        Uninformed _ _ _ _ _ Well-informed
        Inappropriate _ _ _ _ _ Appropriate
        Not used _ _ _ _ _ Used frequently

6. Opinions of other students
        Uninformed _ _ _ _ _ Well-informed
        Inappropriate _ _ _ _ _ Appropriate
        Not used _ _ _ _ _ Used frequently

7. Opinions of parents
        Uninformed _ _ _ _ _ Well-informed
        Inappropriate _ _ _ _ _ Appropriate
        Not used _ _ _ _ _ Used frequently

8. Past student records

                    Uninformed _ _ _ _ _ Well-informed
                Inappropriate _ _ _ _ _ Appropriate
                    Not used _ _ _ _ _ Used frequently

9. Checklist of affective characteristics measured:

_____ Seriousness of pur- *Code:*
pose   F = formal assessment con-
_____ Motivation and ef-   ducted
fort   I = informal assessment con-
_____ Attitude   ducted
_____ Learning style
_____ Interests
_____ Values
_____ Preferences
_____ Academic self-concept
_____ Locus of control
_____ Anxiety
_____ Maturity
_____ Social skills
_____ Study skills
_____ Other (specify _____)

10. Relative importance of affective-assessment methods:

Observing individual students   _____
Observing group interactions   _____
Using questionnaires   _____
Using interviews (formal and informal)   _____
Opinions of other teachers   _____
Opinions of other students   _____
Opinions of parents   _____
Past student records   _____
                                                        100%

C. Assessment of Ability

1. Meaning of ability for teacher
    Value of this factor   Unimportant _ _ _ _ _ Important
    for the teacher

Measurement of ability   Measured formally   _____

Measured informally   _____

Not measured   _____

Ingredients considered in assessment of ability, if measured:

FACTOR(S) INCLUDED IN
       ASSESSMENT   MEASURED HOW?

1.

2.

3.

4.

5.

2. Check decisions influenced by results (i.e., change with varying levels of ability).

_____ Instructional objectives
_____ Instructional strategies
_____ Grouping for instruction (within class)
_____ Methods for measuring achievement
_____ Grading standards
_____ Students selected for special services
_____ Other (specify _____)

D. Text Assessments

Checklist of assessment components provided with text:

Available   *Used*

Available	Used	
_____	_____	Oral questions for class use
_____	_____	Homework assignments
_____	_____	General-assessment guidelines for teachers
_____	_____	Paper and pencil tests
_____	_____	Performance assessments
_____	_____	Scoring guidelines
_____	_____	Quality-control guidelines
_____	_____	Other (specify _____)

III. CRITERIA FOR SELECTING
ASSESSMENT METHODS

A. Results fit purpose

      Uninformed _ _ _ _ _ Well-informed

      Unimportant _ _ _ _ _ Important

      Not used _ _ _ _ _ Used frequently

B. Method matches material taught

      Uninformed _ _ _ _ _ Well-informed

      Unimportant _ _ _ _ _ Important

      Not used _ _ _ _ _ Used frequently

C. Ease of development

      Uninformed _ _ _ _ _ Well-informed

      Unimportant _ _ _ _ _ Important

      Not used _ _ _ _ _ Used frequently

D. Ease of scoring

      Uninformed _ _ _ _ _ Well-informed

      Unimportant _ _ _ _ _ Important

      Not used _ _ _ _ _ Used frequently

E. Origin of assessment

      Uninformed _ _ _ _ _ Well-informed

      Unimportant _ _ _ _ _ Important

      Not used _ _ _ _ _ Used frequently

F. Time required to administer

      Uninformed _ _ _ _ _ Well-informed

      Unimportant _ _ _ _ _ Important

      Not used _ _ _ _ _ Used frequently

G. Degree of objectivity

      Uninformed _ _ _ _ _ Well-informed

      Unimportant _ _ _ _ _ Important

      Not used _ _ _ _ _ Used frequently

H. Applicability to measuring thinking skills

        Uninformed _ _ _ _ _ Well-informed

        Unimportant _ _ _ _ _ Important

        Not used _ _ _ _ _ Used frequently

I. Effective control of cheating

        Uninformed _ _ _ _ _ Well-informed

        Unimportant _ _ _ _ _ Important

        Not used _ _ _ _ _ Used frequently

J. Relative importance of criteria

Results fit purpose	_____
Method matches material taught	_____
Ease of development	_____
Ease of scoring	_____
Origin of assessment	_____
Time required to administer	_____
Degree of objectivity	_____
Applicability to measuring thinking skills	_____
Effective control of cheating	_____
	100%

IV. QUALITY OF ASSESSMENTS

A. Percent of *paper and pencil assessments* (teacher-developed or text-embedded) having the following characteristics (need *not* total 100%):

percent

_____ Clear description of assessment specifications

_____ Matches content of instruction

_____ Matches cognitive levels of instruction

_____ Minimizes time required to gather needed information

_____ Item format matches desired outcome

_____ Items clearly written

_____ Items sample domain
_____ Scoring procedures planned
_____ Scoring criteria written for essays
_____ Clear directions
_____ High-quality reproduction
_____ Test scheduled to minimize distractions

B. Percent of *performance assessments* having the following characteristics (need *not* total 100%):

_____ Clear description of trait to be measured with levels of proficiency articulated
_____ Matches intended outcomes of instruction
_____ Minimizes time required to gather needed information
_____ Clear performance criteria
_____ Students aware of criteria
_____ Thoughtful exercises yield performance samples
_____ Exercises sample performance domain
_____ Performance rating planned
_____ Results match information needs

C. Percent of *oral questions* having the following characteristics (need *not* total 100%):

_____ Sampling methods cover range of achievement levels of students
_____ Strategies involve everyone
_____ Teacher waits for response
_____ Student's response given supportive reaction
_____ Questions match cognitive levels of instruction
_____ Written performance records maintained

V. FEEDBACK PROCEDURES

A. For *oral* and *nonverbal* feedback

Percent of feedback delivered to students who are:

_____ Strong (vs. weak)
_____ Correct (vs. incorrect)

_____ Male (vs. female)

100%

Percent of feedback having the following characteristics:

_____ Delivered in class (vs. out of class)
_____ Oral (vs. nonverbal)
_____ Public (vs. private)
_____ Positive (vs. negative)
_____ Fair (vs. unfair)
_____ Focused on achievement (vs. affect)
_____ Germane (vs. irrelevant)
_____ Immediate (vs. delayed)

100%

B. For *written* feedback

Percent of feedback delivered to students who are:

_____ Strong (vs. weak)
_____ Correct (vs. incorrect)
_____ Male (vs. female)

100%

Percent of feedback having the following characteristics:

_____ Comment (vs. symbol)
_____ Positive (vs. negative)
_____ Fair (vs. unfair)
_____ Germane (vs. irrelevant)
_____ Focused on achievement (vs. affect)

100%

Uses samples of performance   Never _ _ _ _ _ Frequently
as feedback

Uses public achievement chart   Never _ _ _ _ _ Frequently
as feedback

C. Feedback to parents   Minimal _ _ _ _ _ Frequent

Relative use of different media:

_____ Grades

_____ Written comments
_____ Consultations
100%

VI. DESCRIPTION OF TEACHER AND ASSESSMENT

A. Teacher's background

1. Teacher experience, number of years: _____ overall
                                            _____ at grade level
                                            _____ in school
                                            _____ with content

2. Relative contributions of various sources to teacher's knowledge of assessment methodology

_____ Teacher-preparation training
_____ Inservice training
_____ Ideas and suggestions of colleagues
_____ Professional literature
_____ Teacher's guide to textbooks
_____ Own experience in classroom
100%

B. Teacher's expenditure of time

1. Proportion of time spent in *teaching* activities

_____ Planning
_____ Teaching (one-on-one)
_____ Teaching (group)
_____ Assessing (see list, immediately below)
_____ Other (specify _____)
100%

2. Proportion of time spent in *assessment* activities (paper and pencil, performance assessment, oral, assignments)

_____ Reviewing and selecting assessments
_____ Developing own assessments
_____ Administering

———— Scoring and recording
———— Providing feedback
———— Evaluating quality
100%

C. Teacher characteristics

Role in the classroom	Curriculum maker and presenter	—	—	—	—	—	Servant of policy delivering required content
Expectations of professional self	Expects little	—	—	—	—	—	Expects a great deal
Structure needs	Rigid	—	—	—	—	—	Flexible
View of high-quality performance	Correctness demanded	—	—	—	—	—	Degrees of quality evaluated
Stereotypic view of students	None	—	—	—	—	—	Expressed often
Attends to exceptional student	Never	—	—	—	—	—	Frequently
Sense of performance norms	Unclear	—	—	—	—	—	Very clear
Orientation to experimentation	No risks	—	—	—	—	—	Risk taker
Orientation to cheating	No concern	—	—	—	—	—	Major concern
Amount of cheating	None	—	—	—	—	—	A great deal
Value of promptness; importance of timely work completion	Unimportant	—	—	—	—	—	Important

Interpersonal environment of the
classroom regarding assessment:

Cooperative	None	—	—	—	—	—	Frequent
Competitive	None	—	—	—	—	—	Frequent

Attributions for reasons of student success/failure:

———— Due to student
———— Due to teacher
100%

Basis for grading students:

    _____   Sense of ability

    _____   Demonstrated achievement

100%

Interpretation of assessment:

    _____   Norm-referenced

    _____   Criterion-referenced

100%

VII. TEACHER'S PERCEPTIONS OF STUDENT CHARACTERISTICS

A. Ability to learn

                Low _ _ _ _ _ High

       No variation _ _ _ _ _ Great deal

    Variation ignored _ _ _ _ _ Addressed

B. Willingness to learn

                Low _ _ _ _ _ High

       No variation _ _ _ _ _ Great deal

    Variation ignored _ _ _ _ _ Addressed

C. Rate of achievement

                Low _ _ _ _ _ High

        Decreasing _ _ _ _ _ Increasing

       No variation _ _ _ _ _ Great deal

    Variation ignored _ _ _ _ _ Addressed

D. Maturity

      Irresponsible _ _ _ _ _ Responsible

       No variation _ _ _ _ _ Great deal

    Variation ignored _ _ _ _ _ Addressed

E. Study skills

      Undeveloped _ _ _ _ _ Developed

No variation — — — — — Great deal
Variation ignored — — — — — Addressed

F. Social skills

Undeveloped — — — — — Developed
No variation — — — — — Great deal
Variation ignored — — — — — Addressed

G. Willingness to perform

Reticent — — — — — Willing
No variation — — — — — Great deal
Variation ignored — — — — — Addressed

H. Feedback needs

Weak — — — — — Strong
No variation — — — — — Great deal
Variation ignored — — — — — Addressed

I. Self-assessment skills

Undeveloped — — — — — Developed
No variation — — — — — Great deal
Variation ignored — — — — — Addressed

J. Sense of fairness

Unclear — — — — — Clear
No variation — — — — — Great deal
Variation ignored — — — — — Addressed

K. Reaction to testing

Tranquil — — — — — Anxious
No variation — — — — — Great deal
Variation ignored — — — — — Addressed

L. Parental expectations

Unclear — — — — — Clear
Low — — — — — High
Unimportant — — — — — Important

No variation _ _ _ _ _ Great deal
Variation ignored _ _ _ _ _ Addressed

VIII. ORIGINS OF ASSESSMENT POLICY

Fill-in description of state, district, and government policies when
and where appropriate:

APPENDIX C

NORTHWEST REGIONAL EDUCATIONAL LABORATORY CLASSROOM ASSESSMENT-TRAINING RESOURCES

As the program of research described in this volume unfolded, the staff of the NWREL Center for Classroom Assessment were able to devise a wide variety of training experiences for teachers that allowed them to face the task demands of classroom assessment with more confidence and a higher degree of assessment competence. The ten workshops currently included in this training program are listed and described below. All workshops are available for presentation by local trainers in preservice and inservice training contexts, as they are available in a video-based presentation format. For details, contact the Center at 101 S.W. Main, Suite 500, Portland, Oregon 97204 (1-800-547-6339).

NORTHWEST REGIONAL EDUCATIONAL LABORATORY (NWREL) CLASSROOM ASSESSMENT TRAINING PROGRAM

Summary of Available Workshops

A Status Report on the Nature and Quality of Classroom Assessment: The complex task demands of classroom assessment are reviewed, essential classroom assessment competencies are described, and the serious and chronic mismatch between teacher training in assessment and the assessment realities of classroom life is described. Specific strategies are offered for improving the quality of teachers' assessments (1-hour workshop)

Understanding the Meaning and Importance of High-Quality Classroom Assessment: Participants engage in a series of brainstorming activities to explore how to become critical consumers of assessments and their results. Attention focuses on what student characteristics teachers assess, why they assess, how they assess, what can go wrong, how to prevent problems and how to evaluate the quality of any assessment. (3-hour workshop)

Measuring Thinking in the Classroom: This session reveals how easy it is to assess higher order thinking when assessments arise out of a clear and specific definition of the target and how difficult it is when the target is out of focus. Participants also learn a variety of strategies of integrating thinking assessments into instruction. (3-hour workshop)

Paper and Pencil Test Development: Teachers learn how to plan tests, select the important material to test, and write sound test items. The workshop provides lots of practice and many ideas for integrating paper and pencil instruments into instruction. (3 hour workshop)

Developing Assessments Based on Observation and Judgment: Participants learn a step-by-step process for designing and constructing performance assessments and they learn how to align those assessments with important behavior and product-related achievement targets. (3-hour workshop)

Assessing Writing Performance: Issues and Options: The focus is on direct assessment of writing based on teacher evaluation of student writing samples. Holistic, analytical, and primary-trait scoring alternatives are demonstrated. (3-hour workshop)

Assessing Writing Performance: Training in Analytical Scoring: Teachers learn to apply a six-trait analytical-scoring model by hearing about each trait and then engaging in extensive practice in the application of each scoring criterion to actual samples of student writing. (7-hour workshop)

Assessing Reading Proficiency: Reading is defined as a dynamic interaction among reader, text, and context. Key attributes of a good reader are articulated and procedures are suggested for using paper and pencil test, performance assessments and personal communication to assess important aspects of the reading process. (3-hour workshop)

Developing Sound Grading Practices: This session explores the purposes for report-card grades, student characteristics that should be factored into grades, appropriate sources of grading data, and ways of combining data over time to determine grades. Teachers explore their own values about grades and grading. (4-hour workshop)

Understanding Standardized Tests: The focus is on norm-referenced standardized achievement batteries. Participants learn how these tests are designed and constructed, and they learn how the norming process provides the basis for score interpretation. Commonly used scores are clearly explained. (3-hour workshop)

All sessions available for video-based presentation or presentation by NWREL training staff.

REFERENCES

Airasian, P. W. 1984. Classroom assessment and educational improvement. Paper presented at the conference Classroom Assessment: A Key to Educational Excellence, Northwest Regional Educational Laboratory, Portland, Oregon.

Airasian, P. W., T. Kellaghan, and G. F. Madaus. 1977. The stability of teachers' perceptions of pupil characteristics. *The Irish Journal of Education* 11(12):78–84.

Airasian, P. W., T. Kellaghan, G. F. Madaus, and J. Pedulla. 1977. Proportion and direction of teacher rating changes of pupil progress attributable to standardized test information. *Journal of Educational Psychology* 69(6):702–9.

Allal, L. K. 1988. Quantitative and qualitative components of teacher's evaluation strategies. *Teaching and Teacher Education* 4(1):41–51.

American Federation of Teachers, National Council on Measurement in Education, and National Education Association. 1990. Standards for Teacher Competence in Educational Assessment of Students. *Educational Measurement: Issues and Practice* 9(4):30–32.

Berliner, D. C. 1987. But do they understand? In V. Richardson-Koehler, ed. *Educator's Handbook*. New York: Longman.

Brophy, J. F. and T. L. Good. 1970. Teachers' communication of differential expectations for children's classroom performance: Some behavioral data. *Journal of Educational Psychology* 61(5):365–74.

———. 1974. *Teacher-student relationships*. New York: Holt, Rinehart, and Winston.

———. 1986. Teacher behavior and student achievement. In M. C. Wittrock, ed., *Handbook of research on teaching* 3d ed. New York: Macmillan, 328–75.

Burstein, L. 1983. A word about this issue. *Journal of Educational Measurement* 20(2):99–101.

Calderhead, T. 1983. A psychological approach to research on teachers' classroom decisionmaking. *British Educational Research Journal* 7(1):51–57.

Calfee, R. C. and P. A. Drum. 1976. How the researcher can help the reading teacher with classroom assessment. Unpublished manuscript, Stanford University, Stanford, California.

Carter, K. 1984. Do teachers understand the principles for writing tests? *Journal of Teacher Education* 35(6):57–60.

Clark, C. M. and P. L. Peterson. 1986. Teachers' thought processes. In M. C. Wittrock, ed. *Handbook of research on teaching*, 3d ed. New York: Macmillan, 225–96.

Coffman, W. E. 1983. Testing in the schools: A historical perspective. Paper presented at the Center for the Study of Evaluation Annual Invitational Conference, University of California at Los Angeles, Los Angeles, California.

Cooley, R. E. 1979. Spokes in a wheel: A linguistic and rhetorical analysis of Native American public discourse. *Proceedings of the Fifth Annual Meeting of the Berkeley Linguistics Society,* 552–58.

Crooks, T. J. 1988. The impact of classroom evaluation on students. *Review of Educational Research* 58(4):438–81.

Dahlof, U. and V. P. Lundgren. 1970. Macro and micro approaches combined for curriculum process evaluation: A Swedish field project. (Research Report). Gotenberg, Sweden: University of Gotenberg, Institute of Education.

Dorr-Bremme, D. W. and J. L. Herman. 1986. *Assessing Student Achievement: A Profile of Classroom Practices.* Los Angeles: Center for the Study of Evaluation, University of California, Los Angeles.

DuMont, R. V., Jr. and M. L. Wax. 1969. Cherokee school society and the intercultural classroom. *Human Organization* 28(3):217–27.

Dunkin, M. J. and B. J. Biddle. 1974. *The study of teaching.* New York: Holt, Rinehart & Winston.

Ebel, R. L. and D. A. Frisbie. 1986. *Essentials of educational measurement,* 4th ed. Englewood Cliffs, N.J.: Prentice-Hall.

Erickson, F. 1977. Some approaches to inquiry in school-community ethnography. *Anthropology and Education Quarterly* 8(2):58–69.

Farr, R. and M. Griffin. 1973. Measurement gaps in teacher education. *Journal of Research and Development in Education* 7:19–28.

Fleming, M. and B. Chambers. 1983. Teacher-made tests: Windows on the classroom. In W. E. Hathaway, ed., *Testing in the schools. New directions for testing and measurement* San Francisco: Jossey-Bass, 19:29–38.

Frisbie, D. A. and S. J. Friedman. 1987. Test standards—some implications for the measurement curriculum. *Educational Measurement: Issues and Practice* 6(3):17–23.

Fyans, L. J. 1985. Teachers as test experts: Hidden talent. Paper presented at the annual meeting of the American Educational Research Association, Chicago, Illinois.

Gall, M. D. 1970. The use of questions in teaching. *Review of Educational Research* 40:707–21.

Gearing, F. and P. Epstein. 1982. Learning to Wait: An ethnographic probe into the operations of an item of hidden curriculum. In G. Spindler, ed. *Doing the ethnography of schooling: Educational anthropology in action.* New York: Holt, Rinehart and Winston, 240–67.

Gil, D. and D. Freeman. 1980. An investigation of the diagnostic and remedial practices of classroom teachers (Research series No. 78). East Lansing: Michigan State University, Institute for Research on Teaching. (ERIC Document Reproduction Service No. ED 192 247).

Goehring, H. J., Jr. 1973. Course competencies for undergraduate courses in educational tests and measurement. *The Teacher Educator* 9:11–20.

Good, T. L. and J. F. Brophy. 1978. *Looking in classrooms,* 2d ed. New York: Harper and Row.

Goslin, D. A. 1967. *Teachers and testing.* New York: Russell Sage.

Gronlund, N. E. 1985. *Measurement and Evaluation in Teaching.* 5th ed. New York: Macmillan.

Gullickson, A. R. 1982. Survey data collected in survey of South Dakota teachers' attitudes and opinions toward testing. Vermillon: University of South Dakota.

_____. 1984a. Matching teacher training with teacher needs in testing. Paper presented at the annual meeting of the American Educational Research Association, New Orleans, Louisiana.

_____. 1984b. Teacher perspectives of their instructional use of tests. *Journal of Educational Research* 77(4):224–46.

Gullickson, A. R. and M. C. Ellwein. 1985. Post hoc analysis of teacher-made tests: The goodness-of-fit between prescription and practice. *Educational Measurement: Issues and Practice* 4(1):15–18.

Gullickson, A. R. and K. D. Hopkins. 1987. Perspectives on educational measurement instruction for preservice teachers. *Educational Measurement: Issues and Practice* 6(3):12–16.

Haertel, E. et al. 1984. Testing in secondary schools: Student perspectives. Paper presented at the annual meeting of the American Educational Research Association, New Orleans.

Hall, G. E., A. A. George, and W. L. Rutherford. 1977. Measuring stages of concern about the innovation: A manual for use of the SoC questionnaire. Austin: University of Texas. Research and Development Center for Teacher Education.

Hall, G. E. and S. Loucks. 1978. Teacher's concerns as a basis for facilitating and personalizing staff development. *Teachers' College Record* 80(1):36–53.

Heath, S. B. 1982. Questioning at home and at school: A comparative study. In G. Spindler (ed.), *Doing the ethnography of schooling: Educational anthropology in action.* New York: Holt, Rinehart and Winston, 102–31.

_____. 1983. *Ways with words, language, life and work in communities and classrooms.* Cambridge, England: Cambridge University Press.

Herbert, G. W. 1974. Teachers' ratings of classroom behavior: Factorial structure. *British Journal of Educational Psychology* 44:233–40.

Herman, J. and D. W. Dorr-Bremme. 1982. Assessing students: Teachers' routine practices and reasoning. Paper presented at the annual meeting of the American Educational Research Association, New York.

Hills, J. R. 1977. Coordinators' accountability view of teacher's measurement competence. *Florida Journal of Education Research* 19:34–44.

_____. 1981. *Measurement and evaluation in the classroom.* Columbus, Ohio: Merrill.

Jackson, P. W. 1968. *Life in classrooms.* New York: Holt, Rinehart and Winston.

Joyce, B. 1979a. Teachers' thoughts while teaching. (Research series No. 58). East Lansing: Michigan State University, Institute for Research on Teaching (ERIC Document Reproduction Services No. ED 057 016).

Joyce, B. 1979b. Teaching styles at South Bay School. (Research series No. 57). East Lansing: Michigan State University, Institute for Research on Teaching (ERIC Document Reproduction Services No. ED 187 666).

Kellaghan, T., G. F. Madaus, and P. W. Airasian. 1982. *The effects of standardized testing.* Boston: Kluwer-Nijhoff.

Kinder, L. H. and P. J. Porwold. 1977. Standards for reporting pupil progress. In Educational Research Service, Reporting pupil progress: Policies, procedures, and systems. Arlington, Virginia: Author.

Labov, W. 1970. *The study of non-standard English.* Urbana, Illinois: National Council of Teachers of English.

_____. 1972. *Sociolinguistic patterns.* Philadelphia: University of Pennsylvania Press.

Lazar-Morris, C., L. Polin, R. May, and L. Barry. 1980. A review of the literature on test use. Los Angeles: University of California, Center for the Study of Evaluation (ERIC Document Reproduction Services No. ED 204 411).

Lortie, D. 1975. *School teacher.* Chicago: University of Chicago Press.

Marland, P. N. 1977. A study of teachers' interactive thoughts. Unpublished doctoral dissertation, University of Alberta, Edmonton.

Mayo, S. T. 1970. Trends in the teaching of the first course in measurement. National Council of Measurement Education Symposium Paper, Loyola University, Chicago (ERIC Document Reproduction Service No. ED 047 007).

Mehan, H. 1979. *Learning lessons: Social organization in the classroom.* Cambridge: Harvard University Press.

Mehan, H. 1980. The competent student. *Anthropology and Education Quarterly* 11(3):131–52.

_____. 1982. The structure of classroom events and their consequences for student performance. *In* P. Gilmore and A. A. Glatthorn, eds. *Children in and out of school.* Washington, D.C.: Center for Applied Linguistics, 59–87.

Mehrens, W. A. and I. J. Lehmann. 1984. *Measurement and evaluation in education and psychology* (3d ed.). New York: Holt, Rinehart and Winston.

Merwin, J. C. 1989. Evaluation. A chapter in M. C. Reynolds, ed. *Knowledge Bases for Beginning Teachers.* Washington, D.C.: American Association of Colleges of Teacher Education.

Michaels, S. and J. Cook-Gumperz. 1979. A study of sharing time with first grade students: Discourse narratives in the classroom. *Proceedings of the Fifth Annual Meeting of the Berkeley Linguistics Society.* Berkeley, California, 647–660.

Morine-Dershimer, G. 1979. *Teacher conceptions of children* (Research series No. 59). East Lansing: Michigan State University, Institute for Research on Teaching (ERIC Document Reproduction Services No. ED 180 988).

Morrison, A. and D. McIntyre. 1969. *Teachers and teaching.* Harmondsworth, Middlesex, England: Penguin Books.

Natriello, G. 1987. The impact of evaluation processes on students. *Educational Psychologist* 22(2):155–75.

Noll, V. H. 1955. Requirements in educational measurement for prospective teachers. *School and Society* 80:88–90.

Pedulla, J. J., P. W. Airasian, and G. F. Madaus. 1980. Do teacher ratings and standardized test results of students yield the same information? *American Educational Research Journal* 17:303–7.

Peterson, P. L. and S. A. Barger. 1985. Attribution theory and teacher expectancy. In J. B. Dasek, V. C. Hall and W. J. Meyer, eds. *Teacher expectancies*. Hillsdale, New Jersey: Laurence Earlbaum, 159–84.

Philips, S. U. 1972. Participant structures and communicative competence: Warm Springs children in community and classroom. In C. B. Cazden, V. P. John, and D. Hymes, eds. *Functions of Language in the Classroom*. New York: Teachers College Press, 370–94.

Quellmalz, E. S. 1985. Developing reasoning skills. In J. R. Baron, and R. J. Sternberg. eds. *Teaching thinking skills: Theory and practice*. New York: Freeman.

Reynolds, W. M. and K. A. Menard. 1980. An investigation of teachers' test construction practices. Paper presented at the annual meeting of the National Council of Measurement in Education, Boston, Massachusetts.

Rist, R. 1970. Student social class and teacher expectations: The self-fulfilling prophecy in ghetto education. *Harvard Educational Review* 40:411–51.

Roeder, H. H. 1972. Are today's teachers prepared to use tests? *Peabody Journal of Education* 59:239–40.

_____. 1973. Teacher education curricula—your final grade is F. *Journal of Educational Measurement* 10(2):141–43.

Rudman, H. E., et al. 1980. *Integrating assessment with instruction: A review (1922–1980)* (Research series No. 75). East Lansing: Michigan State University, Institute for Research on Teaching (ERIC Document Reproduction Services No. ED 189 136).

Salmon-Cox, L. 1980. Teachers and tests: What's really happening? Paper presented at the annual meeting of the American Educational Research Association, Boston.

_____. 1981. Teachers and standardized achievement tests: What's really happening? *Phi Delta Kappan* 62:631–34.

Scates, D. E. 1943. Differences between measurement criteria of pure scientists and of classroom teachers. *Journal of Educational Research* 37:1–13.

Schafer, W. D. and R. W. Lissitz. 1987. Measurement training for school personnel: Recommendations and reality. *Journal of Teacher Education* 38(3):57–63.

Schultz, J. and S. Florio. 1979. Stop and freeze: The negotiation of social and physical space in a kindergarten/first-grade classroom (Occasional paper No. 26). East Lansing: Michigan State University, Institute for Research on Teaching.

Shavelson, R. J., J. Caldwell, and T. Izu. 1977. Teachers' sensitivity to the reliability of information in making pedagogical decisions. *American Educational Research Journal* 14(2):83–97.

Shavelson, R. J. and P. Stern. 1981. Research on teachers' pedagogical thoughts, judgments, decisions and behavior. *Review of Educational Research* 41(4):455–98.

Shulman, L. S. 1980. Test design: A view from practice. In E. L. Baker and E. S. Quellmalz, eds. *Educational Testing and Evaluation*. Los Angeles: Sage, 63–73.

———. 1986. Paradigms and research programs for the student of teaching: A contemporary perspective. In M. C. Wittrock (ed.), *Handbook of Research on Teaching* 3d ed. New York: Macmillan, 3–36.

Simon, H. A. 1957. *Models of man: Social and rational: Mathematical essays*. New York: Wiley.

Standards for Educational and Psychological Testing. 1985. Washington, D.C.: American Eduational Research Association, American Psychological Association, and National Council on Measurement in Education.

Sproul, L. and D. Zubrow. 1982. Standardized testing from the administrative perspective. *Phi Delta Kappan* 62:628–31.

Stetz, F. and M. Beck. 1979. Comments from the classroom: Teachers' and students' opinions of achievement tests. Paper presented at the annual meeting of the American Educational Research Association, San Francisco, California.

Stiggins, R. J. 1984. *Evaluating students through classroom observation: Watching students grow*. Washington, D.C.: National Education Association.

Stiggins, R. J. and N. J. Bridgeford. 1985. The ecology of classroom assessment. *Journal of Educational Measurement* 22(4):271–86.

Stiggins, R. J., et al. 1985. *A feeling for the student: An analysis of the art of classroom assessment*. Portland, Oregon: Northwest Regional Educational Laboratory.

Stiggins, R. J., D. A. Frisbie, and P. A. Griswold. 1989. Inside high school grading practices: Building a research agenda. *Educational Measurement: Issues and Practice* 8(2):5–14.

Stiggins, R. J., K. Wikelund, and M. Griswold. 1989. Measuring thinking skills through classroom assessment. *Journal of Educational Measurement* 26(3):1–14.

Stinnett, T. M. 1969. Teacher certification. *In* R. L. Ebel, ed. *Encyclopedia of educational research*, 4th ed. New York: Macmillan, 614–18.

Terwilliger, J. S. 1971. *Assigning grades to students*. Glenview, Illinois: Scott, Foresman.

Tobin, K. G. 1983. Management of time in classrooms. *In* B. J. Fraser, ed. *Classroom management*. Perth, Australia: Western Australia Institute of Technology, Faculty of Education.

Tollefson, N., et al. 1985. Teachers' attitudes toward tests. Paper presented at the annual meeting of the American Educational Research Association, Chicago, Illinois.

Watson-Gegeo, K. A. and S. T. Boggs. 1977. From verbal play to talk story: The role of routines in speech events among Hawaiian children. In S. Ervin-Tripp, ed. *Child discourse*. New York: Academic Press, 67–90.

Weiner, B. and A. Kukla. 1974. An attributional analysis of achievement motivation. *Journal of Personality and Social Psychology* 15:1–20.

Weinshank, A. B. 1980. Investigations of the diagnostic reliability of reading specialists, learning disabilities specialists, and classroom teachers: Results and implications (Research series No. 72). East Lansing: Michigan State University, Institute for Research on Teaching (ERIC Document Reproduction Services No. ED 189 574).

Whitmer, S. P. 1983. *A descriptive multimethod study of teacher judgment during the marking process* (Research series No. 122). East Lansing: Michigan State University, Institute for Research on Teaching (ERIC Document Reproduction Services No. ED 234 052).

Wolmut, P. 1988. On the matter of testing misinformation. A paper presented at the SRA, Inc., Invitational Conference, Phoenix, Arizona.

Yeh, J. 1978. Test use in the schools. Los Angeles: University of California at Los Angeles, Center for the Study of Evaluation.

Yinger, R. 1977. A study of teacher planning: Description and theory development using ethnographic and informal process methods. Unpublished doctoral dissertation, Michigan State University, East Lansing.

Zahorik, J. A. 1975. Teachers' planning models. *Educational Leadership* 33:134–39.

INDEX

.